Judie Geise's New Northwest Kitchen

Judie Geise's
New
Northwest
Kitchen

Madrona Publishers   Seattle

Published by
Madrona Publishers, Inc.
P.O. Box 22667
Seattle, WA 98122

10 9 8 7 6 5 4 3 2 1

Library of Congress Cataloging-in-Publication Data

Geise, Judie
    Judie Geise's new Northwest kitchen.

    Includes index.
    1. Cookery—Northwest, Pacific. I. Title.
II. Title: New Northwest kitchen.
TX715.G319 1987   641.5   87-3352
ISBN 0-88089-024-X

Design by Stephen Herold.
Typography by Lasergraphics.

This book is dedicated to all of the wonderful cooks I know, especially Gayle, Brad, David, Annie, Roberto, Raymond—and Jerry, too.

CONTENTS

Acknowledgments

I would like to acknowledge a debt of gratitude to Pamela Hinckley for her sensitive and very sensible wine suggestions—she is one of the rare wine people, completely devoid of snobbery, who unerringly knows just what wine is needed to complete not only a meal but a mood; to Dan and Sara for making this book possible; and most of all to S.G.A. for his understanding and loving encouragement.

Judie Geise's New Northwest Kitchen

CHAPTER ONE

THE NEW NORTHWEST KITCHEN

A fter decades of depending upon Europe for culinary guidance and di-
rection, America has finally declared its independence. We've investi-
gated and absorbed the finest of the world's cuisines and culinary traditions
and are now applying what we've learned to our own rich and varied
heritage. We have turned our attention from expensive and exotic foods
imported from every corner of the globe and begun to explore the vast, and
in many cases virtually untapped, natural resources of our own country.

Our restaurants are now staffed with a proud, ambitious, and inventive
group of chefs who have been trained not abroad, but in America. As they
take their place among today's superstars, cooking as a profession has taken
on a more attractive image. In the home, cooking has become one of the
nation's most popular pastimes for a number of reasons: working with one's
hands in this age of the almighty machine is both challenging and relaxing;
preparing a meal or a dish produces an immediate result and instant
gratification; and, perhaps most important, good food is still one luxury that
we don't have to be rich to enjoy.

We are now at the beginning of a gastronomic revolution, the development of a national American cuisine and, at the same time, distinctive
regional cuisines. A few regional styles have existed for some time in certain
areas—the Southwest, New England, and California, for example—but
those are still in an early stage. The only regional cuisine that is instantly
recognizable and fully formed is that of a relatively tiny area of Southern
Louisiana, where a cohesive style, Creole/Cajun, has developed from several
influences: the French and Spanish contributed techniques and traditions,
while the American and West Indians, the Africans, and the Mexicans
introduced new seasonings and ingredients. What could be more American
than this blending of widely diverse cultures? Creole/Cajun cooking has a
distinct character that relies on certain techniques as well as on particular
foods indigenous to the area. But so far, aside from this single example, we

have been able to view only the tip of the iceberg regarding the development of regional cooking in America.

When Nouvelle Cuisine first appeared in France a few years ago, it was viewed as a fad, but its consequences were far-reaching. First, it freed the French from the tyranny of Haute Cuisine, a method of cooking that had become excessive and outdated. Also, it allowed American cooks to question their blind dependence on a method of cooking that neither suited our palates nor our lifestyle. And finally it provided us with a working theory on which to base our experiments: the use of fresh and local ingredients; replacement of elaborate sauces with the "new" reductions (a technique our grandmothers knew as pan sauces); combining elements from other cultures within a single dish; and rethinking our ideas on presentation. Once aware of our capabilities and resources, we found an awakening of our culinary conscientiousness; we began to rediscover and redefine what we had known up to then as "just plain cooking."

The growth of a regional cuisine in the Northwest has progressed steadily, if slowly. Years ago, serious gastronomes would have dismissed the idea that such a thing could exist. That is no longer the case. The already wonderful abundance of our natural resources is being supplemented by the products of aquaculture, game farms, fish hatcheries, and vineyards, as well as by the products of hundreds of cottage industries that provide our tables with everything from organically-grown flowers to wild greens to home-made preserves. Local farmers now cultivate on a wider scale those rarities that they once grew only for themselves: the white Babcock peach, for example, intensely fragrant and delicately flavored, and the tiny Finnish potato with its rich butter-colored flesh. And although still quite young, the Northwest's wine industry has already amassed a goodly share of awards and accolades throughout the world. The microbreweries, still young (the first opened in 1982), have created a market for their hand-crafted beer that is said to be the largest in the nation.

The Northwest, even in its urban centers, still has a feeling of the frontier, of staunch individualism and openness. So there is an honesty and straight-forwardness to the cooking here that is a direct reflection of those who do it. All these influences have been incorporated into a cuisine that is solidly based on a single outstanding principle: quality. The finest ingredients require no more than the simplest of cooking techniques to allow their innate goodness to shine through. This is the essence of good cooking: unpretentious, unadulterated, and completely honest in flavor.

It is no coincidence that James Beard, for decades one of the foremost authorities on and champions of American cookery, was also a native of the Pacific Northwest. In analyzing the complex development of our cuisine, he commented:

> What interests me is how the quality of cooking in this country can be followed from a period of simplicity and function to one of goodness and bounty, then to an age of elaboration and excess; finally, we hope, we are now in another epoch of gastronomic excellence.

Composing a Meal

Since the first edition of this book was published in 1978, my concerns about food and cooking have greatly changed. Like so many people today I have little time to spend in the kitchen and, much as I love to cook, I firmly believe that the processes involved should be as direct and as uncomplicated as possible. If a particular technique or seasoning in a recipe makes no difference in the final results, it should be eliminated. I once wrote that one *must* peel asparagus before cooking. But peeling asparagus stalks is drudgery, and the damned things cook just as well when one snaps off the stalk at the point where it forms a natural break between tough and tender.

Cooking is no fun when one spends time on a tedious task that can be simplified or performed more quickly and efficiently with the aid of a machine. This does not mean that meals should emerge from the kitchen so uniformly chopped, diced, and sliced that they appear to have come from a factory. Although I've owned a food processor for many years I still prefer to use a good knife or a mortar and pestle, especially when dealing with fresh herbs; food processors, aside from being too large for the job, tear away at the delicate leaves of herbs, and much of their flavor is lost or spoiled. I believe the two most important elements in good cooking are quality and love. One can buy the first, but the second must be given, and its absence is always apparent.

While cooking skills can be learned, only personal sensitivity can create a beautiful meal. This, for me, is the quality that sets the great cooks apart from those who are merely adequate. This begins with common sense: one would not, for instance, serve a meal consisting of oysters Rockefeller, tournedos Rossini, asparagus hollandaise, potatoes au gratin, and chocolate Bavarian cream unless one wished the untimely demise, or at the very least the immediate discomfort, of one's guests. A well-prepared meal should be nutritionally sound, please the eye with its presentation, and offer contrasting tastes and textures.

There should also exist within such a meal the element of surprise. The usual should be made unusual. Imagine corn bread formed into small shells through the use of a madeleine mold or bread sticks made into the shape of stalks of asparagus or wheat. Colette wrote, "If you are not capable of a little magic, it is not worth the trouble for you to get involved in cooking."

The first step in composing a meal is to let the season dictate what foods will appear on your table and how they should be presented. Cold winter months, for example, call for hearty, sustaining fare that will warm and nourish: soups, stews, and the like. This is the time to make use of fresh produce that appears only at that season, such as fennel, celeriac, and chestnuts. In the summer, palates should be teased with dishes both cooling and appetizing. Chicken roasted with rosemary and garlic, or a gratin of red peppers layered with herbs and thick slices of tomato, left to rest until they reach room temperature, become excellent summer fare.

Being mindful of the seasons is both economically sound and realistic. You might find raspberries in December, but they have traveled a long way. The farther produce has traveled, the more it has lost in freshness and flavor. Above all, purchase only the freshest and finest. Be flexible when shopping; be willing to substitute when a certain ingredient cannot be found. No technique or sauce will successfully disguise inferior ingredients.

Take inventory of your personal skills and local resources. If you have neither the time nor inclination to make your own bread, find a good commercial bakery. If you are fortunate enough to live in an area rich with treasures from the sea, use them; get a good book (there are many) on seafood and begin to experiment. Be realistic about time. A menu of dishes that are all sautéed at the last minute can be a harrowing experience for even the most accomplished cook. Remember that many dishes become more flavorful if prepared in advance: soups, stews, vegetables in a vinaigrette, braised meat or poultry, sauces, or frozen desserts—to name only a few.

Cookbooks specializing in menus abound, lavishly illustrated with color photographs, loaded with ideas for table and flower arrangements and, of course, chock full of recipes. The ideas are there, but the reasons behind them are seldom made explicit. The primary consideration in preparing a meal is recognizing which flavors work together. Some simple examples are fish and lemon, tomato and basil, chocolate and coffee. Keeping in mind these basics, one needs only to substitute one complementary element for another to enliven the original idea: fish and orange (or fish and sherry-wine vinegar); tomato and mint (basil is a member of the mint family); or chocolate and a nut-flavored liqueur such as Frangelico.

Once you have identified the natural affinities between certain foods, expand on what you've learned. Suppose your main course is salmon simply grilled or poached and served with a light sauce, accompanied by asparagus. Instead of the usual lemon vinaigrette, try a sauce maltaise (a hollandaise made with orange) for the asparagus. Serve the salmon with steamed leeks, tossed while still warm with sherry-wine vinegar and olive oil. If the fish dish is a rich or spicy one like paella or bouillabaisse, accompany it with a salad of peeled and thickly sliced oranges drizzled with a bit of olive oil or garnished with tiny Niçoise olives.

Color, too, is important when composing a meal. Think of the colors of autumn: the browns and russets of wild mushrooms, the golds and yellows of squash, pumpkins, and peppers. In summer there are brilliant reds: tomatoes and berries; the rich purple of eggplants; the verdant greens of lettuce, cress, arugula, and herbs. The background on which the meal is presented should also be taken into consideration. White plates, or occasionally black ones, are my choice.

Just as flavor and color balances are essential to a meal, so is texture—a quality often overlooked. Texture can transform a dish from just ordinary to extraordinary. For example, there is a sauce for fettucine that is made with three or four cheeses melted in a reduction of heavy cream. The pasta is of a rather soft consistency, the sauce is smooth and creamy—the dish is basically good, but it lacks something. Add coarsely chopped pistachios or walnuts; now you have a contrast of textures that adds interest to the dish.

And last, the most important ingredient that can be added to a meal is thought. I'll close with this one from *Food for the Rich* by Paul Reboux, published in 1927:

> To entertain well means to see that your guests have a gay evening, a good night's sleep, and wake after it feeling rested and restored. There is so very little hospitality of this kind that one is forced to conclude that very few people know how to entertain.

CHAPTER TWO

APPETIZERS

Crab and Fennel Vinaigrette
serves four

T his combination of raw strips of fennel bulb and sweet Dungeness crabmeat dressed with lemon juice and olive oil makes a delightful first course. Serve with a dry Riesling.

1 small fennel bulb
4 ounces Dungeness crab, cooked
Salt and freshly ground pepper

$1\frac{1}{2}$ to 2 tablespoons lemon juice
4 tablespoons fruity olive oil

Cut the stems from the fennel bulb and reserve them for another use. Remove and discard any outside sections of the bulb that are discolored. Cut the remaining fennel into julienne, put in a mixing bowl with the crab, season with the salt and pepper, add the lemon juice and olive oil, and toss well. Chill for about 1 hour before serving.

Stuffed Mussels
serves six as a first course

T hese mussels go very nicely with linguini; you can use some of their broth in making the sauce. They also make a good first course for game hens. Try this with Pouilly-Vinzelles as the accompanying wine.

2 pounds mussels, cleaned (as in Steamed Mussels in Their Broth)
4 shallots, minced
1 tablespoon olive oil
$1\frac{1}{2}$ teaspoons grated lemon rind

2 tablespoons parsley, minced
1 cup freshly made bread crumbs
4 tablespoons grated Parmesan cheese
Dash dried hot red pepper flakes

2 egg whites, lightly beaten
Salt

Preheat the oven to 350 degrees.

Steam the mussels not longer than 5 minutes, remove from pot, extract meat, chop coarsely, and reserve. Reserve the empty shells, also. While the mussels are steaming, sauté the shallots in the olive oil for 3 or 4 minutes.

Put the chopped mussels into a bowl and add the sautéed shallots with their oil, the lemon rind, parsley, crumbs, 2 tablespoons grated cheese, pepper flakes, and egg whites; mix thoroughly, tasting for salt.

Separate the shells, stuffing each half with a bit of the mussel mixture. Place the stuffed shells in a shallow ovenproof dish. Sprinkle the tops of the mussels with the remaining 2 tablespoons grated cheese and bake for 15 minutes, running under the broiler for the last few minutes to brown the tops lightly.

Smoked Salmon Tartar
serves four as a first course

T his is a simple and straightforward recipe for those times when simply serving a plate of good smoked salmon is not quite enough. The work involved is minimal and the presentation can be varied; for example, mound a bit of the fish in the hollows of small cooked new potatoes, halved, with the skins left on. Use a melon-baller to scoop out the potatoes—but only after they are completely cool.

¹/₂ pound smoked salmon
1 tablespoon chopped shallots
1 to 1¹/₂ tablespoons lemon
    juice

Liberal grinding of black
    pepper, coarse grind
Garnish: thin slices of lemon,
    cut in half

Remove and discard the skin and any dark flesh from the smoked salmon. Chop the remaining salmon, by hand, until coarse. Sprinkle the chopped shallots over the salmon and continue to chop until the mixture is very fine and the shallots almost unidentifiable. Put the salmon into a small mixing bowl and add the pepper and enough lemon juice to sharpen the taste (the amount will vary greatly, depending upon the type of smoked salmon used, but be aware that too much lemon juice will make the mixture salty). Mix together lightly, mound the tartar in the middle of a small serving plate, and surround it with the lemon slices. Serve with thin slices of pumpernickel bread spread with a film of unsalted butter and accompanied by small glasses of iced Russian vodka.

Salmon Seviche

serves six

A n unusual treatment for salmon. The lime juice neutralizes the oiliness of the fish and refines its flavor. The green peppercorns used in the marinade should be packed in water; avoid those packed in vinegar, as they have an undesirable tart aftertaste. Serve as a first course with a sparkling Brut Prosecco as the accompanying wine.

$1\frac{1}{2}$ pounds salmon
$2\frac{1}{2}$ tablespoons green peppercorns (water-packed)
1 cup onion, sliced paper-thin
Juice of 6 limes

1 teaspoon salt
Dash Tabasco
$\frac{1}{4}$ cup plus 3 tablespoons
   olive oil

Remove the skin from the salmon; carefully remove and discard any bones. Cut the fish into 1-inch cubes.

Pound the green peppercorns lightly with a mortar and pestle (about half of them should be mashed). Put them in a shallow nonmetallic bowl with the onion, lime juice, salt, Tabasco and $\frac{1}{4}$ cup olive oil; mix together well. Add the salmon and turn it in the mixture so that the fish is coated with the marinade. Cover with plastic wrap and refrigerate for 24 hours.

Before serving, drain the fish in a sieve, reserving a tablespoon or 2 of the marinade. Dress the salmon with a mixture of 1 tablespoon of the marinade and 3 tablespoons olive oil. Taste and add the other tablespoon of marinade if desired. Serve the seviche on lettuce with wedges of lemon and hard-boiled egg.

Potted Salmon
makes about two and a half cups

May also be prepared from leftover poached salmon. A bit of tarragon or chives may be added to the salmon mixture if desired, but chives should be used only if fresh—dried chives have little or no flavor. A dry Riesling accompanies this dish well.

1 ½-pound piece of salmon, center cut	Dash Tabasco
Lemon juice to taste	6 to 8 tablespoons butter, cut into chunks

Prepare a court bouillon (see Bayou Bisque) and bring to a boil in a large enamel casserole with lid. Reduce the heat and simmer for 45 minutes.

Wrap the salmon in cheesecloth and tie the ends tightly with string. Lower the fish into the simmering liquid. Cover, bring to a boil, and cook over high heat for 2 minutes only. Immediately remove the casserole from the heat and allow the fish to cool, covered, in the bouillon. This is an absolutely foolproof way to poach fish of any size to perfection.

Remove the salmon from the casserole when cooled; remove and discard the cheesecloth. Clean off the skin and remove all bones, flaking the fish as you go along. Place the cleaned salmon in a food processor or blender and blend until it is smooth. Add the lemon juice, Tabasco, and the butter, bit by bit, while the machine is running. Blend until the butter is totally absorbed into the salmon. Taste for seasoning, adding salt if necessary. Pack tightly into a serving container and chill 2 to 3 hours before serving. Serve with thinly sliced rye bread or pumpernickel. If potted salmon is to be kept longer than a day, cover the top with a half-inch layer of clarified butter.

Variation: Substitute ½ pound cooked shrimp for the salmon. Put the shrimp (cut into pieces, if they are large) in a food processor and blend just until the shrimp is shredded, then follow instructions above.

Marinated Smelt with Fennel

serves four to six

T his is a variation on an old Italian recipe, typically part of an antipasto platter, and originally made with sardines. The marinade combines the pleasing sweet but tart flavors of orange and fennel, with the addition of sherry wine vinegar. The fish must marinate overnight for the best flavor, but be sure to bring the dish back to room temperature before serving; the subtleties would be totally lost if served ice-cold. A wine such as Orvieto Secco goes well with this dish.

1 1/2 pounds fresh smelt, the smallest possible, left whole (uncleaned)

Flour seasoned lightly with salt and pepper

Vegetable oil

3 tablespoons olive oil

1 heaping cup thinly sliced onion

1 heaping cup thinly sliced fresh fennel bulb

Zest of 1 orange

1 to 2 tablespoons orange juice

2/3 cup sherry wine vinegar

Garnish: orange slices and chopped fresh fennel leaves

Dust the smelt with the flour, shaking off any excess. Heat the vegetable oil in a skillet and fry the smelt over moderately high heat until crisp and brown. Remove to paper toweling and allow to drain without crowding.

Discard any vegetable oil left in the skillet and wipe it clean. Heat the olive oil over moderate heat, then add the onion and fennel. Sauté until tender but still crisp. To the vegetables add the orange zest, juice, and the sherry wine vinegar; cook over high heat until the liquid is slightly reduced and a little syrupy. Arrange the fish in a dish shallow enough to hold them in a single layer and pour the sauce over all. Refrigerate overnight but allow the dish to come to room temperature before serving. Garnish with the orange slices and sprinkle with fennel leaves. Because they are so small, the smelts are eaten whole, like sardines.

Squid with Balsamic Vinegar and Bread Crumbs
serves four

This simple and satisfying dish makes a delightful prelude to any rich meal. Its flavors and textures are most pleasing when prepared right before serving; this should be no hardship for the cook, as the total cooking time for this recipe is only a minute or two. The wine to accompany it could be a good zesty Sauvignon/Semillon blend.

2 pounds small squid, cleaned (see Squid Salad)
3 to 4 tablespoons fruity olive oil
4 to 5 large cloves garlic, finely chopped
Salt and freshly ground pepper

$1\frac{1}{2}$ tablespoons balsamic vinegar
$\frac{1}{2}$ cup coarse, toasted home-made bread crumbs (a firm-textured bread like sour-dough is excellent)

Slice the cleaned squid into the thinnest possible rings. Cut the tentacles in half, or in quarters if they are large.

Heat the olive oil in a large skillet and sauté the garlic over low heat until slightly softened. Raise the heat to moderately high, add the squid, season with salt and freshly ground pepper, and sauté for only 1 or 2 minutes—until the squid is tender. Remove from the heat, sprinkle with the balsamic vinegar, and toss with the bread crumbs.

Herbed Cheese
serves six to eight

This is one of my favorite summer appetizers, an herbed cream cheese much like Boursin but without the accompanying price tag. Fresh herbs are essential; even if you add only two or three of those recommended, you will be amazed by the fine flavor. I like a mixture of thyme, summer savory, chives, sage, and parsley. The addition of feta cheese takes the taste beyond the ordinary as well as giving a slight tang that you will find most appealing. With a good cracker or bread and a fragrant white Bordeaux this dish serves well on the summer patio or more formally as a first course.

2 tablespoons fresh herbs,
  minced
$\frac{1}{2}$ pound feta cheese (Greek
  style)
$\frac{1}{2}$ pound cream cheese
1 tablespoon heavy cream

  (optional)
Freshly ground black pepper
Dash of cayenne pepper
1 large clove garlic, put through
  a press

Put the feta cheese, cut into chunks, in a food processor and process until creamy. Add the cream cheese and blend together until well combined. Remove and place in a serving bowl, adding the cream if the mixture seems too thick (remember that it will thicken when it is chilled).

Add the black pepper and cayenne to taste, the garlic, and minced fresh herbs; mix thoroughly. (Herbs minced by hand are far superior in flavor.) Chill for at least $\frac{1}{2}$ hour. This mixture will keep, tightly covered in the refrigerator, for about a week.

Variations: Use 2 tablespoons coarsely chopped green peppercorns (packed in water) instead of the fresh herbs. Or, instead of feta cheese, use a creamy mild or medium-flavored goat cheese; a Montrachet or Bucheron would be excellent choices.

Montrachet Marinated in Fennel, Orange, Garlic, and Olive Oil
serves four

I've always found the blend of orange and fennel especially pleasing— sweet yet tart. The combination particularly complements goat cheese, but you will also come across it in the Marinated Smelt as well as in the Orange and Fennel Salad. I first discovered this delightful marriage of flavors in a Sicilian recipe for marinated black olives (I use Calamatas, firm Greek olives cured in a red wine vinegar) that combines the strips of orange peel, fennel seed (slightly bruised to release more of the flavor), crushed cloves of garlic, a few crumbled bay leaves, and enough olive oil to moisten the whole affair. Serve with the best Champagne you can afford.

Olive Oil

How does one learn about olive oils? My answer to that is: the same way you learn about wines. However, since olive oil tastings have not come into fashion, this means purchasing olive oil in small quantities until one becomes educated on the subject. The extravagance of olive oils displayed in food specialty shops these days is mind-boggling, but here are a few facts that will make selection easier.

First, country of origin. Italy, with fourteen major olive-oil-producing regions, makes the finest oils; France ranks second. French and Italian oils are lighter in flavor, as well as in the way they feel on your tongue, than the robust and strongly flavored oils of Spain and Greece.

Second, method by which the oil is extracted. There are three grades of olive oil: extra virgin, virgin, and pure. Ideally, the first two are made in the following fashion. After being harvested by hand, the olives are ground by stone wheels into heavy paste. This is placed in trays which fit into a press that extracts the liquid. Oil and water are allowed to separate naturally or by centrifugal force, and the oil is then clarified by filtering through cloth or poured into huge ceramic jars to allow the sediment to settle on the bottom. This is the first cold-pressing and, according to the level of acidity, the oil will be graded as extra virgin (maximum of 1 percent acidity) or virgin (maximum of 3 percent acidity). A first pressing done by machinery does not always compare in quality to that done by hand-operated stone wheels, because the metal in machines tends to heat up, which is injurious to the oil. Since the making of these fine oils is done completely by hand, they are the most expensive.

5-ounce log of Montrachet or any other mild-flavored, creamy goat cheese

Very fruity, extra-virgin olive oil

$1/2$ teaspoon fennel seeds, lightly bruised (use a mortar and pestle)

Good amount coarsely ground pepper

Zest of $1/2$ orange

Orange juice

2 large cloves garlic, peeled and thickly sliced

Garnish: a few Nicoise or Gaeta olives

Pure oil is chemically refined from the residual pits, skins, and pulp of the first cold pressing, and this produces a pale bland oil that must be blended with virgin oil to give it flavor and color. This oil is excellent for general cooking purposes. The refining process raises its smoking point to 400 degrees. Cold-pressed oils, on the other hand, have a smoking point of less than 300 degrees and should not be used for high-heat cooking (sautéing, deep-frying, etc.). In Tuscany, where the very best olive oils are produced, the oil is almost never used to cook with. It is kept on the table as a seasoning or condiment.

Third, intensity of flavor. Olive oil may be separated into three categories: mild, semifruity, and fruity.

Here is a brief listing of oils that can generally be found in quality grocery stores and in specialty shops throughout the U.S., although obviously this will vary from city to city.

Mild—Grade extra virgin: Louis de Regis, France; Poggio al Sole, Italy. Grade pure: Sasso, Bertolli, Berio, all from Italy.

Semifruity—Grade extra virgin: Old Monk, France; Kimberly, California. Grade pure: James Plaignol, France.

Fruity—Grade extra virgin: Antinori and Badia a Coltibuno, Italy.

After pondering the above, you will realize that the selection of an olive oil depends very much on personal taste. If you are uncertain where to begin, you might start with a small container of one of the milder oils and begin your experiments from there. In any case, you will find that the extra virgin oils are best used simply, as in the Montrachet Marinated in Fennel, Orange, Garlic, and Olive Oil.

Using a thin piece of kitchen string, cut the log of goat cheese into approximately 1-inch rounds. If the cheese is at room temperature, it can be cut successfully with a knife. Place the rounds in a shallow serving dish. Drizzle olive oil over all, until there is a thin layer of it in the bottom of the dish. Sprinkle with the fennel seed and pepper. Cut the orange zest directly over the cheese, allowing the thin strips to fall at random. Cut off a small portion of the orange, and squeeze the juice over the cheese. Add the garlic and garnish with the olives. Allow to stand for at least 40 minutes, and serve. Serve with a crisp French or Italian bread, or cream or table-water crackers.

Roquefort Strudel
serves twelve to fourteen as an hors d'oeuvre

Filo dough is a paper-thin pastry available at any shop specializing in Middle Eastern foods. Because of its extreme thinness it should be handled with care. Small tears in the sheets are not a problem because usually many layers of them are used, but remember when working with them that leaves that are out but not in use should be rolled in a slightly dampened towel so they do not dry out and become brittle.

Do not confine Roquefort Strudel to the hors d'oeuvres tray; serve it with fresh, very ripe pears for a savory dessert. Those of your guests who are not overly fond of sweets will find it delightful, and you should pair it with a good vintage Port.

$\frac{1}{2}$ pound cream cheese
3 tablespoons unsalted butter, softened
$\frac{1}{4}$ pound Roquefort cheese, crumbled
2 egg yolks
Dash cayenne pepper or

Tabasco
A few grindings black pepper
8 sheets filo dough
$\frac{1}{2}$ cup (1 stick) unsalted butter, melted
$\frac{1}{2}$ cup bread crumbs

Cream together the cream cheese and the butter; beat in the crumbled Roquefort and the egg yolks until the mixture resembles a smooth and very thick batter. Season with the cayenne and black pepper. Chill for 1 hour. Remove filo dough from the refrigerator and allow to stand for 1 hour.

Preheat the oven to 375 degrees.

Spread a towel over your working space. Place a sheet of filo in the center of it. Brush the sheet with a light coating of butter and sprinkle it lightly with bread crumbs. Place another sheet of dough over the first and repeat this procedure until 4 sheets have been used.

Spread half the cheese mixture in an even mound along the longest side of the pastry nearest you. Fold in the flaps of dough at the sides of the filling. Lift up the end of the towel and roll the pastry over the filling and continue to roll until the filling is completely enclosed.

Transfer the strudel to a lightly greased baking sheet and brush the top with butter. Repeat this with the remaining ingredients to form a second strudel.

Bake the strudels for 35 to 40 minutes, until golden brown. Allow to cool slightly, cut into 2-inch slices with a serrated knife, and serve warm.

Terrine of Rabbit
for a one-and-a-half-quart terrine

A terrine, strictly speaking, is an earthenware or porcelain container with straight sides that is found in both oval and rectangular shapes. It is used for baking patés of meat or game. The name of the utensil has also come to describe its contents, indicating that the paté has been cooked and served in a terrine rather than in a crust. The ground meats used in patés are very often marinated in cognac, but I find this gives the paté an undesirably strong flavor, so I have eliminated this step. Serve with crisp French bread and cornichons. Medium red wines like Burgundy (Mercurey is nice) would make a suitable accompaniment.

1 pound pork fatback, cut into thinnest possible slices
1 ½ pounds rabbit, boned and coarsely ground
½ pound lean pork, coarsely ground
½ pound veal, coarsely ground
½ pound pork fatback, cut into small dice, not ground
2 tablespoons butter
½ cup onion, finely chopped
1 large clove garlic, finely chopped
½ teaspoon dried thyme
3 teaspoons salt
Freshly ground pepper
2 to 3 juniper berries, crushed
Pinch allspice
¼ cup toasted hazelnuts, coarsely chopped
¼ cup cognac or good brandy
½ cup heavy cream
2 egg yolks
2 bay leaves

Preheat the oven to 350 degrees.

Line a 1½-quart terrine or loaf pan with fatback slices, reserving a few for the top. Place the ground rabbit, pork, veal, and fatback dice in a large mixing bowl.

Heat the butter in a small skillet; add the onions and sauté them over moderate heat for about 10 minutes, stirring occasionally. Do not allow them to brown. Pour the onions with their fat into the meat mixture. Add the salt, pepper, crushed juniper berries, allspice, and hazelnuts.

Combine the cognac with the heavy cream and the egg yolks and blend well. Pour this mixture over the meats and, using your hands, mix well. To test the seasoning bring a small skillet of water to a boil, add a teaspoon of the meat mixture, and simmer it for a few minutes. Chill it quickly in the freezer and taste, then adjust seasoning if necessary.

Pour the meat mixture into the prepared terrine, cover the top with the reserved fatback slices, and place the 2 bay leaves on top. Cover the terrine with its lid (substitute a double layer of foil if you are using a loaf pan) and place it in a pan with water that reaches halfway up the sides of the terrine.

Bake in the center of the oven for about 1½ hours. The terrine is done when its juices run clear. Remove the lid, place a weight on top, and allow to cool. Then refrigerate, with the weight still in place, for 2 or 3 days. Before serving, remove the terrine from the refrigerator and allow to stand at room temperature for at least 1 hour.

Variation: Substitute the same amount of blanched sliced green olives for the hazelnuts.

Poor Man's Paté en Croute
serves six

T his savory creation of curried ground beef mixed with a purée of leeks is wrapped in filo pastry. Filo resembles strudel dough: paper-thin sheets that are almost transparent in their lightness and are usually brushed with butter and layered. The end result is a pastry that explodes into crisp, golden flakes when bitten into, very much like a good croissant. Filo can be purchased at any shop that carries Middle Eastern foods. Serve this paté with a first course of Crab and Fennel Vinaigrette, or Fennel Soup, or Potted Shrimp. A Gamay from California would mesh nicely with any or all of these.

4 small leeks
Dash of vinegar
1 tablespoon butter
$\frac{1}{2}$ tablespoon vegetable oil
2 tablespoons onion, finely chopped
3 cloves garlic, finely chopped
2 pounds lean ground beef
Salt

Dash of cayenne pepper
$\frac{1}{4}$ to $\frac{1}{2}$ teaspoon curry powder or paste (depending on strength of brand used)
2 eggs
4 ounces sour cream
12 sheets filo pastry
6 tablespoons melted butter

Preheat the oven to 375 degrees.

One hour before preparation, remove the filo from the refrigerator and wrap it in a damp towel. (Filo dries out rather quickly, and it should be left in the towel throughout preparation.)

Cut the tops off the leeks, leaving 2 to 3 inches of green. Slice them in half almost to the root and wash thoroughly under cold running water, spreading the leaves to rinse out all grit. Cut off and discard the root end. Slice the leeks into 1-inch lengths and drop them into a pot of boiling salted water to which a dash of vinegar has been added. Cook for about 10 minutes, drain well and purée in a food processor. Remove purée, place in a mixing bowl, and set aside.

While the leeks are cooking, sauté the onion in the butter and oil until it has softened but not browned, add the beef and garlic, and sauté until the meat has separated and browned lightly. Season to taste with salt, cayenne, and curry, drain off any excess fat, and place in mixing bowl along with the leek purée.

Combine the eggs with the sour cream and add to the meat, blending well. Taste for seasoning. You may wish to add more curry powder to bring out the flavors of the filling, but curry should not be the dominant flavor.

Spread a large towel over your working space. Place a sheet of filo pastry in the middle of the towel, with the long side nearest you; brush it with a light coating of melted butter. Directly on top of this, place the next sheet, brush with butter, and continue until all 12 sheets have been used. Mound the filling along the side nearest you, leaving a 1-inch border along each of the short sides. Using the towel as an aid, roll the pastry once over the filling, fold the sides over, and roll to close.

Paint the bottom of the roll with a light coating of butter; place a large pastry sheet on top of this, grasp the ends of the towel firmly, and invert. Baste the top of the roll with more butter and place in the oven. Bake for 30 to 40 minutes or until the top of the roll is browned and crisp. Serve immediately, using a serrated knife to slice diagonally.

Country Paté
for a two-quart terrine or paté mold

Country patés are usually identified by their coarse texture and robust seasoning. The small amount of bread crumbs and the egg help to counteract crumbling. Bacon should never be substituted for the fatback; it will lend the paté a definite smoky flavor that is undesirable. If you cannot find pancetta in your area, substitute a good-flavored baked ham instead. Serve with French bread and cornichons. A Moulin-à-Vent completes the impression a fine country paté makes.

1½ pounds lean pork, coarsely ground

1 pound veal, coarsely ground

½ pound pancetta, coarsely ground

¼ pound pork fatback, cut into small dice, not ground

2 tablespoons butter

1 cup onion, finely chopped

4 large cloves garlic, peeled

$^1/_2$ teaspoon thyme
$^1/_4$ teaspoon allspice
Pinch ground cloves
Salt and freshly ground pepper
$^1/_4$ cup cognac or good brandy

2 eggs
$^1/_4$ cup soft breadcrumbs
$1^1/_2$ pounds pork fatback, cut
   into thinnest possible slices
2 bay leaves

Preheat the oven to 350 degrees.

Combine the ground pork, veal, pancetta, and diced fatback in a large mixing bowl.

Heat the butter in a skillet; add the onions and sauté them over moderate heat for about 10 minutes; do not brown. Pour into the mixing bowl with the meat. Put the cloves of garlic through a press and into the bowl; add the thyme, allspice, cloves, and salt and pepper to taste.

Combine and blend the cognac, eggs, and bread crumbs; add this mixture to the meats and work the meats and seasonings together with your hands. To test for seasoning, bring a small skillet of water to a boil, add a teaspoon of the meat mixture, and simmer it for just a few minutes. Chill the bit of paté quickly in the freezer and taste; adjust the seasoning if necessary.

Line a 2-quart paté mold or terrine or loaf pan with the slices of fatback, reserving a few of them for the top. Pour in the meat mixture, cover the top with the reserved fatback slices, and top with the bay leaves. Cover the mold with its lid (or use a double thickness of foil) and place it in a pan containing water, enough to reach halfway up the sides of the terrine. Bake in the center of the oven for about $1^1/_2$ hours; the paté is done when its juices run clear.

Remove the lid, place a weight on top, and allow to cool. Refrigerate with the weight still in place for 2 to 3 days. Before serving, remove the paté from the refrigerator and allow to stand at room temperature for at least 1 hour.

Chicken Liver Mousse
makes approximately two cups

An extremely simple recipe that may be prepared a day or two in advance. If you wish to keep it longer, cover the top with half an inch of clarified butter. Serve it with a French, Italian, or sourdough bread, cornichons, and a dry Madeira.

1 pound chicken livers
8 tablespoons butter
6 medium shallots, coarsely
  chopped
1 large clove garlic, coarsely
  chopped
A few sprigs each of fresh
  parsley and thyme (if no
  fresh thyme is available,

substitute $\frac{1}{4}$ teaspoon
  dried)
1 small bay leaf
$\frac{1}{3}$ cup Madeira
$\frac{1}{4}$ teaspoon each powdered
  ginger and allspice
$\frac{1}{2}$ teaspoon salt
Freshly ground pepper

Clean the chicken livers and cut each in half. Melt 2 tablespoons butter in a 10-inch skillet; when sizzling, add the shallots and sauté over moderate heat for 1 minute. Add the livers, garlic, parsley, thyme, and bay leaf and season the mixture lightly with salt and pepper. Cook the livers until they are firm but still pink in the center, 6 to 8 minutes. Pour the Madeira over the livers, raise the heat to high, and reduce the pan juices to a glaze.

Remove the mixture from the heat and allow to cool for a few minutes. Remove the bay leaf, place the contents of the skillet in a food processor (if using a blender, purée the mixture in 2 batches), and blend into a smooth purée. Add a bit more Madeira to taste, the ginger and allspice, salt, and the remaining 6 tablespoons butter, cut into chunks. Blend the mousse until completely smooth. Taste and adjust seasoning if necessary. Chill the mousse for 2 to 3 hours before serving.

Crostini Roberto (Chicken Liver Canapés)
serves four to six

C rostini are Italian canapés; this excellent version made of chopped chicken livers is a specialty of Tuscany. The livers are blanched for two reasons: to rid them of any bitterness and to make them easier to chop. The chopping must be done by hand to obtain the correct consistency: tiny, but still recognizable pieces of liver. A food processor or meat grinder will turn the liver into too fine a paste.

The vodka used in this recipe is a deviation from the classic style; it gives the dish a lift without adding any flavor. Cognac, Marsala, or Madeira may be substituted, but the quantity should be reduced. The crostini should be served on rounds of sturdy bread, Italian or French, which are neither fried nor toasted. This allows the liver mixture to soak lightly into the bread.

Crostini are a first course, but they are rich, so be careful not to overburden your guests later in the meal. A light main dish like the Veal and Pepper Sauté is ideal. Serve with a Tuscan white wine like Galestro or stick to icy vodka.

$\frac{1}{4}$ cup olive oil
2 tablespoons carrot, finely chopped
1 cup onion, finely chopped
1 small stalk celery, finely chopped
1 tablespoon each fresh rosemary and sage, finely chopped, or $\frac{1}{2}$ teaspoon each dried

1 clove garlic, finely chopped
$\frac{1}{2}$ pound chicken livers, cleaned and halved
3 tablespoons capers
3 tablespoons anchovy paste
1 tablespoon tomato paste mixed with 2 tablespoons water
Freshly ground pepper
$\frac{1}{3}$ cup vodka

Heat the olive oil in a heavy, deep 10-inch skillet, add the carrot, onion, celery, and herbs; sauté over moderate heat for 10 minutes until golden; do not brown.

Meanwhile bring a small saucepan of lightly salted water to a boil, add the chicken livers, and allow them to blanch for 4 to 5 minutes. Drain immediately, run under cold water, and dry thoroughly. Chop very finely together with the capers.

Add the garlic to the sautéed vegetables and continue to cook 2 to 3 minutes. Add the chicken liver and caper mixture to the vegetables; stir in the remaining ingredients, blending well. Do not add any salt at this point.

Sauté this mixture for about 15 minutes or until all excess moisture is absorbed and the mixture resembles a thick paste. Taste for seasoning, adding salt if necessary. Remove mixture from the heat and immediately spread onto thin rounds of Italian or French bread. The mixture may also be allowed to cool and gently reheated later, but it should be kept covered.

Curried Stuffed Eggs
makes forty-eight stuffed halves

In true East Indian fashion, a mélange of spices flavor these eggs rather than a curry powder out of a jar.

1 1/2 tablespoons vegetable oil
1/2 teaspoon black mustard seeds
1/2 teaspoon cumin seeds
2 tablespoons fresh ginger, finely chopped
2 tablespoons onion, finely chopped

1 teaspoon salt
1 teaspoon turmeric
Pinch of cayenne pepper
2 dozen hard-boiled eggs
2 tablespoons Major Gray's chutney, finely chopped
2 to 3 tablespoons mayonnaise

In a small skillet heat the oil over moderate heat till a light haze forms over it. Stir in the mustard seeds and cumin seeds and immediately add the ginger and onion; sauté for 2 minutes.

Add the salt, turmeric, and cayenne and continue to sauté until the onions are soft and lightly colored.

Remove the yolks from the eggs and place them in a mixing bowl; cut the whites in half lengthwise and reserve. Combine the yolks with the onion and ginger, put the resulting mixture in a blender or food processor, and blend to a paste.

Remove to a bowl and add the chutney and enough mayonnaise to lighten the texture; blend thoroughly. Place the stuffing mixture in a pastry bag fitted with a number-2 star tip and pipe it into the reserved egg-white halves.

Chestnuts Flavored with Fennel Seeds
serves four to six

A favorite in the Appenine mountain district of Italy; the fennel seeds impart a delightful aroma to the chestnuts. Serve them with a light red wine.

40 to 50 imported Italian chestnuts
Small pinch of salt

2 tablespoons fennel seeds

Cut a cross into the skins of the chestnuts at the pointed end. Bring a large pot of water to a boil, add the salt and the fennel seeds, and continue to boil for 5 minutes. Add the chestnuts and boil for about 20 minutes more or until they are tender. Drain, let cool to room temperature, and serve.

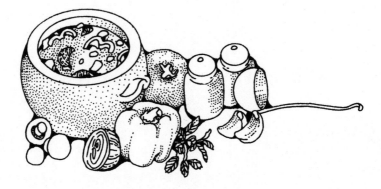

CHAPTER THREE

SOUPS

Chanterelle Soup
serves six to eight as a first course

T his recipe is based on my grandmother's mushroom soup, but since she never wrote down the recipe, perhaps I should call it a variation of her soup. In any case, one variation is clear: the use of chanterelles, among the most delicious of all the Northwest's mushrooms. Like other mushrooms, chanterelles tend to absorb liquid rather easily, so wash them only if they're really dirty. Wash them quickly under cold running water, and dry them thoroughly. One of the best utensils for drying them is a lettuce-drier or spinner, available in most kitchen or hardware shops. Serve the soup with a woodsy scented wine like an Italian Tocai or a white Rhone.

1 pound fresh chanterelles
5 tablespoons butter
Squeeze of lemon juice
Salt and freshly ground pepper
    to taste
2 leeks, thoroughly washed and
    finely chopped
1 large clove garlic, peeled and
    minced

$1\frac{1}{2}$ cups potato, peeled and
    diced
$6\frac{1}{2}$ cups chicken stock, lightly
    seasoned
1 tablespoon fresh thyme or
    parsley, finely chopped
1 cup sour cream
1 tablespoon red wine vinegar

Clean and dry the chanterelles. Reserve 2 or 3 of the best-shaped ones; chop the remainder coarsely. Sauté them in a large heavy skillet with 2 tablespoons of butter and season them with lemon juice, salt, and pepper. The heat must be high enough to allow the mushrooms to release their juices, but take care not to brown them; do not cook them longer than 3 or 4 minutes. Remove the mushrooms with a slotted spoon and reserve the liquid.

Heat 3 tablespoons of the butter in a heavy enameled soup pot (about a 4-quart size); add the leeks, garlic, and potatoes, and sauté them over medium heat for 10 minutes. Add the reserved mushroom juices, chicken stock, and thyme or parsley, bring to a boil, reduce the heat, and simmer for 15 to 20 minutes or until the potatoes are soft. Add the chopped and cooked mushrooms at this point and simmer gently for about 30 minutes.

Pour the soup through a fine sieve into a large mixing bowl, reserving all liquid. Let the chanterelles and vegetables cool slightly, then purée them in a blender or food processor. Rinse out the soup pot with hot water and pour the reserved liquid into it. Add the purée and mix with a wire whisk. Set the pot over low heat and add the sour cream and vinegar, allowing the soup to simmer gently. Meanwhile, slice the reserved mushrooms and add them to the soup to warm. Taste for seasoning and serve.

If you wish, the soup may be thickened slightly with a bit of beure manié (equal parts of softened butter mixed with flour) added at the end. If the soup is to be reheated, do not bring it to a boil or it will curdle. This soup can be prepared a day or two in advance.

Fennel Soup
serves eight as a first course

This is a delicate soup using both the bulb and the leaves of the fennel. The anise flavor of fennel is further accentuated by the addition of Pernod. An Alsatian wine—Pinot Gris or Gewurztraminer—will make the beginning of the meal even more memorable.

2¹/₂ tablespoons butter
1 cup onion, finely chopped
2 cups potato, peeled and diced
2 cloves garlic, peeled and
    finely chopped
Salt and freshly ground pepper

2 fennel bulbs with leaves
1¹/₂ cups dry white vermouth
    or dry white wine
2 quarts chicken stock, mildly
    seasoned
2 tablespoons Pernod

Melt the butter in a heavy 4-quart soup pot; add the onion, potato, and garlic, season lightly with salt and pepper, and sauté for about 10 minutes, until the vegetables are soft but not brown.

While they are cooking, prepare the fennel: cut off the stems and leaves close to the base of the bulb and reserve. Peel away and discard any discolored outer sections of the bulb; cut it in half and wash under running water to remove all grit. Chop the fennel bulb into coarse pieces and add to the soup pot with the vegetables. Pour over this the vermouth or wine and the chicken stock, bring to a boil, reduce heat, and simmer for about 45 minutes or until the fennel is tender. Pour the soup through a sieve into a bowl; reserve vegetables. Rinse the soup pot with hot water and pour the liquid back into it. Place the vegetables in a food processor, reduce them to a fine paste, and add the resulting purée to the soup pot.

Take the reserved fennel stems and strip from them about 2 tightly packed cups of leaves; chop them finely and add them to the soup. Put the pot back on the stove, simmer for 5 or 10 minutes to warm, add the Pernod, correct the seasoning, and serve.

Onion Soup
serves six to eight

This onion soup depends on a stock flavored primarily with chicken rather than beef, which gives a lighter flavor to the finished dish. I like to serve it in wide, shallow soup plates and float large cheese-covered croutons in the middle. You can substitute water for part of the vermouth or wine, but the stock will be just that much less richly flavored.

You might precede this soup with Chicken Liver Mousse or Celery Root Remoulade if you are planning on it as a main course. The underlying sweetness of the onions demands that the accompanying wine be dry and fruity: a full, rich sherry—Amontillado.

1 1/2 pounds beef knuckle or shank bone
1 large onion, peeled and cut in half
4 1/2 cups dry white vermouth and/or dry white wine
5 pounds chicken backs and necks with excess fat removed

3 ribs celery, with leaves
Bouquet garni
Salt and freshly ground pepper
Small handful parsley
2 bay leaves
1 small loaf day-old French bread
3 tablespoons butter

¼ pound salt pork, blanched
   and cut into small dice
6 cups onions, cut in half and
   sliced thin
2 or 3 cloves garlic, minced
Pinch of sugar

2 tablespoons fresh thyme,
   minced, or ½ teaspoon
   dried thyme
½ pound Swiss cheese, grated
   coarsely
1½ tablespoons flour

Preheat oven to 450 degrees.

Place the beef bone and onion in a shallow baking pan and put in the oven. Bake them for 45 minutes or until they are a deep, rich brown. Remove the pan from the oven and place the beef bone and the onion in a large (12- to 14-quart) stock pot. Pour off any fat from the pan used to bake the bone, add ½ cup of the vermouth, and set pan over high heat to deglaze and reduce for a few minutes. Add this liquid to the stock pot. Add the chicken parts, celery, bouquet garni, salt and pepper, parsley, bay leaves, 2 cups vermouth, and enough water to cover all. Bring to a boil, skimming off any foam from the surface, and reduce the heat to simmer. The stock should be simmered for 2 to 3 hours. Take care not to oversalt at the beginning, for as the stock reduces the flavor becomes more concentrated.

While the stock simmers, cut the French bread into slices an inch thick. Place in an oven set at 200 degrees and bake until it is completely dried out, 30 to 45 minutes.

Remove all bones from the stock and strain the liquid through a fine sieve; skim off all fat with a bulb baster. You should have approximately 3 quarts of stock. The soup may be made in advance to this point; any stock not used immediately may be frozen.

In a heavy 5-quart soup pot, melt the butter over medium heat, add the cubed salt pork, and lightly brown. Remove, drain on paper towels, and reserve.

Into the rendered fat put the sliced onions and garlic, sprinkling them with a pinch of sugar, salt, pepper, and thyme. Cover the pot and steam over medium heat for 20 to 30 minutes. Stir the flour into the onions with a whisk and cook for 5 minutes until it is incorporated. Add the remaining 2 cups of vermouth, stirring constantly, and cook for 5 minutes more. Add the

---

The Soup Pot

Because the soups here have such definite flavors, they do not
depend entirely on stocks for their flavor. With soups like these, the old
maxim, "Throw the leftovers into the soup pot," is quite preposterous.
Where a certain harmony of flavors is the ultimate goal, care must be
taken not to upset the balance. Soup-making for many cooks suffers
most from indiscriminate additions of spices and herbs, compatible or
not—thus changing the entire character of the dish.

---

prepared stock, bring to a boil, reduce heat, and simmer for 30 minutes. Stir
in the reserved pork bits and taste for seasoning.

When you are ready to serve the soup, preheat the broiler, set the slices
of bread on a baking sheet, cover each with some grated cheese, and put
under the broiler until the cheese is completely melted. Remove from oven;
put 1 or 2 croutons in each bowl of soup and serve.

Potato Leek Soup
serves four to six

This humble preparation, most enjoyable in itself, can be used as the
basis for a myriad of variations. When watercress is in season, reduce
the quantity of leeks and add a bunch of the peppery greens with stems
removed and proceed as outlined, floating a fresh sprig of watercress in each
bowl as a garnish. With the addition of heavy cream, added just before
serving, this soup is served chilled as vichyssoise, the creation of Louis Diat,
the chef who once made the Ritz-Carlton Hotel in New York a gathering
place for those who appreciated fine food. An elegant garnish for this soup
when served chilled is a tiny spoonful of red or black caviar placed on the top
of each portion.

There is no reason not to serve this soup as a cool-weather main course,
especially when accompanied by a first course of Swiss Chard Tart or Terrine
of Rabbit. A good white Burgundy like a Macon or Saint Veran would make
a fine complement for this soup.

6 leeks
4 tablespoons butter
3 cups potatoes, cut into large
  dice
$\frac{1}{2}$ cup onion, coarsely chopped
1 large clove garlic, sliced
Salt and freshly ground pepper
1 cup dry white vermouth

5 cups chicken stock, mildly
  seasoned
1 small potato, cut into
  quarters and thinly sliced
  (about $\frac{1}{2}$ cup)
Dash freshly grated nutmeg
$\frac{1}{2}$ cup milk (optional)

Cut off and discard all but 2 inches of the green leaves on the leeks. Peel off and discard any discolored outer skin and cut lengthwise, almost in half, to the root end. Wash under cold running water to remove any sand or grit. Cut off the root ends and discard. Put aside one of the smallest leeks and slice the rest into $\frac{1}{4}$-inch slices.

Melt 3 tablespoons of butter in a 3-quart pot; add the leeks, diced potatoes, onion, and garlic, and season with salt and pepper. Cook over high heat, stirring constantly until the vegetables are coated with butter and are slightly softened, about 5 minutes. Add the vermouth and the stock, bring to a boil, reduce the heat, and simmer for 30 minutes.

While the soup is cooking, cut the reserved leek into pieces about the length and thickness of a wooden matchstick (julienne). Melt the remaining tablespoon of butter in a small skillet; add the leek and the thinly sliced potato. Sauté the vegetables over low heat for about 5 minutes and reserve.

Remove the soup from the heat and allow to stand for 10 minutes to cool slightly. Strain off the liquid and reserve. Place the vegetables in a food processor and purée. Rinse the soup pot with hot water, return the stock to it, add the purée, and stir in with a wire whisk. Add the sautéed leek and potato slices with their butter and stir together. Place the soup over low heat and warm it slowly. Add the nutmeg and taste for seasoning. If the soup is too thick for your liking, add the optional $\frac{1}{2}$ cup of milk and blend in with a whisk. Serve immediately.

Warren's Gazpacho
serves four to six

W hat this recipe lacks in authenticity, it more than makes up for in flavor and originality. It should be presented as a first course in a glass container (a two-quart glass soufflé dish would be suitable), showing each of the vegetables in its individual layer. Use only your finest chicken stock and degrease it thoroughly. Accompany the gazpacho with a white wine such as a Rioja.

1 teaspoon saffron
4 cups chicken stock
2 small green or red bell peppers, seeded and cut into small dice
2 medium new potatoes, peeled and cut into small dice
2 bunches scallions, thinly sliced (use only a little of the green tops)
2 large ripe tomatoes, peeled, seeded, and cut into small dice

2 small unwaxed (local) cucumbers, not peeled but seeded and cut into small dice, or an English cucumber with an unwaxed skin
Salt and freshly ground pepper
6 tablespoons mild white wine vinegar
4 cloves garlic, put through a press
Olive oil
Lemon wedges

Heat $\frac{1}{2}$ cup of the chicken stock and pour it over the saffron; allow to steep for 1 hour.

There should be about 2 cups each of the peppers, potatoes, tomatoes, and cucumbers and $1\frac{1}{2}$ cups of scallions. Layer the vegetables, in any order you prefer, in a 2-quart or larger glass container, seasoning each layer lightly with salt and pepper. Combine the saffron in its stock with the remaining $3\frac{1}{2}$ cups of stock and stir in the vinegar and the garlic pulp. Pour the stock carefully over the vegetables so as not to disturb the layers and refrigerate overnight to marinate.

Serve the gazpacho in small individual bowls and pass a cruet of olive oil and the lemon wedges so that guests may season their own servings.

Green Gumbo
serves eight

S pring in the Northwest heralds the arrival of tender and verdant delights
upon the greengrocer's tables: thin spears of crisp asparagus, tiny
bouquets of young radishes, and of course a myriad of greens: collards,
mustard greens, turnip tops, watercress, arugula, spinach, dandelion greens,
chard, kale, chicory, escarole, rape, and sorrel. Greens are one culinary item
the Northwest produces in abundance and that we use less than we might.
Collards, mustard greens, rape and turnip tops, which are consumed in great
abundance in the South, are part of the cabbage family and have been eaten
in Europe for thousands of years. The Romans and the Greeks believed that
collards had great digestive powers. Turnip tops have been brewed into
potions and restoratives since the sixteenth century, and various powers were
attributed to them, from curing hangovers to "awakening slumbering
desires in even the most quiescent spouse," to quote John Milton. The
dandelion, a cousin of the sunflower, marigold, and zinnia, was used by the
Romans in salads and as an herb in stews. Early settlers brought its seeds to
North America as part of their herbal pharmacy; they believed that it had a
cleansing and renewing effect on the body. Our forebears were wise in
making use of this wealth of greens, for all are low in calories, high in
potassium, and extremely rich in vitamin A.

A most delightful and satisfying use of these greens is presented here in
green gumbo, known in the South as "gumbo z'herbes." Traditionally
served on Good Friday, it was thought to give the rejuvenation needed after
many days of abstinence and fasting. Legend has it that for every green put
into the gumbo, a new friend would be made in the succeeding year. This,
like gumbo z'herbes (a Creole contraction for *gumbo aux herbes*), should be
made with no fewer than six different greens.

This particular dish breaks the rules of gumbo—it uses neither okra nor
filé powder for thickening, it is the only gumbo in which the roux is not prepared first, and it does not have you cooking the greens for a long time. The
unique flavor comes from the use of so many greens, and the addition of
coarsely chopped greens at the end gives a fresh flavor and pleasing color.
Green gumbo is best served as a main dish, accompanied with an English ale
or a Sauvignon Blanc.

Stock

2 meaty ham hocks
2 to 3 large carrots, unpeeled
  and sliced thick
2 medium-size yellow onions,
  unpeeled and sliced thick

A few whole allspice berries
A few whole black peppercorns
1 to 2 small hot dried red
  peppers

Combine all ingredients in a large, deep stock pot and cover with cold water. Add no salt, for both the ham and the greens are high in sodium. Bring the stock to a boil and simmer until the meat is falling away from the bone. While the stock is cooking, prepare the roux and the greens.

Roux

$^1/_3$ cup vegetable oil
$^1/_3$ cup flour

Combine the oil and flour in a skillet set over low heat and stir constantly until the roux turns from white, to blond, to a rich light brown—very like the color of roasted nuts. Allow the roux to cool and pour off any excess oil.

Greens—choose at least 6, a bunch of each

Collards
Mustard greens
Turnip tops
Beet tops
Watercress
Arugula
Rape
Spinach
Dandelion greens

Swiss chard
Kale
Chicory
Escarole
Sorrel
Parsley
Carrot tops (young leaves only)
Radish tops (young leaves
  only)

Remaining ingredients

1 large boiling potato, peeled
  and cut into small dice
Coarsely ground black pepper

Cayenne
Salt

Select only the freshest and the greenest leaves; because greens have a high water content they wilt easily and are difficult to revive. Wash them thoroughly, and remove and discard any tough stems. Chop two-thirds of the greens finely and the remainder coarsely.

When the stock is finished, strain off and discard the solids, reserving the ham hocks. Thoroughly degrease the stock (if you place it in the refrigerator for a short time, the fat will solidify and be easy to remove). Discard the bone and skin from the hocks and cut the meat into small pieces.

Place the stock in a large soup pot, stir in about half the roux, and simmer over moderate heat until the gumbo begins to thicken slightly. Add more roux, if necessary, to achieve this slight thickening. To the gumbo add the ham, the finely chopped greens, and the potato cubes. Season with a good amount of coarsely ground black pepper and cayenne, and add salt if necessary. Simmer the gumbo for 20 to 30 minutes. At this point, stir in the reserved coarsely chopped greens and continue to simmer for another 15 minutes. You will find that the last-minute addition of greens gives the gumbo a fresher color, a more sprightly flavor, and a pleasing texture.

Serve the gumbo in shallow soup bowls, each of which contains a mound of steamed rice that has been liberally seasoned with thinly sliced scallions and a pinch of thyme. Corn bread makes a traditional and wonderfully satisfying accompaniment.

Fresh Cranberry Bean and Pasta Soup
serves six

Beans, to most Americans, mean either green beans or dried beans, but cranberry beans—which can be found in supermarkets or at farmers' markets—are fresh beans that have pink speckles on the pods and the beans.

Since garlic is readily available at any time of the year, it is not often thought of as having any specific season. But there are, in fact, certain months—August to October—when garlic is freshest. It just so happens, and a happy coincidence it is, that both garlic and fresh cranberry beans are at their peak during late summer, providing the perfect opportunity to try this ambrosial soup.

Season the soup with fresh herbs: summer savory, sage (both classically paired with these beans in Italy) as well as thin ribbons of basil stirred in at the end. The soup is best served on its own with bread; for wine, try a Dolcetta d'Alba.

2 tablespoons fruity olive oil
1 cup panchetta (Italian bacon, cured with spices and rolled), cut into small dice
½ cup carrot, cut into small dice
¾ cup celery, cut into small dice
1½ cups onion, cut into small dice
½ tablespoon fresh sage, chopped
1 tablespoon fresh summer savory, chopped
Freshly ground pepper
4 large cloves garlic, peeled and finely chopped
3 cups fresh cranberry beans, shelled (about 2½ pounds)
6 cups chicken stock
2 cups rotini (small corkscrew-shaped pasta)
6 to 8 large fresh basil leaves
½ cup grated imported Romano cheese

Heat the oil in a heavy soup pot. Add the panchetta and sauté until transparent and just beginning to brown around the edges. Stir in the carrot, celery, and onion; cook over moderate heat for about 5 minutes. Add the sage, savory, pepper and garlic; continue to cook for about 10 minutes more until the vegetable mixture is softened and very aromatic.

Add the shelled beans; stir to mix with the vegetables, and pour in the stock. Bring the soup to the boil, reduce the heat and simmer, partially covered, for about 1 hour, or until the beans are tender. The soup may be made ahead to this point, refrigerated until ready to serve.

Using a skimmer or slotted spoon, remove approximately ½ of the vegetables and beans. Place in a food processor and purée. Stir the purée back into the soup, adding 1½ to 2 cups water if the soup is too thick.

Bring 4 quarts of water to the boil, salt, and add the pasta. Cook until the pasta is still very firm. Drain and add to the soup. Continue to cook the soup at a simmer until the pasta is al dente. At this point, take the basil leaves, place them one on top of another, and roll lengthwise. Using scissors, cut thin shreds of the basil directly into the soup. Stir in the cheese and simmer for another 5 minutes until the cheese has melted. Taste for seasoning, and serve.

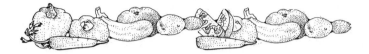

Provençal Bean Soup
serves six to eight

T his is a peasant soup popular in the south of France. It is composed of a number of the freshest seasonal vegetables, which always include at least two or three different varieties of beans: string beans, cranberry or broad beans, shell beans, chickpeas, or whatever. (See preceding recipe in regard to cranberry beans.) The dish is seasoned lightly with saffron and thickened at the table with a basil, garlic, cheese, and olive oil paste that is not for the faint of heart.

I have used a small amount of salt pork to give the vegetables a slightly richer flavor without imparting a definite meat taste to the soup. The fresh shell beans are important: there is a great difference in taste between these and the dried variety. Serve this dish with a light red wine from Provence.

Soup

2 tablespoons olive oil
$\frac{1}{2}$ cup diced salt pork, blanched
2 medium onions, coarsely
    chopped
2 medium red peppers, coarsely
    chopped
2 cups carrots, peeled and
    diced
2 cups potatoes, peeled and
    diced
1 pound (weight before shell-
    ing) fresh cranberry or
    other beans, shelled
3 large very ripe tomatoes,
    peeled, seeded, and coarsely
    chopped

$\frac{1}{4}$ teaspoon saffron
$\frac{1}{8}$ teaspoon salt
Freshly ground pepper to taste
Bouquet garni composed of 2
    bay leaves, 2 sage leaves,
    sprig of thyme
3 small zucchini, diced
$\frac{1}{2}$ pound string beans, cut
    into $\frac{1}{2}$- inch lengths
$\frac{1}{2}$ pound Roman or broad
    beans, cut into $\frac{1}{2}$-inch
    lengths
3 ounces vermicelli, broken
    into 1-inch lengths

Pesto (or pistou)

1 bunch fresh basil (about 3
  cups), cleaned
4 large cloves garlic, peeled
1 teaspoon salt

$^1/_2$ cup fruity olive oil
1 cup freshly grated Parmesan
  or mixture of Parmesan and
  Romano cheeses

In a heavy enameled 6-quart soup pot, place the olive oil and the salt pork cubes; sauté over medium heat until the pork is becoming brown and crisp at the edges. Add the onions and red peppers and sauté for 5 minutes until the onions are golden; then add the carrots, potatoes, and shelled beans. Stir until all the vegetables are coated with fat, then sauté them over low heat for an additional 5 minutes. Add the tomatoes, saffron, salt, pepper, and bouquet garni, and cover all with water. Bring to a boil, reduce the heat, and simmer for about an hour. The soup can be made ahead to this point.

To the simmering soup add the zucchini, string and Roman beans, and vermicelli and continue to cook for 15 minutes more, until the beans and the pasta are both tender. Taste for seasoning, remove bouquet garni, and serve.

While the soup completes this last simmering, prepare the pistou: put into a food processor the basil, garlic cloves, and salt, and blend to a coarse paste. While the machine is running, add the olive oil in a thin stream. Remove the basil paste to a small bowl, stir in the grated cheese, and mix thoroughly. If the pistou is not to be used immediately, cover it completely, placing plastic wrap directly on the surface.

Serve the pistou separately in a bowl, allowing each person to add a tablespoon or more to the individual serving. An additional bowl of grated cheese may also be passed if desired.

Late Summer Bean Soup
serves four to six

A delicious combination of shell and green beans flavored with bits of ham.

2 pounds shell beans
1 small ham shank, about $1\frac{1}{2}$ pounds
1 large onion, peeled and stuck with 4 cloves
Small bunch of celery leaves
2 bay leaves
Salt
3 tablespoons butter
1 cup carrots, peeled and coarsely chopped
1 cup celery, coarsely chopped
2 leeks, cleaned and coarsely chopped
Freshly ground pepper
2 cups green beans, cut into 1-inch lengths
A few sprigs of fresh thyme, minced, or $\frac{1}{4}$ teaspoon dried thyme or summer savory

Remove the beans from their shells and put them into a 5-quart soup pot with the ham shank, onion, celery leaves, bay leaves, and salt. Cover all with water, bring to a boil, reduce heat, and simmer for 1 to $1\frac{1}{2}$ hours, until the beans are tender. Remove the ham and reserve; discard the onion, celery, and bay leaves.

Pour the beans into a sieve over a mixing bowl to catch the cooking liquid; reserve it.

Remove the ham from its bone and chop it into small dice; sauté the meat in the butter for 2 or 3 minutes until it is lightly browned. Add the carrots, celery, leeks, and half of the cooked beans; season with salt and freshly ground pepper and sauté over medium heat for 5 minutes. Add the reserved cooking liquid from the beans (saving about $\frac{1}{2}$ cup) to the vegetables. Cook the soup for about 45 minutes. Purée the remaining reserved beans with the $\frac{1}{2}$ cup of cooking liquid in a blender or food processor. Stir the purée into the soup and add the thyme or summer savory and the green beans. Cook over medium heat for another 10 minutes or until the green beans are just tender. Taste for seasoning and serve.

Oyster Stew
serves two

A good oyster stew is one of the world's most simple dishes to prepare. The only essentials are impeccably fresh oysters, butter, heavy cream, and a bit of milk; all other ingredients, including seasonings, are extraneous.

Matching a wine to a dish as delicately flavored as oyster stew is a ticklish problem, but a Pinot Bianco or Pinot Blanc would go well.

1 to 2 dozen fresh oysters in the shell (choose the smallest)
3 tablespoons butter
1 whole shallot, peeled (optional)
1 cup fresh or canned clam nectar

1 cup milk
$\frac{1}{2}$ cup heavy cream
Dash Worcestershire sauce
Pinch each of celery salt and cayenne
Freshly ground pepper

Shuck the oysters, reserving their juice. Melt the butter in a small enameled saucepan. Add the oysters and their juice and the shallot; cook over low heat until the edges of the oysters curl: 1 or 2 minutes. Add the clam nectar, heavy cream, milk, Worcestershire, celery salt, and cayenne, and bring just to the boil over low heat. Remove the shallot and serve immediately, topping each bowl with freshly ground pepper to taste.

Bayou Bisque
serves six to eight

W hile the combination of crab and yams must at first glance seem odd, it produces an undeniably delicious taste. Live crab is desirable because the difference in flavor and texture is worth the extra effort involved.

This soup is extremely rich: if used as a first course a little cup will suffice for each serving and will make a wonderful prelude to roast beef. Even as a main course, a ladle or two will suffice when accompanied by a simple green salad or vinaigrette. Choose a dry Chenin Blanc to go with the meal.

Court bouillon

1 lemon, sliced
1 small onion, sliced
A few sprigs parsley
6 small dried red peppers

2 bay leaves
A few peppercorns
Salted water sufficient to cover crab

Bisque ingredients

1 ½ pounds yams, boiled whole, skinned, and cubed

1 live crab, approximately 2 pounds

2 tablespoons butter

4 tablespoons finely chopped shallot or onion

1 ½ tablespoons flour

1 ½ cups dry white vermouth or dry white wine

¼ teaspoon sweet paprika

4 cups milk

Pinch of cayenne pepper

Salt

½ pint heavy cream

2 or 3 drops Tabasco

Grating of fresh nutmeg

French bread cut into small cubes and sautéed in butter until brown

In a large stockpot combine the ingredients for the court bouillon: lemon, onion, parsley, red peppers, bay leaves, peppercorns, and salted water; bring to a boil and cook for 30 minutes.

While the stock is flavoring, boil the yams in their skins until done, about 10 minutes. When they are cool enough to handle, peel them and cut them into large pieces. Add the crab to the boiling stock and cook for about 6 minutes to the pound. (If your crab is an especially lively one, you may find it easier to wrap it in cheesecloth and then toss it into the pot.) Remove the crab, allow it to cool, clean it, and reserve the meat; there should be about ½ pound.

Melt the butter in a heavy 5-quart soup pot and sauté the shallot or onion over medium heat until golden; add the flour, blending with a whisk, and cook for 5 minutes. Whisk in the wine, add the paprika, and cook a few minutes more. Add the milk, yams, and cayenne and salt to taste, and bring to a boil, stirring occasionally. Simmer for 5 minutes and drain through a colander, reserving all liquid.

Cool the solids for a few minutes and then purée in a food processor. Blend the purée into the reserved liquid; set over low heat and add the crabmeat and cream, stirring constantly. Simmer the soup for about 10 minutes; season to taste with Tabasco and nutmeg. Serve in soup bowls or large soup plates and top each serving with the croutons.

Mussel Chowder
serves six to eight

With Curried Stuffed Eggs as a first course and broccoli as a vegetable, this hearty, rich soup is a meal in itself. A wine that would go well with it would be a Northwest Chardonnay.

2 pounds mussels, cleaned
1 tablespoon butter
3/4 cup salt pork, blanched and cut into small dice
2 leeks, including 2 inches of the green top, cleaned and finely chopped
3/4 cup celery cut into small dice

1 1/2 cups potatoes, cut into small dice
Pinch cayenne pepper
1/4 teaspoon powdered saffron or 1/4 teaspoon turmeric
1/2 teaspoon salt
3 1/2 cups milk
1/2 pint heavy cream
3 tablespoons parsley, minced

Steam the mussels for not longer than 5 minutes, extract the meat, chop coarsely, and reserve. Reduce the cooking liquid over high heat to 1 cup and reserve it too.

Melt the butter in a heavy 5-quart pot; add the salt pork and sauté until crisp and golden brown. Remove the pork bits, drain on paper towels, and reserve.

In the rendered fat left in the pot, sauté the leeks, celery, and potatoes over high heat for 5 minutes. Sprinkle the vegetables with cayenne, saffron or turmeric, and salt; add the reserved broth, bring to a boil, and cook for a few minutes.

Remove the pot from the heat and add the milk and heavy cream, stirring well. Over low heat cook the chowder for about 1/2 hour till the potatoes are soft; then add the reserved mussels and pork bits and simmer for a few minutes to warm the shellfish and blend the flavors.

Serve immediately, topping each bowl with parsley. If the chowder is to be reheated, do not boil or it will curdle.

Salmon and Sorrel Chowder
serves six

A few dishes are considered quintessentially American: apple pie, fried chicken, corn bread, and chowder, among others. Truth is, each of those can be directly traced to another country. Chowder is actually French. The word *chowder* is a corruption of *chaudière*, a large cauldron used by Breton fishermen as a communal stew pot for their daily catch.

Chowder recipes vary widely, but most cooks agree that among the ingredients there should be pork of some kind, onions, potatoes, and milk. Any sort of fish may be used (although I would avoid those oily, strong-flavored fish such as mackerel) as well as shellfish—all of which produce the most delicious chowders. From here on, it's every cook for herself—or himself, as the case may be.

This salmon and sorrel chowder seemed to come together naturally on a blustery summer day when there was an abundance of that green available in the garden, along with a few fresh salmon steaks in the refrigerator. I was once of the opinion that the flavor of salmon was too overpowering for chowder but this recipe convinced me that that was not so. Sorrel, which is tart and lemony, grows like the proverbial weed, but it has been unavailable in any of our markets, so the cook who likes its flavor will either have to cultivate it in the garden, or cultivate gardeners who grow it. Serve this chowder with a wine like Saucerre or Pouilly Fumé.

2 to 2¹⁄₂ pounds fresh salmon
  fillets or steaks
2 to 3 slices lemon
2 to 3 slices onion
1 bay leaf
6 slices bacon, cut into small
  cubes
3 to 4 small leeks, white part

only, cut into julienne
2 cups raw new potatoes,
  peeled and cut into cubes
2 good-size handfuls of sorrel
  (about 8 to 10 ounces)
3 tablespoons butter
3 to 4 cups unpasteurized
  heavy cream

Pan-poach the salmon: place enough water to cover the fish, along with the lemon, onion, bay leaf, and a little salt and pepper, in a skillet large enough to hold the salmon in a single layer. Bring the liquid to a boil, add the fish, reduce the heat to a simmer and poach the fish until just tender.

Remove and clean away any bones or skin. Flake the fish into bite-size pieces and reserve. Reduce the poaching liquid by half over high heat. Strain and reserve.

In a soup pot, sauté the bacon until brown and crisp. Remove and reserve. To the fat remaining in the pan, add the leeks and the potatoes, and season with salt and pepper. Sauté over moderate heat until slightly softened and evenly coated with the oil; do not brown. Add the poaching liquid and cook until the vegetables are tender.

Meanwhile, trim away the stalks of the sorrel. Cut the leaves cross-wise into thick ribbons. Heat the butter in a small skillet, and add the sorrel. Sauté over low heat only long enough for the sorrel to soften; it has a tendency to "melt" rapidly. Remove from the heat and hold.

Add the heavy cream to the vegetables and heat long enough for it to warm through. Add the salmon and the sorrel with its butter, and heat to warm. Taste, adjusting seasoning if necessary and serve garnished with the bacon bits.

Scallop Chowder
serves six to eight

Serve a Vouvray with this dish—not an inexpensive one!

6 ounces thickly sliced bacon, cut into cubes	1 teaspoon fresh thyme, finely chopped (or $\frac{1}{2}$ teaspoon dried)
2 leeks, including 2 inches of the green tops, cleaned and chopped	Salt and freshly ground pepper
$\frac{1}{2}$ cup celery, cut into small cubes	A few drops Tabasco sauce
	3 cups half-and-half
$1\frac{1}{2}$ cups potatoes, peeled and cut into small cubes	$\frac{3}{4}$ cup very dry white wine
	1 pound fresh bay scallops
	Butter

Fry the bacon cubes until crisp and brown. Remove and reserve the bacon and pour 2 tablespoons of the fat into the soup pot. Place over moderately high heat. Add the leeks, celery, and potatoes. Sauté, stirring so that the vegetables are coated with the fat, for about 5 minutes, taking care not to brown. Sprinkle the vegetables with the seasonings and pour in the half-and-half. Cook the chowder over low heat for about 15 minutes, or until the potatoes are cooked through.

While the chowder is cooking, heat the wine in a skillet. When it has come to a simmer, add the scallops and poach them for 1 minute. Remove with a slotted spoon and add the poaching liquid to the chowder.

When the potatoes in the chowder are cooked, add the scallops and the bacon pieces to it. Taste, and adjust seasoning if necessary. Serve immediately, placing a small knob of butter on top of each serving.

CHAPTER FOUR

FISH AND SHELLFISH

Fish and Cucumber Sauté
serves four

S autéed cucumbers often accompany fish; when they are combined in the same dish the results are uncommonly pleasing. Firm-fleshed fish fillets must be used here; they will keep their shape better than the more delicate varieties. You may substitute heavy cream for half the wine called for, adding it after the wine has reduced a bit in the skillet. Serve with a green salad or, if it is in season, Asparagus with Ginger. The wine should be a Chardonnay with little or no oak.

2 small cucumbers
3 tablespoons butter
$1/4$ cup onion, finely chopped
Salt and freshly ground pepper
2 pounds firm fish fillets (cod, sea bass, snapper, halibut cheeks, striped bass, etc.)

Flour seasoned with salt and pepper
4 tablespoons vegetable oil
$3/4$ to 1 cup dry white wine
Squeeze of lemon juice
1 tablespoon parsley, finely chopped

Peel the cucumbers, cut each in half, and remove the seeds. Cut the flesh into cubes $1/2$ inch square. Melt the butter in a small skillet, add the onion, and sauté 1 to 2 minutes until it begins to take on color. Add the cucumber cubes, sprinkle lightly with salt and pepper, and sauté for about 5 minutes, stirring occasionally, until just tender. Set aside.

Cut the fish fillets into strips about 3 inches wide. Flour the fish lightly, shaking off any excess. Immediately place in a skillet containing the hot vegetable oil. Quickly fry the fish over moderately high heat, about 1 minute to a side, removing each piece as it finishes cooking. When all the fish is done, pour off any excess oil from the pan, taking care not to disturb the browned particles on the bottom. Pour in the wine and stir constantly until it begins to thicken. Add the fish and the cucumber-and-onion mixture to the skillet and mix gently until all is coated with sauce. Season with salt, pepper, and lemon juice to taste, stir in the parsley, and allow to cook for an additional minute or 2 until the fish is heated through. Serve immediately.

Poached Salmon with Black Butter Sauce
serves two

Too often a small cut of fish, such as a fillet or steak, is grilled or broiled because the cook doesn't realize it can be poached. But small cuts are easy to poach in a skillet or sauté pan, and in fact the technique makes it easy to watch for doneness. To deduce the correct cooking time, measure the fish at its thickest point and poach 10 minutes for each inch or fraction thereof; for example, if the fish is $1\frac{1}{2}$ inches thick, cook for 15 minutes. With this poached salmon serve a Northwest Pinot Gris or Beaujolais.

2 fresh salmon steaks	Salt and freshly ground pepper
$\frac{1}{2}$ medium onion, sliced	2 tablespoons butter
$\frac{1}{4}$ teaspoon dried thyme	2 tablespoons balsamic vinegar

Place the salmon steaks in a skillet wide enough to hold them in a single layer. Scatter the onion slices on top; season with the thyme, salt, and pepper. Cover with cold water and bring gently to a boil, with the pan uncovered. Reduce the heat and allow the salmon to poach, at a simmer, for about 10 minutes, or until it is quite firm to the touch. When cooked, remove the fish to a serving platter and drain it thoroughly. Place in a warm oven.

Heat the butter over moderately high heat in a small skillet until it foams and begins to turn brown. Remove the pan at once from the heat and pour the butter over the fish. Place the still-hot pan back on the heat and pour in the vinegar, which will immediately bubble. Reduce this for a few seconds and then pour this, too, over the salmon. Serve immediately.

Aioli Banquet, Northwest Style
serves ten

A typical scene in the south of France on Christmas Eve is a table laden with an immense platter containing a poached salt cod, surrounded by tender rings of squid or octopus, wedges of hard-boiled egg and tomato, and a large variety of steamed or boiled vegetables. There may also be, on another platter, the beef from a pot au feu or a few poached or roasted chickens, and always a shallow dish of snails poached in a court bouillon of white wine and fragrant herbs. And in the center of all, the supreme complement for all this bounty, is a deep bowl piled high with the golden "butter of Provence": aioli.

This is a repast for those who have a deep and abiding passion for that "truffle of the poor," garlic. Aioli is, in essence, a garlic mayonnaise. It is prepared classically with two cloves of garlic for each serving (this quantity may be cut in half as the garlic in France is much milder than our own), egg yolks, and a good, fruity olive oil.

A lighter version of the same sauce can be made by substituting a boiled and rather mealy potato for the egg yolks. The aioli may be prepared in a food processor or blender, but I find it tastes best when done by hand with a mortar and pestle in the traditional manner.

This version of the legendary banquet substitutes a whole poached salmon for the salt cod and Hood Canal shrimp for the squid or octopus, although you may include either or both if you wish. The snails, albeit costly, lend a definite note of festivity to the dish and those who are fond of them already know their marvelous affinity for garlic.

As for the vegetables, the selection listed here includes ones most often used in this dish, but you may substitute whatever you think suitable. At the end of this feast, you may wish to serve fresh sprigs of mint or parsley or squares of dark chocolate to those guests who fear dragon breath. Those who want wine with this banquet might try a White Graves or a Sauvignon Blanc.

Aioli sauce

8 to 10 cloves of garlic, peeled
3 egg yolks at room temperature
Pinch salt
2¼ cups fruity olive oil (or a

mixture of half olive oil and
   half corn oil)
Lemon juice
Freshly ground pepper

Aioli garni

1 pound dried chickpeas
6-pound whole salmon, poached
1 bay leaf
1 large onion, peeled and stuck
   with 3 cloves
2 pounds French-style carrots,
   peeled
2 pounds small Finnish potatoes, not peeled
2½ pounds green beans, cut
   into 3-inch lengths
2 small cauliflowers, divided
   into flowerets
1 cup dry white vermouth or
   dry white wine

½ teaspoon fennel seeds
A few sprigs fresh thyme or ½
   teaspoon dried thyme
1 bay leaf
3 dozen canned snails, rinsed
   thoroughly under cold water
2 fennel bulbs or 1 head celery,
   cut into thick strips
5 hard-boiled eggs, peeled and
   cut in half lengthwise
5 tomatoes, cut into wedges
2 to 3 pounds Hood Canal
   shrimp or other shrimp,
   cooked
Parsley and lemon wedges

The night before, cover the chickpeas with cold water and allow to stand at room temperature.

The next day, prepare the aioli first. Put the garlic cloves through a press into a large mortar. Add the egg yolks and beat them into the garlic with the pestle or a wire whisk until they are a light yellow in color. Add the pinch of salt and begin to beat in the oil, at first adding it very slowly, drop by drop. This will take longer than a plain mayonnaise sauce because the garlic thins out the yolks. When half the oil has been added and the sauce is quite thick, add the lemon juice to taste and continue to beat in the remaining oil. When all the oil has been added, taste for seasoning, adding a bit more salt or lemon juice if necessary and a grinding or 2 of black pepper. Cover the sauce and refrigerate.

About 3 or 4 hours before serving, poach the salmon (see Bayou Bisque) and allow it to cool in the court bouillon.

Two hours before serving, drain the chickpeas, place them in a large pot, and add the bay leaf, the onion stuck with cloves, and some salt. Cover them with water, bring them to a boil, reduce the heat, and simmer for about $1\frac{1}{2}$ hours, until tender.

The simplest way of preparing the vegetables is to first steam the carrots for 10 to 15 minutes; then add the potatoes to the same pot and continue to steam for another 10 minutes, depending on the size of your potatoes. The green beans and cauliflower should each be boiled separately in their own pots until tender.

While the vegetables are cooking, combine the white vermouth or wine with the fennel seeds, thyme, and bay leaf in a saucepan. Add a quart of water and bring this court bouillon to a boil; add the snails, reduce the heat, and simmer them for about 15 minutes, until tender.

Place the salmon on a large serving platter; remove the skin if you wish. Surround the fish with the potatoes, carrots, and cauliflower, and garnish the platter with the tomato and egg wedges. Place the chickpeas in a bowl and surround them with the green beans, garnishing with parsley.

Place the drained snails in a shallow serving dish and surround with the fennel or celery strips; garnish with parsley. Place the shrimps, still in their shells, on a serving platter and garnish with parsley and lemon wedges. Mound the aioli in the mortar or a deep serving bowl and place in the center of the table. Serve at once.

Kulebiaka
serves six to eight

K ulebiaka, one of the world's most elegant dishes, has its origins in the peasant kitchen. It began as a coarse mixture of salmon, rice, mushrooms, and eggs (sometimes cabbage, onions, and eggs) encased in a breadlike pastry. The French took this dish some degrees higher by adding refinements to the filling and using a brioche dough for the casing. My version uses a cream-cheese pastry, which has a rich and flaky texture somewhat like puff paste. This is a tricky pastry to handle; it must be kept chilled and worked quickly or it becomes sticky.

I have suggested adding the fillings in layers, giving a more pleasing visual effect and allowing each ingredient to stand on its own while subtly blending with the others.

If there is any pastry left over, it can be frozen and used to make miniature pirozhkis, small turnovers filled with ground lamb or beef, minced onion, and minced hard-boiled egg and seasoned with a bit of curry powder.

This is an ideal dish for spring or summer picnics, served with a semi-dry Northwest Riesling.

Pastry

12 ounces cream cheese
3 sticks sweet butter ($^3/_4$ pound)

3 cups unbleached white flour
$^1/_2$ teaspoon salt

Filling

Salmon mixture

2-pound piece of fresh salmon, poached
Juice of 1 lemon

2 tablespoons capers, coarsely chopped

Duxelles mixture

3 tablespoons butter
1 cup onions, peeled and finely chopped
1 clove garlic, peeled and finely chopped
Pinch of sugar
$^1/_2$ pound mushrooms, cleaned and finely chopped

2 tablespoons flour
1 cup reserved poaching liquid from the salmon
1 tablespoon lemon juice
2 tablespoons fresh dill, finely chopped
Salt and freshly ground pepper

Rice mixture

¹/₂ cup rice, cooked
1 tablespoon butter
1 tablespoon fresh dill, finely

chopped
Salt and a dash of cayenne
  pepper to taste

Topping

2 hard-boiled eggs, shelled and
  coarsely chopped
1 tablespoon melted butter

mixed with
¹/₄ teaspoon mild curry
  powder

Egg glaze for pastry

1 egg yolk mixed with
1 teaspoon water

The night before, make the pastry. Mix together until creamy the thoroughly chilled butter and cream cheese (both cut into chunks), using a pastry blender or an electric mixer. Sift in the flour and salt and work it in with a pastry blender until a dough is formed. Divide the dough into 2 parts, 1 slightly larger than the other, sprinkle with a little flour, wrap in waxed paper, and chill overnight in the refrigerator.

The next day, poach the salmon (see method for small cuts in Poached Salmon with Black Butter Sauce), reserving 1 cup of the poaching liquid for later use. Skin and carefully bone the fish and break into large flakes. Mix the salmon with the lemon juice and capers and set aside.

Now prepare the duxelles mixture. Melt the 3 tablespoons butter in a skillet, add the onions and garlic, sprinkle with a pinch of sugar, and sauté over medium heat for about 5 minutes. Add the mushrooms, turn the heat to high, and sauté until all excess moisture is drawn off the mushrooms, taking care not to burn the mixture.

Remove from heat and add the flour, mixing it well into the mushrooms, then add ¹/₂ cup of the reserved poaching liquid. Place the skillet back over medium heat and stir until the mixture becomes thick. (The consistency should be a loose paste; if it is too thick, add a bit more broth.) Add the lemon juice, dill, salt, and pepper and mix well; set aside.

Allow the cooked rice to cool slightly. Mix in the butter, dill, salt, and cayenne and mix well. Reserve.

While you prepare other things, let the pastry sit at room temperature for about 15 minutes. Preheat the oven to 400 degrees. Roll out the smaller piece of dough, using a floured pastry cloth and floured rolling pin cover. (This pastry tends to become extremely sticky if handled in any other manner.) The dough should be about $\frac{1}{8}$ inch thick when rolled out. You may cut it into any shape desired: I usually make it into a circle about 11 inches in diameter. Place the dough directly on a greased rimless baking sheet.

Spread the rice mixture evenly over the circle to within $\frac{1}{2}$ inch of the edge. Over the rice spread half of the duxelles mixture, using a wet metal spatula to facilitate spreading. Cover this with all of the salmon, mounding it slightly in the center. Cover with the remaining half of the duxelles. Top this with the chopped eggs and sprinkle with the curry butter.

Roll out the remaining pastry, using the same methods, and cut into a 13-inch circle. Moisten the exposed $\frac{1}{2}$-inch rim of the base with a little water and place the 13-inch circle on top, pinching the upper and lower layers together with your fingers or a fork to seal. Trim off any excess. Using a pastry brush, paint the dough with the egg glaze. This will allow the pie to turn a lovely golden brown when baked. Cut a small circle out of the top of the pie and insert an inverted pastry tip to act as a funnel.

Bake about 25 minutes or until golden brown. Remove from the oven and let cool for 45 minutes before serving. The entire pie may be assembled and baked earlier in the day and lightly warmed in a 300-degree oven for 20 minutes before serving.

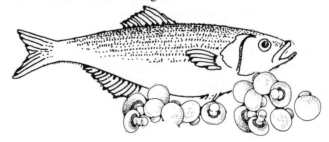

Matelote of Sturgeon
serves four

A specialty of the province of Touraine in France, this dish, usually prepared with eel, is sauced with a rich blend of red wine, cognac, small white onions, and mushrooms. The Columbia River sturgeon, with its dense texture and meaty flavor, responds beautifully to the same treatment. Serve this with Asparagus with Sauce Maltaise as a first course or side dish; the flavors complement each other beautifully. For wine, I suggest a red Bandol.

$1\frac{1}{2}$ pounds fresh Columbia
    sturgeon
3 tablespoons butter
1 teaspoon vegetable oil
$\frac{1}{4}$ cup blanched salt pork, cut
    into small dice
$1\frac{1}{2}$ cups whole, tiny white
    onions, boiled for 5 min-
    utes, skins removed
$\frac{1}{2}$ pound mushrooms, thickly
    sliced
Squeeze of lemon juice

Salt and freshly ground pepper
Seasoned flour for dredging
$\frac{3}{4}$ cup onion, finely chopped
1 large clove garlic, finely
    chopped
$\frac{1}{4}$ cup cognac or other good
    brandy
$1\frac{1}{4}$ cups young earthy red
    wine
$\frac{1}{4}$ cup parsley, finely chopped
Toasted slices of French bread

Preheat the oven to 325 degrees.

Remove skin from the sturgeon and discard. Cut the flesh from the bones and slice it against the grain into 2-by-$\frac{1}{2}$-inch rectangles. Set aside.

In a large heavy skillet melt 2 tablespoons of the butter with the oil, add the salt-pork cubes, and sauté over moderately high heat until they have browned and rendered their fat. Remove them to paper towels to drain.

To the rendered fat, add the parboiled small white onions and brown on all sides, shaking the skillet occasionally so they do not stick. Remove them when done and place in a shallow ovenproof container.

To the same skillet add the mushrooms, seasoning lightly with salt, pepper, and a little lemon juice; sauté over high heat for about 3 minutes until golden brown. Remove and place in the container with the onions.

Assemble the pieces of fish and a shallow bowl of flour (seasoned with salt and pepper) for dredging near the stove. Add the remaining tablespoon of butter to the fat in the skillet and set over moderately high heat. When the fat is hot, coat each piece of fish lightly with flour and put it in the skillet to brown on all sides. When the fish is browned, scatter the chopped onion and garlic over it, reduce the heat, and cook for about 3 minutes, stirring occasionally. Pour cognac over the fish and allow it to heat for a minute; then flame. When the flames have subsided, immediately add the wine and cook for a few minutes more. Remove the fish and place in the dish containing the onions and mushrooms; scatter the salt-pork bits over all.

Reduce the sauce over moderate heat for about 10 minutes, adding the parsley during the last 5 minutes. Add salt, pepper, and a bit of lemon juice to taste. Pour the sauce over the fish, onions, and mushrooms and place in the oven just long enough to heat through. Serve over thin slices of toasted French bread.

Trout Grilled with Fennel Butter
serves four

The trout is wrapped in foil to keep in the succulent juices, whether the fish is grilled outdoors or baked in the oven. Fennel butter also complements other fish: salmon, snapper, bass, etc. Serve with Steamed Potatoes in Parsley Sauce or Green Beans Sautéed with Lemon or Peppers and a dry Riesling or Pinot Gris.

2 teaspoons fennel seeds
1 large clove garlic, finely
    chopped
Pinch salt
1 tablespoon lemon juice

Pinch cayenne pepper or dash
    Tabasco
Freshly ground pepper
4 tablespoons butter, softened
4 fresh trout

First prepare the fennel butter: place in a mortar the fennel seeds, garlic, and salt, and grind into a coarse paste. Add the seasonings and the butter and blend well.

Stuff the cavity of each fish with one quarter of the fennel butter. Tightly wrap each trout in a double layer of foil. When the coals are red-hot, place the trout on the grill and cook for 8 or 9 minutes per side. Remove from the heat when done and serve in the foil.

Variation: This can also be baked. In an oven preheated to 325 degrees, bake the wrapped trout for about 30 minutes, or until done

Fennel-Butter Sauce for Fish
serves four

A butter sauce to which has been added chopped fennel leaves and a dash of Pernod. It is wonderful on poached or grilled fish.

6 tablespoons butter	finely and tightly packed
¼ cup fennel leaves, chopped	1 to 2 teaspoons Pernod

Melt the butter slowly in a small saucepan or skillet, add the fennel leaves and the Pernod, stir, and serve immediately.

Bouillabaisse Northwest Style
serves six to eight

T here are many arguments against attempting to make a true bouilla-baisse outside the south of France, but there is no reason we can't produce a superb fish soup from local products. The stock for this version is made from crayfish and ocean perch (though any such inexpensive, light-flavored fish would do as well) along with a selection of aromatic vege-tables. When fresh fish is not available at reasonable prices for stock-making, frozen will do quite well; the main thing is that the stock be fragrant and highly seasoned. The toasted rounds of French bread and the sauce rouille (made, for the sake of lightness, with a bread rather than an egg-yolk base) are necessary accompaniments. This pungent bouillabaisse is nearly a meal in itself; you might begin with an antipasto of red peppers and feta cheese. Serve with a Sauvignon Blanc or a Southern French red wine.

Stock

4 tablespoons olive oil
1 ½ medium onions, peeled and coarsely chopped
1 small fennel bulb, coarsely chopped (substitute 2 or 3 stalks of celery, if unavailable)
3 cloves garlic, peeled but left whole
2 or 3 small leeks, cleaned and coarsely chopped
1 carrot, peeled and coarsely chopped
1 small boiling potato, peeled and coarsely chopped
Salt and freshly ground pepper

2- to 2½-pound whole ocean perch, cleaned and cut into large chunks (including bones and head)
1 pound crayfish in the shell
4 large ripe tomatoes, peeled, seeded, and coarsely chopped
2 cups dry white wine or dry white vermouth
½ teaspoon fennel seeds, bruised with a mortar and pestle
3-inch piece of dried orange peel
2 bay leaves
1 teaspoon saffron threads

Sauce rouille

2 small dried hot red peppers (each about 2 inches long)
1 small piece pimento (optional)
1 piece of French bread, about 2 inches thick

6 large cloves garlic, peeled and put through a press
3 tablespoons olive oil
½ cup fish stock
Salt

Bouillabaisse

1 ½ pounds Columbia River sturgeon, trimmed of skin and bones, cut into 2-inch cubes
1 ½ pounds sea bass fillets, cut into 2-inch cubes
1 ½ pounds halibut cheeks (or cod fillets) cut into 2-inch cubes

12 to 14 small shrimp, peeled if you wish
1 ½ pounds mussels, scrubbed, with beards removed
Toasted rounds of French bread

To make the stock, heat the olive oil in a heavy 6- to 8-quart enameled soup pot. Add the onions, fennel or celery, garlic, leeks, carrot, and potato and sprinkle lightly with salt and pepper. Sauté over medium heat for about 10 minutes, stirring occasionally to coat the vegetables with oil.

Add the pieces of perch and the crayfish and sauté for another 10 minutes; then add the tomatoes, white wine or vermouth, fennel seeds, orange peel, and bay leaves. Add enough water to cover all, bring to a boil, reduce heat, cover, and simmer for about an hour.

With a slotted spoon skim off about 2 cups of the vegetables—removing any bones or crayfish—and purée the vegetables in a food processor. Set them aside. Pour the rest of the stock through a fine sieve; discard the remaining vegetables, bones, and crayfish. Rinse the pot with hot water, return the stock to the pot, keeping aside 1 tablespoonful, and mix in the puréed vegetables. Add the saffron to the set-aside tablespoon of stock and allow to steep for 10 minutes; add this to the pot. The bouillabaisse may be made ahead to this point.

Make the rouille sauce: put the dried red peppers into a small Pyrex bowl and cover with boiling water; allow them to soften for 5 minutes. Drain and place in a blender or food processor with the pimento. Soak the bread briefly in the fish stock, squeeze out excess moisture, and add to the peppers along with the pressed garlic. Blend for a few seconds until a paste is produced. Add the olive oil slowly with the blender at low speed; remove to a serving bowl and stir in $\frac{1}{2}$ cup of fish stock; taste for seasoning and add salt if necessary.

Now make the bouillabaisse. Bring the stock pot to a boil, taste and correct seasoning if necessary; add the sturgeon, sea bass, halibut cheeks (or cod), and simmer for about 5 minutes; then add the shrimp and mussels and cook for another 5 to 8 minutes until all the fish and shellfish are tender. Serve immediately in large shallow bowls over rounds of toasted French bread topped with a spread of sauce rouille.

Jambalaya
serves six

Jambalaya is a lovely one-dish meal, great for entertaining. Serve with a
Northwest Semillon.

1½ tablespoons butter
1 pound mild Italian sausage
   (casings removed), coarsely
   chopped
1½ cups onion, finely chopped
2 medium green peppers,
   seeded and cut into julienne
2 cups lightly seasoned chicken
   or fish stock
1½ cups short-grain white
   rice (Italian rice is excellent)
28-ounce can plum tomatoes,
   thoroughly drained and
   coarsely chopped
2 cloves garlic, minced

½ teaspoon dried thyme
Small pinch powdered cloves
½ teaspoon chili powder
Small pinch cayenne pepper or
   2 to 3 drops Tabasco
Small pinch allspice
Small pinch powdered saffron
   (optional)
Salt and freshly ground pepper
¾ pound cleaned crabmeat
2 dozen medium oysters,
   shucked (reserve liquor and
   add to stock)
Garnish: lemon wedges

In a heavy casserole (I prefer cast iron with enamel) heat the butter, add
the sausage meat, and cook over medium heat till all fat is rendered. There
should be about 3 tablespoons; if there is more, remove it and discard.

Add the onions and green pepper and sauté over medium heat till the
onions are limp and golden.

Heat the stock in a saucepan. While it is warming, add the rice to the
onions and green pepper and cook it, stirring constantly, until it turns
lightly brown—about 5 minutes. This coats each grain of rice with the fat,
sealing it so that it keeps its shape and texture during the cooking, as in the
technique used in preparing Italian risotto.

Add the tomatoes, garlic, spices, salt, and pepper to taste and cook for a
few minutes until the excess liquid from the tomatoes is absorbed into the
rice.

Add the stock, $\frac{1}{2}$ cup at a time, stirring lightly with a fork. Cover the casserole partially and lower the heat to simmer. The rice must totally absorb each addition of stock before any more is added, and a close watch must be kept so that it does not dry out and stick to the bottom of the pot. The dish can be done ahead to this point.

When the rice is done, taste for seasoning; then add the crab and oysters, cover, and cook over medium heat till the crabmeat is warmed through and the edges of the oysters have just begun to curl—approximately 10 minutes. Serve immediately, garnished with lemon wedges.

Paella
serves eight to ten

T he technique used in this recipe for cooking the rice is similar to that used for risotto. In a departure from tradition, the tomatoes are omitted and the dish is seasoned with paprika and Pernod, along with the traditional saffron. Serve with a green salad on the side. For wine, serve a Spanish white or a light Spanish red, perhaps from Rueda.

$\frac{1}{4}$ pound salt pork or bacon (blanched), cut into small dice
1 tablespoon olive oil
$1\frac{1}{2}$ pounds shrimp, shelled
$1\frac{1}{2}$ pounds scallops (if sea scallops are used, halve them)
8 hot Italian sausage links, cut into $\frac{1}{2}$-inch rounds
10 chicken drumsticks
1 medium onion, coarsely chopped
3 cups Italian (short-grain) rice
3 cloves garlic, finely chopped

$\frac{1}{4}$ teaspoon powdered saffron
$\frac{1}{4}$ teaspoon sweet paprika
Pinch of cayenne pepper or dash of Tabasco
$\frac{1}{2}$ cup dry white vermouth
5 to 6 cups chicken broth
$\frac{1}{2}$ cup cooked chickpeas
15 small steamer clams, well cleaned
15 fresh mussels, cleaned and bearded
1 to $1\frac{1}{2}$ tablespoons Pernod
$\frac{1}{4}$ cup parsley, finely chopped
2 tablespoons whole capers
Lemon slices

Place the salt pork or bacon with the olive oil in a heavy 6-quart enameled soup pot or paella pan. Sauté over high heat till the pork is crisp and the fat is rendered. Remove the pork bits and reserve them. In the remaining fat, sauté the shrimp for about 3 minutes over medium heat until just done; remove and reserve them. Do the same with the scallops, then the sausage and the chicken, adding more olive oil if needed.

In the remaining fat, sauté the onion for about 5 minutes. Add the reserved salt pork or bacon, rice, garlic, saffron, paprika, and cayenne or Tabasco; stir with a wooden spoon until the grains of rice are coated with the oil and spices and have become slightly opaque.

Pour in the vermouth and 1 cup of the chicken broth and cook over medium heat until the liquid is absorbed, stirring all the while with a fork. Add the remaining broth as needed, 1 cup at a time, stirring frequently until the rice is almost cooked. The dish may be done ahead to this point.

Preheat the oven to 350 degrees.

Gently mix the cooked and reserved shrimp, scallops, sausage, and chicken with the chickpeas, steamer clams, mussels, and Pernod into the cooked rice. Cover the pot with a lid (if using a paella pan, cover with foil) and place in the oven for 10 to 15 minutes or until the shellfish open. Remove from the oven and sprinkle the top with parsley and capers. Rim the dish with lemon slices.

Crayfish Boil
serves four

It is difficult to say just exactly how many crayfish constitute one serving; a good rule of thumb is to serve a dozen for each person and, if your guests are true crayfish fanciers, to add another dozen or two "for the pot." Serve with Caesar Salad with mint. This dish is great with Orvietos or Fumé Blancs.

4 lemons, cut in quarters
2 large onions, peeled but left
   whole, each stuck with 3
   cloves

2 stalks celery, coarsely chopped
4 dried hot red chilies, left
   whole
6 cloves garlic, left whole with

skins intact
6 bay leaves, crumbled
2 tablespoons whole allspice
$\frac{1}{4}$ cup mustard seeds
1 small handful fresh thyme

(substitute parsley if
unavailable)
$\frac{1}{4}$ cup sea salt
48 live crayfish

In a 12- to 14-quart stockpot combine all ingredients except the crayfish and cover with 8 quarts of water. Bring to a boil over high heat, cover tightly, reduce heat to a simmer, and cook for 45 minutes.

While this is cooking, rinse the crayfish in plenty of cold water—this may be done in batches in your kitchen sink. When the court bouillon is ready, add the crayfish—about 2 dozen at a time—and boil them uncovered for about 5 minutes. Remove with a large skimmer and repeat the procedure with the remaining crayfish.

Place all the crayfish in a large colander to drain. When they are cool enough to handle, arrange them on your largest platter, claws facing out, and allow to cool a bit longer. Garnish the platter with slices of lemon and parsley sprigs.

Crayfish

I once thought that crayfish could only be found in the bayous and marshlands of Louisiana. Not so: there are crayfish in the lakes and rivers of Wisconsin, Minnesota, Oregon, Washington, and many other places. There isn't much meat on them, since they are usually three to six inches long, but what there is is succulent and sweeter-tasting than lobster. They are obtainable at Seattle's Pike Place Market for only a short time, mid-July to September or October, depending on the vagaries of the weather or the fishermen.

These delicious morsels are almost as versatile as eggplant and can be used in many ways: in gumbos or jambalayas, mixed with other seafood in a salad, in paella, and in cioppino or other fish stews. One of the tastiest methods of preparation is simply to cook them as a spicy court bouillon, better known as a Louisiana Boil. It's a pity these wonderful crustacea have been almost ignored by local restaurants and cooks; they are one of the chief splendors of the Northwest summer.

Steamed Mussels in Their Broth

Mussels must be well cleaned before they are used. With a sturdy, short-bladed knife, remove the barnacles that often encrust mussels, then wash the mussels under cold running water, rubbing the shells together with your hands. Pull off the "beards" with your fingers or using a knife. While removing the beards, squeeze each mussel; if it does not close its shells tightly, discard it.

Put the mussels into a large bowl, cover with water, and add a bit of sea salt. Sprinkle the top of the water with a handful of corn meal or flour and allow to stand a few hours or overnight. This last process may be omitted when using cultivated mussels.

Serve these mussels with a delicate wine like a Muscadet.

3 slices lemon	1 1/2 cups water
2 thick slices onion	1/4 cup dry white vermouth
1 bay leaf	A few peppercorns
Sprig each of thyme and parsley	Pinch of salt
	2 pounds mussels

In a pot large enough to hold all the mussels, put the lemon, onion, bay leaf, thyme, parsley, water, vermouth, peppercorns, and salt. Bring to a boil and cook a few minutes. Add the cleaned mussels, cover, and steam over high heat for 5 to 8 minutes, until all the mussels have opened. Remove the mussels from the pot, put into soup plates, and strain broth over all.

Octopus in Tomato Sauce
serves four

This is delicious served with steamed rice and a green salad; it is also very good chilled, served in individual portions as a first course. Purchase cooked octopus at your fish market; if it is not as tender as you'd like, simmer it in water to which you've added a dash of vinegar. A Bardolino or young Chianti would go well with this dish.

4 tablespoons olive oil
2 pounds cooked octopus, cut
   into $1/4$-inch slices
1 cup onion, finely chopped
2 cloves garlic, peeled
1 teaspoon grated lemon rind
4 sprigs parsley
2 cups tomatoes, peeled,

   seeded, and coarsely chopped
Pinch sugar
Pinch allspice
Salt and freshly ground pepper
$1/4$ cup dry white vermouth or
   dry white wine
2 tablespoons Pernod

Heat the olive oil in a heavy 12-inch skillet; add the octopus and sauté quickly over moderately high heat until lightly browned. Remove and reserve. To the remaining oil, add the onion and sauté for 5 minutes.

While the onion is cooking, finely chop together the garlic, lemon rind, and parsley. Add this to the skillet and cook together with the onions for 1 to 2 minutes; do not brown. Add the tomatoes, sugar, allspice, salt, pepper, and vermouth.

Raise the heat and reduce the sauce for 5 minutes. Lower the heat to simmer and cook for an additional 30 minutes, adding the Pernod during the last 5 minutes. Taste the sauce and adjust the seasoning, if necessary; add the octopus. Cook only long enough to heat the octopus through.

Curried Scallops
serves four

The flavor of this quickly prepared dish depends on the quality of the seasonings used. Curry paste gives a richer and more savory taste than dry powder. Fresh ginger root is specified; an excellent way to keep fresh ginger handy is to wrap the whole unpeeled root tightly in foil and keep it in the freezer. Then, when it is needed, simply take it out and grate what you need directly into the dish you are preparing. Black mustard seed is found in shops specializing in East Indian foods; do not substitute the larger yellow mustard seed.

This is a mild curry; serve it with steamed rice mixed with butter and a little lime juice. Grated Carrot Salad makes a refreshing side dish. Try a German Kabinett from the Rhinegau as an accompanying wine.

3 1/2 tablespoons vegetable oil

1/2 teaspoon black mustard
   seeds

1 1/4 cups onion, finely chopped

1 teaspoon curry paste (or to
   taste)

1 1/2 tablespoons flour

1 cup clam juice or lightly
   seasoned fish stock

1/2 cup heavy cream

1 teaspoon fresh ginger root,
   grated

1 1/2 pounds scallops (if sea
   scallops are used, cut each in
   half)

2 tablespoons sour cream or
   unflavored yogurt

Pinch of sugar (optional)

Heat 2 tablespoons of oil in a heavy 10-inch skillet; add the black mustard seeds and stir to coat them with oil. Immediately add the onion and sauté over medium heat for about 5 minutes. Add the curry paste, blending it with the onion, and cook for 1 to 2 minutes; then add the flour, stir well, and cook over low heat for 5 minutes.

When the flour has browned lightly, add the clam juice or fish stock and stir till the liquid thickens. Pour in the heavy cream, add the ginger, and cook the sauce over low heat for about 10 minutes.

While the sauce is cooking, heat the remaining 1 1/2 tablespoons oil in a skillet over high heat; add the scallops and sauté them briefly, 3 to 4 minutes—only long enough to just cook them. Add the scallops with their pan juices to the curry sauce, stir in the sour cream or yogurt, taste for seasoning, and add a small pinch of sugar if desired. Serve at once.

Scallops with Cream
serves four

T his recipe is based loosely on an old French formula for mussels steamed in their shells with shallots, garlic, and a drop of wine. When the mussels are tender, they are removed to a serving platter and kept warm. The broth remaining in the pot is enriched with a dollop of heavy cream and just the smallest amount of curry powder. This is reduced until it thickens sufficiently to coat the ever-handy wooden spoon, and then is poured over the shellfish.

The dish is garnished with freshly toasted bread crumbs and parsley. The use of bread crumbs adorning a cream sauce seems to have fallen out of use in recent French cookery. What a shame, for their crispness lends interest to the closely related textures of the cream and the fish.

The curry powder, only the smallest pinch, serves to color the sauce a pale, golden yellow. Its flavor should be unobtrusive; if you can taste it in the sauce, you've added too much. I've specified using unpasteurized cream because of its superb thickening qualities and, of course, its fine flavor. Serve with a dry French Colombard or Chenin Blanc.

1 small hard roll
5 tablespoons butter
1 $\frac{1}{2}$ pounds fresh bay scallops
Salt and freshly ground pepper
2 tablespoons shallots, finely
   chopped
1 large clove garlic, finely
   chopped
Tiny pinch of curry powder or
   powdered saffron
$\frac{1}{2}$ cup heavy cream, preferably
   unpasteurized
Garnish: chopped parsley

With the aid of a food processor or blender, chop the roll into coarse crumbs. Place them in a shallow baking pan and toast in a 250-degree oven for 20 minutes. Remove from oven, melt 2 $\frac{1}{2}$ tablespoons butter in a small skillet and add crumbs. Sauté over medium heat until the crumbs have absorbed all the butter and are a rich, golden brown. Reserve.

Heat the remaining butter in a skillet just large enough to hold the scallops in a single layer. When the butter is hot, add the scallops and sauté over moderately high heat for no more than 2 minutes. Season with salt and pepper, remove the scallops with a slotted spoon, and reserve. To the oil remaining in the pan, add the shallots and garlic. Cook for about 1 minute, taking care not to brown. Add the curry powder, stir, and continue to cook for 1 minute more. Pour in the cream and reduce the sauce over high heat until it has thickened considerably. Adjust seasoning if necessary, then add scallops and leave them over the heat just long enough to warm through.

Pour the scallops and their sauce into a serving dish and scatter enough bread crumbs on the top to cover the surface. Lightly sprinkle the parsley over all and serve immediately.

Scallops with Cucumbers and Coriander
serves four

This is actually a variation of the Fish and Cucumber Sauté, which proves how easy it is to completely change a recipe by using different (and in this case, much more assertive) seasonings. Wonderful with Sicilian Orange Salad. Serve with a Northwest Semillon.

2 small cucumbers
4 tablespoons vegetable oil
Salt and freshly ground pepper
1½ pounds sea scallops
½ cup onion, finely chopped

2 cloves garlic, finely chopped
4 tablespoons fresh coriander, finely chopped
Juice of 2 large limes
Dash Tabasco sauce

Peel the cucumbers, cut each in half, and remove the seeds. Cut the flesh into cubes about ½ inch square. Heat a tablespoon of the oil in a skillet, add the cucumber, season with salt and pepper, and sauté for a few minutes over moderate heat. The cucumbers should be just tender and offer no resistance when pierced with a knife. Remove and reserve.

Dry the scallops thoroughly. Heat the remaining oil in the skillet over high heat. Quickly brown the scallops, cooking about a bare minute to a side, and remove when done. Pour off all but about 1 tablespoon of oil. Over moderate heat sauté the onion and garlic until soft but not brown. Add the coriander, lime juice, and season with a few drops of Tabasco. Stir in the cucumbers and the scallops, cooking only long enough to heat all the ingredients through. Taste for seasoning and serve immediately with buttered rice seasoned with grated lime rind and lime juice.

Squid and Fish Stew Mediterranean Style
serves six

Served with an antipasto of roasted red and green peppers with feta cheese, good crusty bread, and a green salad, this makes a real Mediterranean feast. Serve with a light red Dolcetto wine or a dry Pinot Noir Blanc.

3 pounds squid, cleaned (see
    Squid Salad)
4 tablespoons olive oil
3 tablespoons onion, finely
    chopped
3 tablespoons fennel, finely
    chopped
2 cloves garlic, minced
$^1/_4$ cup parsley, finely chopped
1 cup dry white vermouth
2 cups Italian plum tomatoes,
    drained and coarsely chopped

Salt and freshly ground pepper
Small pinch hot red pepper
    flakes
$^1/_2$ teaspoon dried oregano
Pinch powdered saffron or
    curry powder (optional)
2 pounds firm-fleshed fish
    fillets: red snapper, cod,
    halibut, or striped bass
Thick toasted slices of French
    or Italian bread

Cut the bodies of the squid into rings, 1 inch wide; cut the tentacles in half if they are large. Reserve.

Heat the olive oil in a 4-quart soup pot; add the onion and fennel and sauté over medium heat until the onion is golden. Add the garlic, parsley, and vermouth, raise the heat to high, and reduce the mixture for about 4 minutes. Add the tomatoes, squid, seasoning, and spices; cover, reduce the heat, and simmer for about 30 minutes, or until the squid is tender.

Add the fish fillets, cut into bite-size pieces; cover again and simmer for about 10 minutes, until the fish is just flaky. Taste for seasoning and serve over thick, toasted slices of Italian or French bread.

CHAPTER FIVE

POULTRY & RABBIT

Roast Chicken Stuffed with Chanterelles
serves four

D o not substitute canned imported chanterelles for the fresh ones; they are overpriced and have a distinct metallic taste. Serve with Watercress and Snow Pea Salad or with Leeks Vinaigrette. For wine try a French Chablis.

4 tablespoons butter
1 tablespoon oil
1 cup French bread cut into
   1- inch cubes
1 pound fresh chanterelle
   mushrooms, cleaned and
   coarsely chopped
Squeeze of lemon juice

Salt and freshly ground pepper
2 tablespoons dry white
   vermouth
$\frac{1}{2}$ cup onion, finely minced
3 to 4 sprigs fresh thyme or
   parsley, finely minced
1 whole chicken ($2\frac{1}{2}$ to 3
   pounds)

Preheat the oven to 450 degrees.

Heat 1 tablespoon butter with the oil in a heavy skillet; add the bread cubes and sauté them over medium heat on all sides until they have turned crisp and golden. Remove from pan and allow to drain on paper towels.

Heat 2 tablespoons butter in a large skillet; add the chanterelles, lemon juice, salt, and pepper and sauté over high heat until the mushrooms have released their juice and have softened, 3 to 4 minutes. Remove the mushrooms with a slotted spoon and set them aside. Add the vermouth to the liquid left in the pan and reduce over high heat to $\frac{1}{2}$ cup. Reserve. Heat 1 tablespoon butter in a small skillet and sauté the minced onion in it until soft and golden, 5 minutes.

Put the reserved croutons, mushrooms, onions, and thyme in a mixing bowl and mix gently; add 1 tablespoon of the reserved pan juices and check the seasoning. Use this mixture to stuff the cavity of the chicken, sewing the opening closed.

Truss the chicken tightly, place it in a shallow roasting pan, and paint it lightly with the pan juices. Roast the chicken for about 1 hour, basting every 15 minutes with the remaining pan juices. Remove from oven when the bird has a crisp, golden-brown skin; remove the trussing and allow the chicken to stand for 5 minutes before carving.

Variation: Substitute fresh morels in season (early spring) for the chanterelles.

Roast Chicken with Rosemary and Garlic
serves four

Although most roast chicken recipes call for tarragon, you will find that the combination of rosemary and garlic used here lends a delicious, subtle, and highly aromatic flavor. This chicken is roasted at a slightly higher temperature than usual, which results in a beautifully brown, crisp skin and moist, tender meat. It can be served hot from the oven, but I find it most appealing when just slightly warm.

This is one of the most flexible of dishes: try it with Baked Artichoke Hearts for one effect, with a Salad Nicoise for another, with Potatoes in Pesto or Rice Salad for yet others. A young Brunello is a superb complement.

2 $\frac{1}{2}$- to 3-pound chicken
$\frac{1}{2}$ lemon
3 or 4 sprigs fresh rosemary
4 cloves garlic, unpeeled and
    left whole

3 tablespoons butter
Salt and freshly ground pepper
1 tablespoon dry white ver-
    mouth

Preheat the oven to 450 degrees.

Wipe the chicken inside and out with the cut side of a lemon. Dry the outside of the bird with paper toweling. Into the cavity put 1 or 2 sprigs of fresh rosemary, the cloves of garlic, 1 tablespoon butter, and a light sprinkling of salt and pepper.

Truss the chicken tightly, making sure the legs and wings are tied close to the body. Sprinkle the outside of the bird with a little salt and pepper and the remainder of the rosemary, finely chopped. Place the chicken in a shallow ovenproof roasting pan.

In a small pan melt the remaining 2 tablespoons butter with the vermouth. Baste the chicken with a little of this mixture and put in the oven. The chicken will take about an hour to roast and must be basted with the butter and vermouth every 10 or 15 minutes. Remove from the oven when done, cover (not too tightly) with foil, and let stand for an hour before serving.

Country-Style Roast Chicken
serves two to four

This is a wonderful example of just how delicious very simple ingredients can be. The combination of chicken roasted with onions and potatoes is an unbelievably satisfying one and is also child's play to prepare. You will notice that the chicken is roasted at the very high heat of 450 degrees. This technique produces a bird that is moist and tender within and skin that is crisp and beautifully browned. Serve the chicken on its own and follow with a salad of greens. An appropriate wine would be a medium-weight brambly Zinfandel.

3- to 3 1/2-pound whole
  chicken
3 to 4 cloves garlic, peeled but
  left whole
Salt and freshly ground pepper
Small bunch fresh thyme

Unsalted butter
2 medium-size yellow or white
  onions
12 to 14 small new potatoes (a
  little larger than walnuts)
Chicken stock

Preheat the oven to 450 degrees.

Clean the chicken and stuff with the garlic, season with salt, pepper, and a few sprigs of the thyme. Truss the chicken and place in a shallow, ovenproof dish large enough to hold the onions and potatoes, which will be added later. Season the outside of the chicken with salt, pepper, and some of the thyme leaves (removed from their stems). Melt 3 or 4 tablespoons of the butter in a small pan; brush the chicken with a little of it and place in the oven to roast. Baste the chicken every 10 to 15 minutes with the melted butter.

Meanwhile, peel the onions and cut into thick wedges. Cut the potatoes in half, or in quarters if they are large; the idea is that both the onion and potato pieces be approximately the same size. After the chicken has been in the oven 30 minutes, place the onions and potatoes all around the bird, sprinkling with the remaining thyme leaves.

Add enough chicken stock to the dish to come halfway up the sides of the vegetables and continue to roast, basting the chicken with the pan juices, for about another 30 minutes or until the chicken is a golden brown and the onions and potatoes are tender. Serve at once.

Poule au Pot
serves four

This dish is composed of a chicken poached whole and served in its own broth with a selection of seasonal vegetables. Such simplicity does not prepare you for the subtleties of flavor the dish contains. It deserves a medium-weight California Cabernet.

$3^1/_2$- to 4- pound chicken
$^1/_2$ lemon
4 cloves garlic, not peeled
A few sprigs of fresh thyme
  and/or parsley
1 small onion, peeled and
  coarsely chopped
1 carrot, peeled and coarsely
  chopped
1 celery stalk, coarsely chopped
White wine or dry white
  vermouth
2 cups chicken broth (optional)
Salt and a few black peppercorns

1 bay leaf
4 leeks, thoroughly washed but
  left whole
3 to 4 large carrots, peeled and
  cut into wedges about 4
  inches long
3 small turnips, peeled and cut
  into quarters
8 small potatoes, peeled and
  cut in halves or quarters
4 stalks celery, each cut into
  thirds, or 1 small celeriac
  peeled and cut into large
  cubes

Wash the chicken thoroughly under cold running water, remove any fat found within the cavity, and rub it inside and out with the cut side of a lemon.

Stuff the belly with the garlic, thyme, and parsley and truss well. In a 6-quart soup pot put the chopped onion, carrot, and chopped celery; cover the bottom of the pot with an inch of white wine or dry vermouth. Add the optional chicken stock and enough water to cover the chicken; add the salt, peppercorns, and bay leaf; bring to a boil, reduce the heat, and simmer for about 40 minutes.

Remove the chicken carefully and put the stock through a sieve. Discard the cooked vegetables, put the stock back into the pot, add the chicken, leeks, carrot wedges, turnips, potatoes, and celery or celeriac, and simmer for 20 to 25 minutes more until all the vegetables are tender.

When done, remove the chicken, skin it completely, and cut into serving pieces. Into large soup plates place a serving of chicken and an assortment of vegetables; ladle some broth over all and serve at once with Green Sauce (following).

Green Sauce
for Poule au Pot

A piquant sauce usually served with boiled or poached dishes in Italy. You may want to use it only over the chicken or perhaps stir a small amount of it into the broth, too.

$^1/_4$ cup coarse fresh bread crumbs

$^1/_2$ cup parsley, loosely packed, stems removed

2 tablespoons capers

1 large clove garlic

1-inch squeeze anchovy paste

or 2 flat anchovy fillets, finely chopped

$^1/_2$ tablespoon red-wine vinegar

$^3/_4$ cup olive oil

Salt and freshly ground pepper

Soak the bread crumbs for 10 minutes in just enough chicken stock to cover them. Squeeze out excess moisture and place bread pulp in a small mixing bowl.

Finely chop the parsley, capers, and garlic together; stir into the bread mixture along with the anchovy paste and the vinegar. Stirring constantly, pour in the olive oil slowly until the sauce is of a creamy consistency. If it is too thick for your taste, add a bit more oil. Add a few grindings of pepper, taste for seasoning, and add salt if necessary. The sauce may be made hours in advance and held covered until serving time. Refrigerate if to be held overnight.

Roast Capon with Noodle Dressing
serves six

A superb dish for the holidays: roast capon stuffed with egg noodles and bits of chicken liver and served with a sour-cream-and-tarragon sauce. Accompany with Braised Celery Root. A fairly concentrated white Burgundy would serve well as a wine.

5- to 6-pound fresh capon
3 cups $\frac{1}{2}$-inch-wide egg noodles
7 tablespoons butter
4 large shallots, finely chopped
1 clove garlic, finely chopped
$\frac{1}{4}$ pound chicken livers, cleaned and cut in half
$\frac{1}{3}$ cup Madeira

2 tablespoons fresh parsley chopped together with
$\frac{1}{2}$ teaspoon dried thyme
2 tablespoons heavy cream (preferably unpasteurized)
Salt and freshly ground pepper
$\frac{1}{4}$ cup dry white vermouth or dry white wine

Sauce

$\frac{1}{4}$ cup fat from roasting pan
3 tablespoons flour
1 cup stock (see preparation below)

$\frac{3}{4}$ cup sour cream
Salt
Dash cayenne pepper
$\frac{1}{2}$ teaspoon dried tarragon

Prepare a stock for the sauce using the wing tips, giblets, and neck of the capon. You will need about 1 cup.

Preheat the oven to 350 degrees.

To start preparing the dressing, bring a large pot of salted water to a boil, add the noodles, and cook for just 5 minutes. Drain them well, toss with 1 tablespoon butter, and reserve. Melt 2 tablespoons butter in a 10-inch skillet, add the shallots and garlic, and sauté for 3 minutes over moderate heat.

Add the chicken livers and sauté for about 5 minutes more. Remove the livers with a slotted spoon and chop finely. Return them to the pan, raise the heat, and add the Madeira; reduce the liquid in the pan to half. Sprinkle the mixture with herbs, stir in the heavy cream, and pour it over the noodles. Toss this together until it is thoroughly combined and season lightly with salt and pepper.

Stuff the capon with this dressing and truss it well. Melt the remaining 4 tablespoons of butter with the vermouth or wine and baste the bird with a little of it. Place the capon in a shallow baking pan and season the outside lightly with salt and pepper. Roast for 1 hour and 45 minutes or until tender, basting with the butter-vermouth mixture every 15 minutes. When the capon is tender, remove it from roasting pan and keep warm. Pour $^1/_4$ cup fat from the roasting pan into a saucepan and set over moderate heat. When it is hot, stir in the flour with a wire whisk and cook for 5 minutes, making a roux. Take care not to brown it. Stir in the cup of stock, whisking until the sauce thickens.

Reduce the heat to low, add the sour cream, and season with salt, cayenne pepper, and tarragon. Cook this for another 5 minutes, taste, and adjust seasoning if necessary. Place in a heated sauceboat and serve with the roast capon and its dressing.

Grilled Game Hens in Lemon-Pepper Marinade
serves two to four

C ornish game hens are often thought of as having little flavor; usually their only fault lies in being very overcooked. This simple marinade— lemon juice, black and red pepper, salt, and olive oil—gives the birds a zesty flavor. They are grilled for no longer than 40 minutes, allowing the meat to be moist, tender, and most flavorful. Serve with Caesar Salad, along with a young white Bordeaux or young Graves.

2 Cornish game hens, each weighing about 1 ¹/₂ pounds	**1 teaspoon dried hot red pepper flakes**
1 ¹/₂ tablespoons black peppercorns	**Juice of 7 or 8 lemons**
1 teaspoon coarse salt	**¹/₄ cup olive oil**

Wash the hens. Dry them and split each in half.

To prepare the marinade, grind the black peppercorns, salt, and red pepper flakes with a mortar and pestle for a minute or 2; the peppers should be coarsely ground. Combine with the lemon juice and the olive oil in a shallow nonmetal dish large enough to hold the game hens in a single layer.

Place the hens in the marinade, skin side down, and spoon some of the marinade over them. Allow them to stand at room temperature for 4 to 6 hours, turning occasionally. If you wish to marinate them overnight, the dish should be covered tightly and refrigerated.

Heat the coals on the grill to moderately hot. Drain the game hens, reserving the marinade. Place the birds bone side down on the grill. Cook for 30 to 40 minutes, basting every 10 to 15 minutes with the marinade. During the last 10 minutes of cooking, the hens may be turned over to brown on the skin side. Remove from grill when done and baste once more with marinade. Serve at once or allow to cool to room temperature.

If you want to cook the game hens in your oven, they can be either baked or broiled, basted as above.

André Daguin's Roast Game Hen with Garlic and Lemon Sauce
serves six

This recipe was originally published in *Cooking*, the magazine put out by Cuisinart. It is, quite simply, one of the most delicious dishes I've ever had. I have included it here so that those of you who are not familiar with the magazine or the dish may have the chance to taste it. The amount of garlic (five or six large *heads*) seems astounding, but the finished sauce has a mild, mellow, slightly nutty flavor that is produced by cooking the whole cloves of garlic until meltingly tender and then combining the puréed garlic with heavy cream and reducing the mixture. Serve with freshly made buttered noodles and accompany with a French Pinot Noir.

5 1/2 ounces (about 60) unpeeled garlic cloves (1 head
  has 10 to 12 cloves),
  separated
1 1/2 lemons, unpeeled, thinly
  sliced, with seeds removed
Salt
2 cups water
1 1/2 cups heavy cream, preferably unpasteurized
5 tablespoons softened
  unsalted butter

Freshly ground pepper
3 1 1/4- to 1 1/2-pound Cornish
  game hens, defrosted
3 tablespoons port wine
1 cup rich chicken stock
1 teaspoon fresh lemon juice or
  juice to taste
3/4 pound fresh egg noodles or
  fettuccine freshly cooked
  and tossed with salted
  butter

In a heavy 2 1/2- or 3-quart saucepan, combine the unpeeled cloves of garlic, lemon slices, 1 teaspoon of salt, and the water. Bring to a boil; reduce the heat and simmer, uncovered, for about 1 1/2 hours. The liquid in the pan will have evaporated and the garlic cloves will be the color of straw and extremely tender. Cool.

Separate the lemon slices and garlic cloves. Press the garlic through a fine strainer and discard the skins. Return the puréed garlic to the saucepan with the heavy cream and bring to a boil. Simmer, stirring often, until the mixture is reduced to one-half—a thick sauce. Set aside.

Preheat the oven to 425 degrees.

Purée the cooked lemon slices with 3 tablespoons of butter, seasoning the mixture with salt and pepper. Stuff a third of this mixture into the cavity of each game hen and truss tightly with kitchen string. Arrange the trussed hens side by side in a greased roasting pan. Sprinkle each with salt and pepper and rub with the remaining 2 tablespoons of butter. Roast for about 45 minutes, basting the hens every 10 minutes or so. When done, the birds should be a golden brown and when pricked with a fork their juices should run clear.

Remove the trussing strings; arrange the hens on a large heatproof serving dish; cover loosely with foil and return to the turned-off oven to keep warm. Discard the fat in the roasting pan. Deglaze the pan juices with the port wine, stirring to dissolve all brown particles that cling to the bottom of the pan. Add the chicken stock and reduce quickly over high heat to a half. Stir in the reserved garlic and cream reduction. Reduce all together to a thick, creamy sauce. Adjust seasoning, adding a drop of lemon juice if desired. Halve the birds, discard the stuffing, and add to the sauce any new juices that the birds have exuded.

Place half a hen on each heated individual plate, piling the freshly cooked and buttered noodles on the same dish; spoon a few tablespoons of the sauce over each portion of hen and serve at once. Any extra sauce can be passed in a warm bowl.

Roast Pheasant with Dirty Rice
serves two to three

Dirty rice is a mixture of finely chopped chicken livers sautéed with onion, green pepper, and celery and tossed with cooked rice. This gives the rice a brownish and slightly "dirty" color; hence its name. Serve with Chanterelle Soup and Braised Celery Root. A Nebbiolo wine will go well with this dish.

$2\frac{1}{2}$-pound pheasant

Dirty rice stuffing

The pheasant liver plus
5 chicken livers
6 tablespoons butter
1 teaspoon vegetable oil
$\frac{1}{2}$ cup onion, finely chopped
$\frac{1}{4}$ cup each celery and green

pepper, finely chopped
1 large clove garlic, finely chopped
$\frac{1}{2}$ cup short-grain rice, cooked to make $1\frac{1}{2}$ cups
Salt and freshly ground pepper

3 tablespoons parsley, finely   Dash Tabasco
   chopped $\frac{1}{4}$ cup dry Madeira
Pinch allspice

Preheat the oven to 375 degrees.

First, prepare the stuffing. Clean the livers and cut them in half. Heat 2 tablespoons of butter with the oil in a skillet; sauté the livers until firm and lightly browned, about 8 minutes. Remove with a slotted spoon, set aside, and allow to cool slightly.

Add the onion, celery, green pepper, and garlic to the skillet and sauté over moderate heat for 5 minutes. Chop the livers into very fine pieces, add them to the skillet with the onion mixture, and continue to cook for another 5 minutes, browning the mixture slightly. Put the cooked rice in a mixing bowl, add the liver mixture, salt, pepper, parsley, allspice, and Tabasco, and mix well.

Clean the pheasant and stuff its cavity with the rice. Truss the bird tightly and season the outside lightly with salt and pepper. Melt the remaining 4 tablespoons butter with the Madeira and brush the bird lightly with this mixture. Place in a roasting pan and put in the middle of the oven to roast for $1\frac{1}{2}$ hours or until tender. The pheasant must be basted with the butter-Madeira mixture every 10 or 15 minutes so the meat does not become dry. Remove from the oven when done and allow to stand for 10 minutes before carving.

Roast Turkey with Stuffing
serves ten to twelve

The recipe given here for roast turkey with stuffing is based partly on one that has been used by my family for years. It begins with a *fresh* turkey, and those are not as difficult to get as you might think. Almost any supermarket or poultry shop can supply you with one if given enough notice.

The merits of a plump, juicy, untampered-with bird are obvious, as opposed to the frozen variety, shot full of oil because all the natural oil sacs on the skin have been removed, and complete with a built-in thermometer—the very idea is demoralizing.

The stuffing here is a savory preparation of toasted cubes of egg bread, minced chicken livers, onion and celery sautéed to a golden tenderness, ground pork tenderloin, toasted hazelnuts, and herbs, all bound together with eggs, Madeira, and sour cream.

The stuffed bird is roasted at a low heat of 325 degrees; I find this is the only way to achieve a crisp and meltingly brown skin and still have both the dark and light meat done to a turn. The turkey must be basted often when done this way, but the results will be more than satisfactory. For wine try an Oregon Pinot Noir.

Stuffing

1 loaf challah or other egg
 bread
6 tablespoons butter
$1/2$ pound chicken livers,
 cleaned and cut in half
Salt and freshly ground pepper
2 cups onion, finely chopped
$1/2$ cup celery, finely chopped
2 cloves garlic, finely chopped
1 pound pork tenderloin,
 ground

$1/2$ cup parsley, finely chopped
A few sprigs fresh thyme, finely
 chopped, or $1/2$ teaspoon
 dried thyme
$3/4$ cup toasted hazelnuts
 (filberts), coarsely chopped
2 eggs
1 cup sour cream
$1/4$ cup Madeira

The bird

12-pound fresh turkey
1 lemon
Salt and freshly ground pepper
6 tablespoons butter

 melted with
3 tablespoons dry white
 vermouth or dry white wine

Preheat the oven to 200 degrees.

First, prepare the stuffing. Cut the bread into $1/2$-inch cubes, place on pastry sheets, and toast in the oven until the croutons are completely dried; there should be enough to measure 8 cups.

Heat 2 tablespoons butter in a skillet, add the chicken livers, season lightly with salt and pepper, and sauté for 5 to 8 minutes; the livers should be firm but still pink in the middle. Remove the livers with a slotted spoon, chop them finely, and place in a large mixing bowl.

In the same skillet, put the remaining 4 tablespoons butter, and heat. When the butter is hot, add the onions, celery, and garlic and sauté for about 5 minutes over moderate heat. Add the ground pork to the skillet and cook it just until there are no traces of pink in the meat. Place this in the mixing bowl and add the parsley, thyme, hazelnuts, and croutons.

In a small bowl, combine the eggs, sour cream, and Madeira and beat lightly. Pour this over the stuffing and mix together with your hands. Season the stuffing to taste with salt and peper. This may be made a day in advance but the bird should not be stuffed until it is ready for roasting.

Preheat the oven to 325 degrees.

Rub the turkey inside and out with the cut side of a lemon. Stuff both cavities lightly with the dressing (it will expand during cooking) and sew closed with a trussing needle and heavy kitchen string. Truss the bird well, rub it with a bit of the butter and vermouth mixture, and place in the oven.

Baste the bird every half hour with the butter mixture until the skin is a deep golden brown, then cover the turkey and its pan completely with foil and continue roasting. At 325 degrees, the bird should be allowed 25 minutes to the pound; a 12-pound turkey should be done in 5 hours. The dark meat should still have a slightly pink color near the bones and the white meat will be moist and succulent.

I refuse to involve myself in any discussions regarding the uses of leftover turkey. Too many abominable recipes are in existence already. For my taste there is nothing better than cold, thinly sliced turkey on rye bread with a bit of home-made mayonnaise.

There is, however, something wonderful that can be done with the turkey carcass. Cut it into manageable pieces and set it aside; coarsely chop some celery, carrot, and onion, sauté them in a large stock pot until soft but not brown; add a cup or 2 of dry white wine, some parsley, thyme, and bay leaf, and the turkey carcass; and add enough water to cover.

Cook this as you would any stock. The result should be a rich broth, redolent of turkey. After straining off all bones and vegetables, degrease the broth and bring it to a boil. Into the boiling broth, stir a mixture of 2 or 3 eggs that have been beaten with about $\frac{1}{4}$ cup of freshly grated Parmesan cheese and a dash of freshly grated nutmeg. Cook only until the egg mixture forms tiny flakes in the soup. This is called stracciatella, which, roughly translated, means "little rags," and is an old Roman favorite.

Saltimbocca
serves two

S altimbocca, literally transalted, means "jump in the mouth," perhaps because the dish is so delicious it seems to disappear without any assistance from the eater. Classically it is prepared with veal—delicate pink scallops cut from the leg and pounded to transparency—but veal of this character is almost impossible to find in the Northwest so I have substituted chicken breast instead. Before cooking, soak the chicken in milk to achieve a lighter, more delicate meat (I also use this technique very often with fish to "clean up" the flavor). A fine Italian Merlot would complement this perfectly.

1 chicken breast, boned, halved, and lightly pounded
Milk to cover
Flour
Salt and freshly ground pepper
Powdered sage
1 tablespoon butter
1 teaspoon olive oil
2 slices prosciutto
2 slices Italian fontina cheese
$\frac{1}{4}$ cup chicken stock
$\frac{1}{4}$ cup Marsala wine
Lemon juice to taste

Preheat the oven to 450 degrees.

Cover the chicken breast fillets with milk and soak for about $\frac{1}{2}$ hour. Remove, dry thoroughly, dredge with flour, and season on both sides with salt, pepper, and a small pinch of sage. In a 10-inch skillet melt the butter with the olive oil; when the foam subsides, add the chicken and sauté over moderately high heat for 5 or 6 minutes till golden brown and slightly crisp on both sides.

Remove the chicken to an ovenproof platter, reserving the pan juices in the skillet. Cover each piece of chicken with a piece of prosciutto folded to fit, then with a slice of cheese trimmed to fit. Place in the oven.

Working quickly, add the stock to the reserved pan juices in the skillet and reduce slightly over high heat; add the Marsala and reduce to a light glaze. Add the lemon juice to taste and taste for seasoning, adding salt and pepper if desired. The whole deglazing process should take no longer than 3 to 4 minutes, in which time the cheese on the chicken should be melted and lightly browned.

Remove the platter with the chicken from the oven, pour on the pan sauce, and serve.

Breast of Chicken Parmigiana
serves four

If you have everything on hand, this is a very quick and elegant main dish; even the cream sauce is quick to make. Serve with Raw Mushroom Salad. If you're in no hurry with this meal, it is delightful with a good risotto. Drink an Italian Trebbiano with this dish.

Flour seasoned with salt and
　freshly ground pepper
1 egg, lightly beaten
2 cups unseasoned fresh bread
　crumbs (home-made if
　possible)

Breasts of 2 chickens, split,
　skinned, and boned
2 tablespoons butter
1 tablespoon oil

Sauce

2 tablespoons butter
2 tablespoons flour
1 cup chicken stock
$\frac{1}{4}$ cup heavy cream (preferably
　unpasteurized)

Scant $\frac{1}{4}$ cup grated Parmesan
　cheese
Dash each cayenne pepper and
　freshly grated nutmeg
Salt

Place the flour, egg, and bread crumbs in 3 separate shallow bowls. Take the pieces of chicken and dip them, 1 at a time, first into the flour, shaking off any excess, then into the egg, and finally into the crumbs, pressing the crumbs firmly into the meat. If you have time, the chicken may be refrigerated: this will help the crumbs to adhere.

Heat the butter and oil in a skillet large enough to hold the chicken pieces in a single layer. When the foam subsides, add the meat, turn the heat to high, and sauté each side for about 3 minutes until golden brown and slightly crisp. Remove the chicken to a heated platter and place in a 200-degree oven to keep warm.

Now prepare the sauce. In a small saucepan heat the butter. When it has melted add the flour, stirring with a wire whisk. Cook over medium heat, whisking continuously for 3 to 4 minutes, but do not allow the roux to brown.

Add the chicken stock, turn up the heat a bit, and stir constantly until the sauce thickens. Add the cream and all but 1 tablespoon of the grated cheese and mix in with the whisk. Season with the cayenne, nutmeg, and salt.

Remove the platter of chicken from the oven, pour the sauce over it, and sprinkle the last tablespoon of grated cheese over the top. Place under a hot broiler for 1 to 2 minutes to glaze lightly, and serve immediately.

Chicken Curry
serves four

T his recipe for chicken curry uses only the dark meat, more flavorful in this particular preparation than breast meat, which has a tendency to dry out quickly. Melon pieces, stirred in at the end, lend an element of surprise to the dish, their cool flavor a perfect foil for the savory sauce.

Serve the curry with steamed, buttered rice that has been lightly flavored with citrus juice and a little of its zest, either lime, lemon, or orange. Accompany with Peach Chutney (following recipe), coarsely chopped unsalted cashews, ripe tomatoes cut into small dice, and a Northwest dry Gewurztraminer.

6 large chicken thighs (about
  1 $\frac{1}{2}$ pounds)
3 cups chicken stock
3 tablespoons butter
1 large onion, cut into quarters
  and thickly sliced
2 tablespoons fresh ginger
  root, cut into short julienne
  strips

2 cloves garlic, finely chopped
$\frac{1}{2}$ to 1 tablespoon imported
  curry paste
2 tablespoons flour
Juice of 1 lime
$\frac{1}{2}$ cup sour cream or yogurt
$\frac{1}{2}$ small cantaloupe or honeydew melon, cut into small,
  bite-size pieces

Place the chicken thighs in a saucepan, add the stock, and bring to a boil. Reduce the heat and simmer the chicken for about 15 minutes, until tender. Strain and reserve the stock: remove the skin and bones from the meat and discard them. Cut the meat into bite-size pieces and set aside.

Melt the butter in a 10- or 12-inch skillet, add the onion slices, and sauté them over moderate heat for 5 minutes. Add the ginger and garlic; continue to cook for another 5 minutes. Stir in the curry paste, blending it into the vegetables, and sauté for 3 minutes. Stir in the flour with a wire whisk and continue to cook over low heat for 3 minutes more.

Pour in 2 cups of the reserved chicken stock, add the lime juice, and stir until the sauce has thickened. Cook the sauce over low heat, stirring occasionally, for about 20 minutes. When the sauce has reduced a bit, stir in the chicken and simmer for 5 minutes. Add the sour cream, thoroughly blending it into the sauce, stir in the melon pieces, and continue to simmer for 1 to 2 minutes more. Serve immediately.

Peach Chutney
makes fifteen cups

T his recipe for peach chutney begins with a technique that helps solidify the cubes of peach so they do not disintegrate during the cooking process. I've suggested that the garlic and fresh ginger be julienned, since this adds much to the final presentation, but they can be finely chopped, if you wish. The addition of hot pepper flakes gives the chutney a definite bite without being searingly hot—the amount, of course, can be adjusted to individual taste.

12 large ripe peaches
3 tablespoons salt
2 quarts water
3 cups cider vinegar
6 cups brown sugar
2 whole cinnamon sticks
2 tablespoons black mustard
    seeds
1 1/2 tablespoons hot red
    pepper flakes

1 1/2 cups yellow raisins
2 teaspoons ground ginger
Zest of 3 large limes
1 cup lime juice (from about 4
    limes)
3 cups thinly sliced onions
1/2 cup fresh ginger, peeled
    and cut into julienne
8 cloves garlic, peeled and cut
    into julienne

Bring a large pot of water to a boil. Remove from heat, add peaches and allow them to stand in the water for 1 minute. Take the peaches from the water and, when they are cool enough to handle, peel off the skins, which should slide off easily, much like tomatoes. Cut the peaches in half, remove and discard the pits, cut the flesh into cubes, and place in a large bowl. Combine the salt and water, pour over the peaches and allow to stand overnight. This salt solution will firm the peaches so that they will not disintegrate during the cooking.

In a large pot, combine the cider vinegar, brown sugar, and 1 cup of water. Bring to a boil, reduce the heat to a simmer, and add all remaining ingredients. Cook this mixture for 30 minutes. Drain the peaches thoroughly, add to the chutney and continue to cook for 20 minutes more. Spoon into hot sterilized jars and seal at once.

Chicken Hunter's Style

serves four to six

Chicken parts sautéed in a fresh tomato sauce with fresh and dried mushrooms and Italian bacon (pancetta). This is best served over your favorite pasta cooked al dente. It will go best with a vigorous vegetable dish like Green Bean and Pepper Sauté. Barbaresco wine was made to go with dishes like this.

$^1/_2$ ounce dried porcini mushrooms (Italian boletus)
3- to 3$^1/_2$ pound whole
  chicken, cut into serving
  pieces
Seasoned flour for dredging
3 tablespoons olive oil
$^1/_2$ pound fresh mushrooms,
  cleaned and thickly sliced
Squeeze fresh lemon juice
$^1/_3$ cup pancetta, cut into small
  cubes

$^1/_3$ cup onion, finely chopped
$^1/_3$ cup carrot, finely chopped
2 cloves garlic, finely chopped
1 tablespoon lemon rind, finely
  grated
$^1/_2$ cup dry white vermouth or
  dry white wine
2$^1/_2$ pounds fresh ripe tomatoes, peeled, seeded, and
  coarsely chopped
Pinch dried hot pepper flakes
Salt and freshly ground pepper

Rinse the dried mushrooms under cold running water. Place them in a small container, pour boiling water over them to cover, and allow them to soak for 30 minutes.

Dredge the chicken with the seasoned flour and shake off any excess. Heat the olive oil in a large heavy skillet and sauté the chicken until brown on all sides. Remove the chicken to a 4- or 5-quart pot and set aside. In the oil remaining in the skillet, quickly sauté the fresh mushrooms with the lemon juice until golden brown; remove from the pan with a slotted spoon and reserve.

Pour off all but 1 tablespoon oil from the skillet, add the pancetta, and cook over medium heat until it turns brown and begins to release its fat. Add the onions and carrots and sauté for 5 minutes. Drain and coarsely chop the porcini mushrooms; add them, the garlic, and the lemon rind to the onion and carrot mixture and continue to cook for another 5 minutes. Pour in the vermouth, raise the heat, and reduce the liquid slightly.

Add the vegetable mixture and the tomato pulp to the chicken, season with the dried hot pepper flakes, salt, and pepper, and just simmer over very low heat for about 45 minutes or until the chicken is tender. Taste for seasoning, adjust if necessary, and serve immediately over pasta.

Boned Stuffed Chicken Roll
serves six

A delightful presentation: boned chicken rolled around a sausage and spinach stuffing. The roll must be allowed to stand for three to four hours after roasting so that the filling holds together when it is sliced.

Serve this with Rice Salad or Potatoes in Pesto or Roasted Sweet Bell Peppers. For wine try a California Chardonnay.

3- to 3 $\frac{1}{2}$-pound whole plump chicken

2 or 3 sweet Italian sausages, skinned and chopped

5 tablespoons olive oil

$\frac{1}{4}$ cup onion, finely chopped

1 large clove garlic, finely minced

10-ounce package frozen chopped spinach, cooked and drained

Salt and freshly ground pepper to taste

$\frac{1}{4}$ teaspoon marjoram

$\frac{1}{4}$ cup freshly grated Parmesan or Romano cheese

1 egg, lightly beaten

6 ounces pancetta (Italian-style bacon), thinly sliced

2 hard-boiled eggs, peeled

Preheat the oven to 400 degrees.

Cut the chicken down the back and remove all the bones, including the leg bones and the large bone in the wings; reserve the outer two joints of the wings and the carcass for making a stock. Do not remove the skin. Sauté the sausage meat in 1 tablespoon olive oil until browned. Add the onion and garlic and cook for about 5 minutes. Add the cooked spinach and sauté over moderately high heat until all excess moisture is absorbed; season with salt, pepper, and marjoram. Remove from heat and mix in the grated cheese and the beaten egg.

Put the boned chicken on your working space, skin side down. Arrange pieces of leg and wing meat over any holes or thin spots; cover the chicken with waxed paper and pound the meat lightly to produce a more uniform thickness.

Cover the exposed meat with the pancetta. Over this, spread the sausage and spinach mixture, leaving a 1-inch margin on all sides. Place the hard-boiled eggs, end to end, on the short side nearest you. Roll up the chicken, tucking in the sides as you roll. Tie the roll with kitchen string every 2 inches along its length, and season the chicken lightly with salt and pepper.

In a shallow ovenproof dish, pour the remaining 4 tablespoons olive oil, add the chicken, and roll it around in oil until its surface is lightly covered. Put in the oven and roast for about 1 hour, basting every 10 or 15 minutes. Allow the chicken to stand for 3 to 4 hours before serving. Remove strings and slice into $\frac{1}{2}$-inch thicknesses.

Chicken Hash à la Ritz
serves four

C hicken hash was a favorite on New York hotel menus during the early part of this century, and the Ritz-Carlton produced many variations on that theme. The recipe here was inspired in part by those versions and I'm sure Louis Diat himself would heartily approve of it. This dish is simplicity itself; the only trick is to use very moist chicken, so I've specified poached thighs rather than breast meat (which tends to dry out when combined with vegetables and sautéed). This makes an elegant breakfast when accompanied by Corn Bread Madeleines. Serve it with a dry Pinot Noir Blanc.

6 slices bacon, cut into small cubes
2 tablespoons butter
1 cup onion, finely chopped
2 cups cooked new potatoes, cut into small cubes (allow the potatoes to cool thoroughly before attempting to chop them)

6 to 8 chicken thighs, poached, skinned, boned, and cut into small cubes (approximately 2 cups)
$\frac{1}{2}$ teaspoon dried tarragon
Salt and freshly ground pepper
$\frac{3}{4}$ cup heavy cream (preferably unpasteurized)
Dash Tabasco (optional)

Fry the bacon until crisp; remove to paper towels to drain. Pour off all but 2 tablespoons of the bacon fat from the skillet. Add the butter to the fat and place the pan over moderately high heat. When the butter has melted, add the onions and sauté for a few minutes until soft and lightly browned. Add the potatoes and continue to cook until they too are beginning to brown just around the edges.

Stir in the chicken and tarragon; cook only long enough to heat the chicken through. Season with salt and pepper, and stir in the cream. Allow the cream to be absorbed into the hash, which will take about 5 minutes or so.

Taste for seasoning, adding Tabasco if you wish. Stir in the bacon and serve immediately.

Chicken, Shrimp, and Sausage Gumbo
serves six

T he roux used in this recipe forms the basis of many creole dishes; unlike its French ancestors, this roux is browned and then cooked a good deal. Filé powder (ground sassafras leaves) can be purchased in any spice shop; it is used as a thickening agent and care should be taken not to boil the gumbo after it is added or the gumbo will become stringy. Serve with a Lembeger from the Northwest or a good Pilsner.

3-pound chicken
1 medium onion, coarsely chopped
2 carrots, coarsely chopped
2 ribs celery, coarsely chopped
2 cloves garlic, whole and unpeeled
1 bay leaf
Salt and 6 or 8 peppercorns
A few sprigs parsley
$\frac{1}{2}$ teaspoon dried thyme
4 cups chicken stock
$\frac{1}{3}$ cup vegetable oil
1 pound Polish or farmer's sausage, cut into $\frac{1}{2}$-inch slices

1 pound shrimp, shelled and deveined
5 tablespoons flour
1 cup onion, finely chopped
$\frac{1}{2}$ cup green pepper, chopped
2 tablespoons sliced scallions with green tops
2 cloves garlic, finely chopped
Pinch cayenne or dash Tabasco
1 cup tomatoes, peeled, seeded, and coarsely chopped
Salt and freshly ground pepper
1 tablespoon filé powder

Wash and truss the chicken. Place the onion, carrots, celery, garlic, bay, salt, peppercorns, parsley, and thyme in a 4-quart Dutch oven. Place the chicken on top of the vegetables, add the stock and 2 quarts of water, and bring to a boil. Reduce the heat and simmer the chicken for about 1 hour.

When the chicken is tender, remove it from the stock, allow it to cool slightly, and remove the meat from the bones. Put the bones and skin back in the pot and continue to cook for another hour. Then cut the chicken into bite-size pieces and reserve. Drain the stock, discarding everything in the colander; there should be about 2 quarts.

Rinse the Dutch oven with hot water and dry. Add the oil and heat it; add the sausage meat and brown it over moderate heat, stirring frequently. When done, remove with a slotted spoon and reserve. Add the shrimp to the pot, sauté for 3 to 4 minutes until pink, remove with a slotted spoon, and set aside.

Make the roux with the remaining oil; over low heat blend in a tablespoon of the flour at a time, stirring constantly with a wire whisk; when the flour has been absorbed, raise the heat slightly and allow the roux to cook until it takes on a medium-brown color.

When this stage is reached, stir in the chopped onion and green pepper, scallions, garlic, cayenne or Tabasco, and tomatoes and continue to cook over low heat for about 10 minutes, until the vegetables are tender. Stir in the stock, 2 cups at a time; season lightly with the salt and pepper and simmer over low heat for 30 minutes. Add the reserved chicken, sausage, and shrimp and allow them to heat through. Stir in the filé powder, remove from heat, and serve in soup plates over a mound of steamed or boiled rice.

Rabbit in Vinegar Sauce
serves four to six

A vinegar-and-cream sauce may appear at first glance rather odd, but the vinegar in question (balsamic) is used to deglaze the pan and leaves behind only the essence of its flavor. The rabbit is then put back in the pan and braised with a quantity of heavy cream; the resulting sauce tastes smooth and mellow. Serve with a Côte du Rhone.

Rabbit

In his wonderful dictionary *Food*, Waverly Root writes, "I do not suppose that this is the primary function of the rabbit, but it can serve as a touchstone to separate food snobs from those earthy characters who really like to eat." When it comes to dining on rabbit, sometimes it is more a case of squeamishness rather than snobbery and frankly I cannot understand the sentimentality surrounding these creatures.

Rabbits, although commercially raised, stubbornly have retained their fine flavor—a delicious cross between chicken and veal. The meat of a rabbit is close-textured and contains a very low percentage of water, which means that when it is cooked there is little shrinkage. Because the flesh is so lean, the best possible cooking technique is braising—the meat is first browned and then slowly simmered in liquid almost to cover. But this versatile viand may also be stewed, roasted, grilled, fried, or turned into sausages or patés. Rabbit freezes well; its flavor and texture will not be harmed, providing it is defrosted properly (in the refrigerator rather than sitting atop the kitchen counter at room temperature).

Now that I've managed to convince some of the cooks reading this that rabbit shouldn't be ignored, I'll attack the problem of the fussy guest. When asked, "What's for dinner?" hedge. If you must give an answer, mumble something about chicken. I've always been a firm believer in the dictum that most people dislike something because they've never eaten it well prepared.

3- to 3½-pound fresh rabbit, cut into serving pieces
Flour seasoned with salt and pepper
3 tablespoons vegetable oil
½ cup chicken stock
1 tablespoon garlic, finely chopped

1 tablespoon fresh rosemary, finely chopped, or 1 teaspoon dried rosemary, crumbled
¼ cup balsamic vinegar
1 cup heavy cream, preferably unpasteurized
Salt and freshly ground pepper

Lightly flour each of the rabbit pieces. Heat the vegetable oil in a 10-inch skillet until very hot. Add a few of the pieces, making sure that they are not touching, and brown each side evenly. Remove each piece as it browns and continue with remaining meat. When the rabbit is browned, pour off all fat from the skillet and add the chicken stock. Place the browned rabbit in the stock, sprinkle with the garlic and rosemary, cover, and cook over low heat for about 45 minutes, or until tender.

When the rabbit is tender, remove from pan and keep warm. Raise the heat, add the vinegar to the skillet and reduce the liquid by half. Add the heavy cream, turn heat to low and simmer for a minute. Taste for seasoning, adjust if necessary. Add the rabbit to the sauce and cook for a few minutes more, basting the meat with the liquid. Serve immediately with steamed couscous.

Rabbit with Cabbage and Mustard Sauce
serves four

This is a casserole of richly browned rabbit and sautéed cabbage in a mustard sauce. It is an uncomplicated, lusty dish and one that I'm extremely fond of.

I've recommended using a Moutarde à l'Ancienne here, a grainy French mustard from Alsace found in specialty food shops; substitute Pommery or Dijon if you desire. Precede with a first course of Hood Canal shrimp with home-made mayonnaise and serve with Potato Pancakes and a good red Burgundy.

1 medium-size Savoy cabbage, about 3 pounds, cut into 1-inch shreds
5 tablespoons butter
$\frac{1}{2}$ cup salt pork, rind removed, cut into small dice
$2\frac{1}{2}$- to 3-pound fresh rabbit, cut into serving pieces
Flour seasoned with salt, pepper, and paprika
$1\frac{1}{2}$ medium onions, coarsely chopped
2 tablespoons flour
1 cup dry white wine or dry white vermouth
$1\frac{1}{2}$ cups milk
Pinch of freshly grated nutmeg
Salt
Pinch of cayenne pepper
1 tablespoon Moutarde à l'Ancienne

Preheat the oven to 350 degrees.

Bring to a boil a 10- or 12-quart stockpot filled three-quarters full of salted water; add the cabbage and allow to boil for 5 minutes. (This removes much of the overly strong taste and smell of the vegetable.) Put the blanched cabbage in a large colander and refresh it under cold running water. Allow it to drain well and set aside.

In a heavy 12-inch skillet melt 3 tablespoons of butter; add the salt-pork cubes, allowing them to brown and render their fat completely. Remove the solids with a slotted spoon and reserve both them and their fat.

Wash the rabbit quickly with cold water and dry it well. Dust the meat heavily with the seasoned flour, shaking off any excess. Set the large skillet containing the rendered pork fat over high heat and put in only enough pieces of rabbit to just cover the bottom. Brown the meat well, turning only once to brown the other side; continue until all the meat is browned.

To the remaining fat add half the onion and half the cabbage, sprinkling with salt and pepper. Sauté over moderate heat for abut 10 minutes. Remove to a bowl and repeat the process with the rest of the onions and cabbage. Add the salt-pork cubes to the cooked cabbage and set aside.

In the same skillet, prepare a roux; melt 2 tablespoons of the butter, add the flour, stirring well with a wire whisk, and cook over low heat for 5 minutes; do not brown. Add the wine or vermouth and mix in with the whisk until there are no lumps; then add the milk and blend together. Season this with the nutmeg, salt, cayenne, and mustard. (This should be a highly seasoned sauce and the taste of the mustard should be evident; add more mustard if you wish.)

In a 4- or 6-quart Dutch oven, place half the cabbage mixture, mixing it with one-third of the mustard sauce. Put the rabbit on this, spooning half the remaining sauce over it. Finally, add the remaining cabbage and sauce. The casserole should be tightly packed. Cover and bake the dish for $1\frac{1}{2}$ to $1\frac{3}{4}$ hours, then serve directly from the pot.

Rabbit and Sausage Gumbo

serves six to eight

S erve with a big Zinfandel.

$^1/_2$ cup vegetable oil
$^1/_4$ pound panchetta (Italian
    bacon), cut into small dice
5 to 6 hot Italian sausages, cut
    into slices $^1/_2$ inch thick
3-pound fresh rabbit, cut into
    serving pieces
$^3/_4$ cup flour
$2^1/_2$ cups onion, coarsely
    chopped
3 cloves garlic, chopped
2 cups red or green bell pep-
    per, coarsely chopped

5 scallions (trimmed of all but
    2 inches of green), sliced
1 cup parsley, chopped
Salt and freshly ground pepper
6 cups chicken stock
$2^1/_2$ pounds tomatoes, peeled,
    seeded and coarsely chopped
3 bay leaves
Pinch each ground cloves and
    ground allspice
$^1/_4$ teaspoon cayenne pepper
$^1/_2$ teaspoon Tabasco sauce

Heat the oil in a heavy Dutch oven. Add the panchetta and cook over moderately high heat until the fat is rendered and the small cubes have become crisp. Remove with a slotted spoon and reserve. To the fat remaining in the pan, add the sausage, and brown. Remove and reserve.

Dry the pieces of rabbit well, add them to the hot fat remaining in the pot, and brown well on all sides. Remove and reserve.

Prepare the roux. Reduce the heat under the pot to low, slowly whisk the flour into the fat remaining in the pan and cook the roux, stirring constantly, for about 20 to 25 minutes, until it becomes a rich, honey-brown color. The roux must be cooked slowly for the best flavor. If at any time it appears that it may scorch, the pot should be taken off the heat until it has cooled slightly. The roux must not be allowed to burn. Immediately add the onion, garlic, pepper, scallions, and parsley and season lightly with salt and pepper. Stir the vegetables until they are coated with the roux and cook over low heat for about 10 minutes.

Stir in 2 cups of the stock, and when the mixture has thickened add the tomatoes and the reserved panchetta, sausage and rabbit. Pour in the remaining 4 cups stock and season with the remaining ingredients.

Simmer the gumbo about 1 hour, or until the rabbit is very tender. Remove the rabbit, allow to cool slightly, and strip the meat from the bones. Discard the bones and cut the meat into bite-size pieces. Return the rabbit meat to the gumbo, cooking just long enough to heat it through. Taste, and adjust seasoning if necessary. In individual soup plates place a small mound of boiled or steamed rice, ladle the gumbo over the rice, and serve.

Rabbit with Sherry Sauce
serves four

Serve with an earthy Côte du Rhone.

3- to 3 1/2-pound fresh rabbit

Marinade

2 tablespoons red-wine vinegar
3 tablespoons olive oil
4-inch stick cinnamon, broken into several pieces

2 bay leaves, crumbled
3-inch piece of orange peel, cut into 3 or 4 pieces

Place the rabbit in a container just large enough to hold it in a single layer. Combine the marinade ingredients and pour over the rabbit. Cover with plastic wrap and refrigerate overnight.

Cooking and sauce ingredients

2 tablespoons butter
2 tablespoons olive oil
1 cup pale, dry sherry
1/2 cup chicken stock

Garnish: orange slices and 1/4 cup whole blanched almonds lightly browned in a little butter

The next day, drain the rabbit (discarding the marinade) and dry it thoroughly. Heat the butter and oil in a sauté pan. When hot, add the rabbit and brown evenly on all sides. Pour in the sherry and the chicken stock, reduce the heat, and simmer for about an hour until the rabbit is tender, and the liquid in the pan is reduced to a glaze. If the liquid reduces too quickly, a little more stock may be added to it from time to time.

Arrange the rabbit on a serving platter, spooning the pan sauce over it. Sprinkle with the sautéed almonds and surround with the orange slices.

Rabbit with Leeks and Chanterelles
serves four

If fresh chanterelles cannot be found, or are out of season, simply omit them rather than substitute cultivated mushrooms. Serve with buttered noodles, tiny carrots braised in beef stock to which a knob of sweet butter has been added, and, for wine, a Gigondas.

3- to 3 ½-pound fresh rabbit, cut into serving pieces
Flour seasoned with salt and pepper
4 tablespoons vegetable oil
1 ½ cups chicken stock
6 small leeks (trimmed of all but 2 inches of green), cleaned and cut into julienne

5 tablespoons butter
Salt and freshly ground pepper
1 small clove garlic, chopped
½ pound fresh chanterelles, thickly sliced
Lemon juice
1 ½ cups heavy cream, preferably unpasteurized
Grated nutmeg

Dredge the rabbit pieces in the seasoned flour. Heat 3 tablespoons of the oil in a heavy sauté pan and brown the rabbit on all sides. Pour off all oil from the pan, add the chicken stock, cover and simmer for about an hour, until the rabbit is tender.

While the rabbit is cooking, melt 3 tablespoons butter in a skillet, reduce the heat to low, add the leeks and season lightly with salt and pepper. Cover, steam for about 8 minutes, and reserve. Heat 2 tablespoons of butter with 1 teaspoon oil in another skillet. When hot, add the garlic and the mushrooms; cook over high heat for 2 to 3 minutes. Reduce the heat to moderate, add salt, pepper, and a squeeze of lemon juice and continue to sauté for a few minutes more, until the mushrooms are tender. Reserve.

If the chicken stock has not reduced down to a glaze, turn up the heat and reduce it. Lower the heat and scatter the leeks and mushrooms over the rabbit. Pour in the cream and season with just a hint of freshly grated nutmeg. Simmer for about 10 minutes more and serve.

Rabbit with Paprika Sauce
serves four

Although rabbit can be treated almost like chicken in any dish, it will usually need a bit more cooking time. Use only the best imported Hungarian paprika for this recipe. Serve with Brussels Sprouts in Cheese and Bread Crumbs and with a red wine from Pomerol.

3- to 3$^1/_2$-pound rabbit, cut into pieces
Salt and freshly ground pepper
4 tablespoons butter
1 tablespoon vegetable oil
$^1/_2$ cup vermouth or dry white wine
1 cup chicken stock
2 green bell peppers, seeded and cut into julienne
1 large onion, thinly sliced
2 fresh tomatoes, peeled, seeded, and cut into julienne
1 tablespoon imported paprika
$^3/_4$ cup sour cream
$^1/_2$ cup heavy cream (preferably unpasteurized), whipped

Preheat the oven to 350 degrees.

Dredge the rabbit pieces with flour seasoned lightly with salt and pepper. Heat 2 tablespoons of the butter with the oil in a large heavy skillet. Add the rabbit and sauté over moderately high heat until golden brown.

Remove the rabbit and place it in a shallow ovenproof container large enough to hold it in one layer. Pour off all but 1 tablespoon of the fat from the skillet, add the vermouth or wine and the chicken stock, and reduce the liquids over high heat, scraping up any brown particles from the bottom of the pan, for about 5 minutes. Pour this over the rabbit and place the baking dish in the middle of the oven. Bake the rabbit uncovered for about 1$^1/_2$

hours, basting it frequently with the pan juices.

About 10 minutes before the rabbit is done, begin the sauce. Heat the remaining 2 tablespoons of butter in a skillet, add the pepper and onion, and sauté over moderate heat for about 5 minutes; do not brown. Stir in the tomato, season lightly with salt and pepper, and continue to cook for another 3 minutes. Add the paprika, reduce the heat, and cook the vegetables, stirring frequently, for 5 minutes more.

Remove the rabbit from its baking dish to a serving platter and put it in the warm oven. Degrease the pan juices and pour them into the pepper and onion mixture. Stir in the sour cream, using a wire whisk, and cook the sauce over low heat for about 10 minutes.

Slowly beat in the whipped cream and allow the sauce to cook for another 1 to 2 minutes. Pour the sauce over the rabbit and brown the dish lightly under the broiler to finish. Serve with buttered noodles.

Polenta Pie with Rabbit and Mushroom Sauce
serves six

This recipe was originally devised as the main course of a Christmas dinner. Begin the meal with oyster bisque, prepared as for oyster stew and then puréed (a small amount of chopped and seasoned cooked spinach is a delicious addition to this). Follow the main course with Orange and Fennel Salad and end the meal with fresh seasonal fruit and cheese. The wine to serve with this would be a Ghemme.

Polenta

3 cups water	1 tablespoon salt
3 cups milk	2²/₃ cups polenta (1 pound)

Bring the water and milk to a boil and add salt. Lower the heat and slowly sift in the polenta, a little at a time, stirring constantly to avoid sticking. Cook the polenta for about 40 minutes, stirring occasionally. When it has cooked, pour the polenta onto a platter and allow to cool. Cut the polenta into slices ¹/₄ inch thick.

Sauce

1 ½ ounces dried porcini
  mushrooms (Italian boletus)
4 tablespoons olive oil
⅓ pound pancetta (Italian
  bacon), cut into small cubes
1 whole fresh rabbit, cut into
  serving pieces
⅔ cup onion, chopped
2 large cloves garlic, chopped
1 cup plum tomatoes, seeded

  and chopped
Pinch allspice
Salt and freshly ground pepper
Robust dry red wine
1 pound cultivated mush-
  rooms, cleaned and halved
  or quartered if large
½ to ¾ pound Italian fontina
  cheese, coarsely grated
2 tablespoons butter

Rinse the dried mushrooms under cold running water. Place them in a small bowl and add just enough hot water to cover them. Allow to soak for 30 minutes. Drain, reserving liquid, and chop.

In a sauté pan that will be large enough to hold the rabbit in a single layer, heat 3 tablespoons of the oil. Add the panchetta and cook until the cubes of meat have browned around the edges. Remove and reserve. To the oil remaining in the pan, add the rabbit and cook until it is browned on all sides. Remove and reserve.

Pour off and discard all but a tablespoon of the oil remaining in the pan. Add the onion and garlic and sauté over moderate heat until the vegetables have just softened. Stir in the dried mushrooms and the tomatoes; season with allspice, salt, and pepper. Raise the heat and cook only long enough for the liquid from the tomatoes to evaporate. Add the rabbit, panchetta, mushroom liquid, and just enough wine to barely cover the meat.

Cook over moderate heat, braising the rabbit until it is tender. When the rabbit has cooked, remove it from the sauce. Separate the meat from the bones, cut it into bite-size pieces, and put it back into the sauce. Sauté the cultivated mushrooms over high heat in the remaining tablespoon of oil and add to the sauce.

Generously butter a shallow 2-quart baking dish and fill it with alternate layers of sauce, polenta slices, and fontina cheese. Reserve enough cheese to cover the top layer well. Dot with butter and bake in a 400-degree oven for 20 to 25 minutes. Let the pie sit for 15 to 20 minutes before serving.

CHAPTER SIX

MEATS

Boiled Beef Dinner, French Style
serves eight

T his is the legendary French boiled beef dinner; the rich bouillon is served as a first course, followed by the meats mounded on a platter and surrounded with the vegetables. Accompany this sumptuous feast with crisp French bread, cornichons, coarse salt, horseradish sauce, and/or mustard. A good wine with this would be a simple Haut-Médoc (Bordeaux).

2 whole fresh tomatoes (do not use canned)
1 large onion, unpeeled
Pan of boiling water
4 carrots, unpeeled and coarsely chopped
2 celery stalks, coarsely chopped
2 leeks, cleaned and coarsely chopped
1 small turnip, peeled and cut into quarters
4 cloves garlic, unpeeled and left whole
2 bay leaves
4 sprigs parsley
$\frac{1}{2}$ teaspoon dried thyme, or 3 sprigs fresh thyme

1 tablespoon salt
6 peppercorns
4 pounds lean brisket of beef
$1\frac{1}{2}$ to 2 pounds ox tails
3- to $3\frac{1}{2}$-pound chicken, tightly trussed
6 carrots, peeled and cut into quarters
1 small celery root, peeled and cut into 1-inch cubes
6 leeks, cleaned and cut into 3-inch lengths
1 cotechino (a large Italian pork sausage) or Polish or farmer's sausage, cooked separately (optional)

Preheat the oven to 400 degrees.

When the oven is hot, cut the tomatoes and onion in half, place them in a shallow ovenproof container, and bake them for 20 to 30 minutes until they are browned. This adds a rich color to the stock.

Place the baked tomatoes and onion in the bottom of an 8- to 10-quart soup pot. Add a cup of boiling water to the baking pan, scrape off any brown particles from the bottom, and add to the large pot. To the baked vegetables add the carrots, celery, leeks, turnip, garlic, bay leaves, parsley, and thyme; sprinkle the salt and the peppercorns over all and place the beef and the ox tails on top. Cover with very cold water and bring slowly to a simmer, skimming off all brown scum from the surface. Keep the liquid barely simmering for 3 to $3\frac{1}{2}$ hours, until the meat is almost tender.

Remove the brisket and the ox tails, reserving the latter meat for another purpose; strain the broth into a large bowl and degrease it thoroughly. Discard the vegetables. Put the stock back in the pot, add the brisket and the chicken, and simmer over low heat. After 45 minutes, add the quartered carrots; cook for 15 minutes more, then add the celery root and the leeks and continue to cook for an additional 15 to 20 minutes, until all the vegetables are tender.

Remove the meats to a platter, add the sausage, and surround with the cooked vegetables. Keep them warm while serving each person a small bowl of broth; then follow with the meats and vegetables.

Short Ribs Braised with Onions and Beer
serves four

This beef-and-beer stew, a specialty of Belgium, is usually made with boneless meat. The bones from the short ribs, though, add an amazing amount of flavor to the sauce and also aid in thickening the stew. The dish is served classically with boiled or steamed potatoes; buttered noodles are also a good accompaniment.

Serve this with Watercress and Radicchio Salad and a modestly priced California Cabernet Sauvignon.

2 tablespoons butter
$\frac{1}{4}$ pound bacon, cut into
    small dice
4 to 6 pounds beef short ribs
    ("English style"), trimmed
    of any excess fat
Flour for dredging meat
Salt and freshly ground pepper
2 pounds mild onions, peeled,
    cut in half, and thinly sliced

2 or 3 cloves garlic, minced
2 tablespoons flour
3 cups dark beer
1 cup beef stock
2 tablespoons red-wine vinegar
$\frac{1}{2}$ tablespoon brown sugar
$\frac{1}{2}$ teaspoon each dried thyme
    and tarragon
1 bay leaf

Preheat the oven to 350 degrees.

Melt the butter in a 4- or 5-quart ovenproof casserole with lid; add the bacon and sauté over high heat until it is crisp and the fat is rendered. Remove bacon and drain on paper toweling.

While the bacon is cooking, dry the ribs and coat them with the flour, salt, and pepper, shaking off any excess. Brown them in the rendered fat over high heat. Remove them and reserve.

To the remaining fat, add the onions and garlic and cook slowly over low heat for about 15 minutes. Stir in the flour and cook for 3 or 4 minutes, stirring constantly, until it is thoroughly incorporated. Pour in the beer and the beef stock, stirring until the liquid has thickened. Add the vinegar, sugar, and herbs and simmer for about 5 minutes.

Immerse the ribs in the liquid, sprinkle with the reserved bacon bits, cover, and bake for 2 hours until the meat is tender and is separating from the bones.

Florentine Braised Beef
serves six

S ome of the finest beef in the world is raised in Tuscany and while most of it is simply grilled, this specialty of Florence, akin to a pot roast, is extremely popular. Serve some of the sauce spooned over a sturdy pasta first and follow with the meat, sliced and covered with the remainder of the sauce and accompanied by a seasonal green vegetable. Serve a wine to match the ingredients: a Tuscan Cabernet, for example.

1/2 ounce dried Italian mush-
    rooms
3 1/2 pounds beef pot roast,
    rump, chuck, eye of round,
    or shoulder (arm)
Salt and freshly ground pepper
3 large cloves garlic, peeled and
    thinly sliced
3 or 4 sprigs fresh rosemary or
    1 1/2 teaspoons dried
3 tablespoons olive oil
1 cup carrot, peeled and cut
    into small dice
1 cup onion, peeled and finely
    chopped

1/2 cup celery, cut into small
    dice
1 clove garlic, minced
1 teaspoon finely grated lemon
    peel
1 1/2 cups dry red wine (Chi-
    anti Classico, Barolo, or
    Barbera)
1 cup tomatoes, peeled, seeded,
    and finely chopped
8-ounce can Progresso tomato
    sauce
Pinch allspice
1 cup beef stock (optional)

Place the dried mushrooms in a small bowl and cover them with boiling water. Allow them to stand for 30 minutes and drain, reserving 1 cup of liquid; chop the mushrooms into coarse pieces and set aside.

Dry the meat well and season with salt and pepper. Cut small slits in the meat; insert a piece of garlic and a little rosemary into each cut. Heat the olive oil in a heavy 4-quart casserole, add the beef, and brown well on all sides over high heat; remove and reserve. Pour out all but 1 tablespoon of the oil and add the carrot, onion, celery, garlic, and lemon peel. Sprinkle lightly with salt and pepper and sauté over medium heat, stirring, for 5 minutes. Add the reserved chopped mushrooms and continue to cook for 1 to 2 minutes. Turn up the heat, add the wine, and allow to reduce for 1 to 2 minutes. Add the tomatoes, tomato sauce, allspice, a good grinding of black pepper, and the meat. Add the reserved mushroom liquid to the pot. The meat should be halfway covered by sauce; if it is not, add the optional beef stock.

Cover the pot and simmer for about 3 hours or until the beef is tender. Serve as suggested. May be prepared a day in advance.

Beef Stroganoff
serves four

Traditionally this dish is prepared with tenderloin of beef, an extraordinarily expensive cut of meat, but it also can be prepared with flank steak that has been marinated briefly and cut on the bias against the grain. This technique, borrowed from the Chinese, produces very tender meat if it is cooked quickly over high heat. The traditional accompaniment for this dish is buttered noodles; for wine, a Washington or California Merlot.

1½ pounds flank steak	Squeeze of lemon juice
2 tablespoons Madeira	½ cup onion, finely minced
Salt and freshly ground pepper	1 clove garlic, finely minced
6 rashers thick-sliced bacon, cut into large dice	¼ cup dry white vermouth
½ pound mushrooms, cleaned and sliced	1½ cups sour cream
	Small handful parsley, finely chopped

Trim away and discard any fat from the flank steak. Cut the meat lengthwise into strips about 2 inches wide, then cut each strip diagonally against the grain into slices ¼ inch thick. Place the slices in a small bowl, add the Madeira, salt, and pepper, and mix.

In a heavy 10- or 12-inch skillet sauté the bacon over medium heat until brown and crisp; remove and reserve. To the remaining fat add the mushrooms, sprinkle with a little lemon juice, salt, and pepper, and brown quickly over high heat (about 3 minutes); remove with a slotted spoon and reserve.

Set the skillet over high heat and add the flank steak with its liquid and sauté in the hot fat very quickly. This will take only 4 or 5 minutes. Remove to a hot platter and keep warm.

To the remaining fat add the onion and garlic and cook for about 5 minutes over medium heat. Add the vermouth, turn up the heat, and reduce the liquid briefly. Add the sour cream, mushrooms, and bacon bits; reduce heat and simmer long enough to heat all ingredients through. Taste for seasoning, pour over meat slices, garnish with parsley and plenty of freshly grated pepper, and serve over rice or buttered noodles.

Beef and Pork Chili
serves eight to ten

This dish is a favorite of mine and over the years its composition has changed dramatically. Gone is the long list of herbs and spices used to flavor the mixture and in their place is only a savory chili paste made from two different chili peppers. The first is the ancho chili, a dried Mexican pepper with rounded pods 2 to $2^1/_2$ inches in diameter, their rich red-black outside skin a mass of tiny wrinkles. This chili is rather sweet; the heat is added to the paste with the chipolte chili—actually the jalapeno chili after it has been dried, smoked, and packed with a chili paste into cans. The latter is worth seeking out for its marvelous smoky flavor and also its incendiary punch. Both chilies are available in Latin American specialty shops.

Also to be found in such shops is the Mexican chorizo, a fine-ground pork sausage that is highly seasoned and quite hot. If unavailable, omit it from the recipe rather than try to substitute another type of sausage. Personally, I adore beans in chili—but those who cannot abide them should feel free to omit them from this recipe. The addition of unsweetened cocoa powder to the stew may seem odd at first glance until one realizes that this ingredient is a common one in many Mexican recipes; the color and flavor that it adds is subtle but necessary.

A good wine suggestion for this dish would be an Italian Barbera; if you'd like beer instead, go Mexican, of course.

$1^1/_2$ pounds each beef and pork stew meat, cut into small cubes

6 to 8 large cloves garlic, finely chopped

3 to 4 tablespoons fresh coriander, finely chopped

1 teaspoon cumin seed, lightly bruised (use a mortar and pestle)

Salt and freshly ground pepper

$^1/_4$ cup, approximately, vegetable oil

10 to 12 dried ancho chilies

2 chipolte chilies with a little of the liquid from the can (1 or 2 tablespoons)

1 pound Mexican chorizo

6 large onions, cut into wedges

$^3/_4$ cup pinto or black beans, soaked overnight and drained (optional)

3 to 4 cups beef stock

1 bottle Mexican beer

2 tablespoons unsweetened cocoa powder

Garnish: sour cream and Salsa Verde (following recipe)

Combine the beef and pork cubes with the garlic, coriander, cumin seed, salt and freshly ground pepper to taste, and add about a tablespoon of vegetable oil to moisten. Toss the mixture and allow to marinate for a few hours or refrigerate overnight.

Roast the ancho chilies in a dry skillet set over moderate heat until they are slightly puffed and emit an aroma; this should take only a minute or 2. Remove the stems and seeds from the chilies and cover the flesh with hot water. Allow to stand until the chilies soften, about an hour. Drain the chilies (reserving the water if you wish to substitute it for some of the stock) and purée with the chipolte chilies and a bit of their liquid.

Heat 2 tablespoons of the vegetable oil in a skillet, brown the beef and pork cubes, and remove them to a large stew pot. Remove the chorizos from their casings and sauté the meat, adding more oil if necessary, until lightly browned. Add to the beef and pork. Drain off all but 1 tablespoon of oil from the skillet. Cook the ancho paste for a few minutes over moderate heat, stirring so that it does not stick. Add to the stew pot.

Sauté the onions until lightly browned but still crisp and add to the beef and pork mixture. Add the beans to the stew and cover all with a mixture of stock and beer. Stir in the cocoa powder and slowly simmer until the meat and the beans are tender, about 2 hours. Serve with sour cream and Salsa Verde.

Salsa Verde
makes about two cups

4 fresh jalapeno chilies (each about 3 inches long)
1 small onion
2 large cloves garlic
1 small bunch fresh coriander
13-ounce can tomates verdes (Mexican green tomatoes), drained

1 large ripe tomato, peeled, seeded, and quartered
Large pinch sugar
Salt and freshly ground pepper
2 tablespoons mild vinegar (rice-wine vinegar is excellent)
2 tablespoons vegetable oil

Split open each chili and remove the veins and seeds; these are the hottest parts. (If you are not used to handling fresh chilies, you might wish to wear rubber gloves while working with them. Be careful to keep your hands away from your face when working with chilies.) Chop the chilies, onion, and garlic coarsely in a food processor. Add the coriander, tomatoes verdes, and the fresh tomato. Process until finely chopped but not puréed. The sauce should contain recognizable pieces of all its ingredients.

Remove from the processor and mix in the sugar, seasonings, vinegar, and oil. Salsa verde may be served immediately or held in the refrigerator in a covered container.

Note: Four chilies make this a very piquant sauce. The amount of chilies used may, of course, be adjusted to your taste.

Veal and Pepper Sauté
serves four

Here veal and peppers are combined with a light tomato sauce, and since very few of us are likely to have on hand a good home-made sauce, I have recommended using canned: Progresso makes a good one.

Although the tomato sauce is traditional for this dish, a lighter sauce may also be served; simply use the recommended amount of vermouth, omit the tomato pulp, and substitute chicken stock for the tomato sauce. For wine, a hearty Oregon Pinot Noir would go well with this dish.

$1\frac{1}{4}$ pounds veal round steak, boneless

Flour seasoned with salt and freshly ground pepper

4 tablespoons olive oil

2 large cloves garlic, peeled and cut in half

2 green bell peppers, seeded and cut into 1-inch squares

$\frac{1}{2}$ cup onion, sliced

$\frac{3}{4}$ cup dry white vermouth or chicken stock

$\frac{1}{2}$ cup tomato pulp (tomatoes, peeled, seeded, and coarsely chopped)

$\frac{3}{4}$ cup tomato sauce

Pinch of sugar

Pinch of dried oregano

Grated Romano or Parmesan cheese

Trim away and discard any fat on the veal; cut the meat into 1-inch cubes and dust them lightly with the seasoned flour. Heat the olive oil in a heavy 12-inch skillet, add the garlic, and sauté until it turns golden (do not brown); remove and discard. Raise the heat to moderately high, add the veal cubes, and brown them on all sides. Add the pepper squares and sauté for 3 minutes; add the onion and continue to cook for another 3 minutes.

Pour in the vermouth (or chicken stock), scraping up any brown particles on the bottom of the pan, and reduce the liquid until it lightly glazes the veal and peppers. Add the tomato pulp and tomato sauce and season with a small pinch of sugar, oregano, salt, and pepper.

Reduce the heat to low, cover the skillet, and simmer for 10 minutes. Taste and adjust the seasoning, if necessary, and serve over steamed rice. Sprinkle the top of each portion with freshly grated Romano or Parmesan cheese.

Veal Nicoise
serves eight

A dish typical of the region around Nice; the veal is simmered in a fresh tomato sauce seasoned with anchovy, orange peel, onion, garlic, herbs, and black olives. The olives must be the imported kind, either from Southern France or Greece, and they must be quickly blanched to remove excess salt. Serve with saffron rice and a spinach salad. For wine choose a spicy Chateau Neuf de Pape.

5 pounds boneless veal, cut
    from the leg
Flour seasoned with salt and
    freshly ground pepper
6 tablespoons olive oil
32 small white onions, skinned
Pinch sugar
$1\frac{1}{4}$ cups onion, finely chopped
4 or 5 cloves garlic, finely

    chopped
4 anchovy fillets, finely chopped
3 pounds fresh ripe tomatoes,
    peeled, seeded, and chopped
$\frac{1}{2}$ teaspoon dried rosemary
$\frac{1}{2}$ teaspoon dried thyme
$\frac{1}{4}$ teaspoon dried fennel seeds
1 cup dry white vermouth or
    dry white wine

1 $\frac{1}{2}$ cups chicken stock
3-inch piece of dried orange
  peel (optional)

1 bay leaf
6 ounces imported black olives,
  blanched, pitted, and halved

Remove any excess fat and cut the veal into 1$\frac{1}{2}$-inch cubes; dust them lightly with the seasoned flour.

Heat the olive oil in a heavy 12-inch skillet. Add only enough veal cubes to the pan as will fit comfortably in a layer; brown them thoroughly. Remove and put in a heavy 5- or 6-quart Dutch oven; continue until all veal is browned.

Add the whole, peeled onions to the oil remaining in the skillet and sprinkle with a pinch of sugar. Sauté them for about 5 minutes, shaking the pan frequently, until they have browned. Remove and set aside.

Pour off all but about 1 tablespoon oil from the skillet and add the chopped onions. Sauté them over a moderate heat for 5 minutes, then add the garlic and anchovy. Stir well and continue to sauté the mixture for another 5 minutes. Stir in the tomato pulp, raise the heat, and allow all moisture released by the tomatoes to evaporate. Meanwhile, briefly grind the rosemary, thyme, and fennel seed with a mortar and pestle and add them to the tomatoes, along with the vermouth, chicken stock, orange peel, and bay leaf. Bring the sauce to a boil and pour it over the veal. Place the Dutch oven on low heat and simmer the stew for 30 to 40 minutes. (Do not add any salt at this point.)

When the veal is almost tender, add the reserved whole onions and continue to cook for another 15 minutes. When the onions are tender, add the olives and stir them in well; continue to cook for only another 2 or 3 minutes. Taste for seasoning, adding salt and pepper if necessary. Remove the orange peel and bay leaf and serve at once.

Veal and Artichokes in Lemon-and-Cream Sauce
serves four

Although many think of the artichoke as merely a vehicle to propel mayonnaise into the mouth, everyone agrees that the most delectable part of that vegetable is the heart. The artichoke heart may be consumed in countless forms: thinly sliced, lightly battered, and fried to a crisp, golden brown; cut in wedges, drizzled with garlic, mint, and olive oil and baked au gratin; julienned and sautéed with prosciutto, heavy cream, and grated Parmesan for a pasta sauce; or just steamed and sprinkled with Parmesan and a little melted butter.

This recipe combines artichoke hearts with veal in a fresh-tasting reduction of lemon and heavy cream. The preparation of the hearts may appear to be rather time-consuming, but since only two large artichokes are used, it should take no longer than ten minutes to complete that portion of the recipe. When working with artichokes, I find using only stainless steel (rather than carbon) knives to be extremely helpful. Also, keeping your hands dry throughout will help you to avoid staining your fingers. I would not substitute either canned or frozen hearts for the fresh, since the flavor would be entirely different.

A Vino Nobile di Montepulciano would be an appropriate wine.

2 large artichokes, stems left on (when peeled, they're as good as the hearts)
$1\frac{1}{2}$ lemons
1 cup heavy cream (preferably unpasteurized)
$1\frac{1}{4}$ pounds veal steak (round or sirloin)

Flour, lightly seasoned with salt and pepper for dredging
3 tablespoons vegetable oil
3 tablespoons onion, finely chopped
1 large clove garlic, finely chopped

To prepare the artichoke hearts, have ready a bowl of cold water to which you have added the juice of $\frac{1}{2}$ lemon. Use the remaining $\frac{1}{2}$ lemon to rub over each surface of the artichokes as they are cut. Begin by bending back each of the outer green leaves and snapping them off close to the core, allowing only the whitish, tender bottom of each leaf to remain (this is the edible portion). Keep snapping off leaves until you get down to the leaves that are a pale yellow-green. Slice these off close to the core.

Cut the now-exposed core (including the stem) in half lengthwise to facilitate removal of the choke. Place your knife just beneath the choke and carefully trim it away without cutting too deeply into the heart itself. Pare away the green outer parts of the leaves remaining on the outside and also peel the tough skin from the stem, which should always be left on. Slice each heart into $1/4$-inch-thick pieces and immediately drop them into the acidulated water. The cleaned hearts may be kept in this manner for hours in advance.

Combine the heavy cream and the juice of the remaining $1/2$ lemon in a small bowl and allow to stand 30 minutes.

Trim away and discard any bone or fat from the veal. Cut the steaks into 3-by-$1\frac{1}{2}$-inch pieces. Dredge the veal in the seasoned flour, shaking away any excess. Heat the oil in a large skillet. Brown the veal strips over moderately high heat, about 2 minutes on each side or until lightly golden. Remove the veal and pour off all but 1 tablespoon of the oil, taking care not to disturb any browned particles on the bottom of the pan.

Place the pan over moderate heat; when the oil is hot add the onion and sauté until it is soft but not browned, about 3 minutes. Add the garlic and the slices of artichoke (well dried), season lightly with salt and pepper, and sauté the vegetables for 5 minutes, stirring frequently. Pour in the cream and lemon mixture, cover the pan, and continue to cook over low heat until the artichoke slices are tender, about 10 to 15 minutes. When the artichokes are done, stir in the veal slices and cook only long enough to warm the meat through. Serve immediately.

Stuffed Breast of Veal
serves ten

There are many recipes in the Italian cuisine for stuffed breast of veal. The ingredients in the stuffing vary widely from town to town but may all have one thing in common: you will not find these delectable dishes on the menu of any of the grand hotels or restaurants, for the preparation is considered "a dish of the people." It may be found on the Sunday dinner table from Milan to Rome, it may be purchased by the pound in a rosticceria, and it is sometimes even seen in the humble trattoria.

This recipe was given to me by a friend whose expertise in Italian cooking is truly wonderful. I have added a fresh artichoke heart to the stuffing; its green color makes a delicate contrast to the cream color of the meat and it also lends an indescribable flavor to the finished dish. The stuffing also includes whole sausages, julienne of carrot, and pitted black olives; when the veal is sliced you will have a lovely mosaiclike effect.

Preparation for this dish should begin at least six hours before you plan to serve it: the veal must be allowed to cool for four hours if the meat and stuffing are to hold together. Since this is a rather rich main course you should serve it with foods that are light and cool. I like to surround the veal with tomatoes stuffed with a creamy rice salad and garnish the platter with sprigs of Italian parsley or watercress. Accompany with a simple green salad vinaigrette and fruit in season for dessert. For more elaborate meals, add the Rice Salad or Eggplant Salad or Potatoes in Pesto. You should serve a really good but not expensive wine with this; a riserva Chianti is my suggestion.

1 tablespoon olive oil
1 small onion, finely chopped
1 rib of celery, finely chopped
1 large fresh artichoke heart, cut into small cubes (see preceding recipe for preparation)
5 sweet Italian sausages
$1/4$ cup grated Parmesan or Romano cheese
1 egg, lightly beaten
1 boned breast of veal, about 5 pounds

Salt and freshly ground pepper
6 ounces mortadella (Italian-style bologna with bits of pistachio), thinly sliced
6 ounces pancetta (Italian-style bacon), thinly sliced (available, like the mortadella, at good Italian markets)
6 to 8 pitted black olives
4 thin strips of carrot, cut into lengths of 4 to 6 inches and cooked

Preheat the oven to 450 degrees.

Heat the olive oil in a 10-inch skillet, add the onion and celery and sauté over moderate heat for about 3 minutes; then add the artichoke heart and cook for another 5 minutes. Remove 2 of the sausages from their casings, crumble the meat, and add it to the skillet. Sauté the sausage meat until all traces of pink are gone.

Remove the mixture from the heat, add the grated cheese and the egg and mix well. Season the breast of veal lightly with salt and pepper and spread the filling on it, leaving a 1-inch border all around the edges. On top place a layer of mortadella slices, then cover with a layer of the pancetta slices, making sure that all of the sausage mixture is covered. In the middle, place the three remaining whole sausages end to end and surround them with the carrot strips and the olives in any way that suits your fancy. Starting with the shortest end nearest you, roll up the veal tightly and tie together with heavy kitchen string every 2 inches along the length of the meat. Season lightly with salt and pepper.

Pour enough olive oil into a heavy ovenproof casserole just to cover the bottom. Add the stuffed veal, rolling it around in the oil so that the surface is lightly coated. Put in the oven uncovered and roast for 15 to 20 minutes to brown. Reduce heat to 325 degrees, cover and roast for 2 hours. Remove from oven, place meat on a serving platter, and cover loosely with foil. Allow the stuffed veal to rest for at least 4 hours before serving. Remove string and slice the veal into $1/2$-inch thicknesses with a very sharp knife.

Grilled Lamb Chops with Rosemary Paste
serves four

Food grilled over an open fire is one of the oldest forms of cooking, and in many ways it remains the best. There is no meat more succulent when grilled than lamb and it should always be done over a moderate fire for the finest results—beautifully browned on the outside and lusciously pink within. Cooking time differs slightly with the various types of grills and also depends greatly upon the temperature of the meat itself; for example, meat at room temperature will take a shorter time to cook. A tool I've found indispensible when cooking on a grill is the instant-reading thermometer—the kind that does not stay in the meat throughout the cooking but is simply stuck into the meat briefly for a reading. It will give you an accurate temperature within seconds. So, rather than cutting large holes in the meat to test for doneness, you know that at 140 degrees, the chops are medium rare.

The lamb here is flavored with a deliciously scented rosemary and garlic paste that is quickly prepared with a mortar and pestle (the amount is much too small to be prepared in a food processor). The chops may of course be cooked under your oven broiler, if you prefer.

A good wine with these chops would be a Zinfandel.

8 1-inch-thick lamb chops, cut from the loin

Rosemary paste

**2 heaping tablespoons fresh
rosemary, finely chopped
4 large cloves garlic, coarsely
chopped**

**¹/₂ teaspoon grated lemon zest
Salt and freshly ground pepper
1 to 1¹/₂ tablespoons fruity
olive oil**

Loin chops are usually cut so that there is a small strip of meat and fat just loosely attached to the main section. Take this strip and stretch it around the chop as tightly as possible; secure it with a metal skewer or toothpick.

To prepare the rosemary paste, combine the rosemary, garlic, lemon zest, and salt and pepper to taste in a mortar. Grind into a paste, adding only enough oil to make it liquid enough to spread. Spoon a little of the paste on each side of the chops and allow to stand for an hour.

Heat the coals in your grill to a moderately hot fire. Sear the chops over the hottest area for a minute per side. Then move them to the coolest part of the fire and continue to grill them for about 5 minutes per side for medium-rare meat—140 degrees on an instant-reading thermometer. Remove the skewers or toothpicks and serve at once.

Grilled Rack of Lamb
serves two

One of the most delectable of meats when done on an outdoor grill. With a dish so simple and delicious, the possible accompaniments are almost endless, but some suggestions, as starters, would be Roasted Pepper Salad, Baked Artichoke Hearts, Potatoes in Pesto, Eggplant Salad, or Rice Salad. For wine, choose your favorite fleshy red—but be sure to choose one that has some tannins.

**1¹/₄ pounds rack of lamb
Salt and freshly ground pepper**

Score the fat side of the rack of lamb with a sharp knife. Season lightly with salt and pepper and cover the exposed ends of the bones with a piece of foil. Place the rack over very hot coals, fat side down, to sear for 2 minutes. Turn bone side down and allow to cook for 35 to 40 minutes. Remove when an instant-ready thermometer registers 140 degrees for medium-rare meat. Allow to stand for 5 minutes before carving.

Sauté of Lamb in Anchovy Cream
serves two

Serve with a Nebbiolo or Zinfandel wine.

2 1½-inch-thick lamb chops
2 tablespoons vegetable oil
Salt and freshly ground pepper
2 tablespoons robust red-wine
   vinegar, preferably balsamic

¼ cup heavy cream, preferably
   unpasteurized
4 anchovy fillets, finely chopped

Bone the chops and cut away any fat or gristle. Cut the meat into cubes; there should be approximately ¾ of a pound. Dry the lamb thoroughly.

Heat the vegetable oil in a 10-inch skillet. When it is hot, add the lamb cubes and brown them over high heat for 3 to 4 minutes. The meat should not be crowded in the pan; if necessary brown it in 2 batches. As soon as the meat is browned, remove it to a plate. Season lightly with salt and pepper.

Reduce the heat to moderate, add the vinegar to the pan juices and cook until it has almost evaporated. Pour in the cream, add the anchovies, and reduce for a minute or 2 until the cream begins to thicken. Add the lamb, reduce the heat, and cook only until the lamb is warmed through. The cream at this point should be thick enough to coat the cubes of meat. Serve at once.

Sauté of Lamb with Artichoke Hearts
serves four

T his savory sauté combines the best of springtime: tender, young lamb with artichoke hearts in a lemony sauce. Serve it with a risotto or Roast Potatoes with Rosemary and Sage or Steamed Potatoes with Parsley Sauce. An appropriate wine would be a rich Chardonnay.

2 pounds boned leg of lamb
Flour, seasoned lightly with
   salt and freshly ground
   pepper
4 tablespoons olive oil
$\frac{1}{2}$ cup onion, finely chopped
2 cloves garlic, finely chopped
Rind of 1 lemon, finely grated
$\frac{1}{2}$ cup dry white vermouth
1 cup chicken stock

1 sprig fresh rosemary or $\frac{1}{2}$
   teaspoon dried
$\frac{1}{2}$ bay leaf
3 large fresh artichoke hearts,
   each cut into 6 pieces (see
   Artichoke Hearts for
   method of trimming) in
   acidulated water
Lemon juice

Trim off and discard any fat and gristle, and cut the meat into 1-inch cubes. Flour the meat, shaking off any excess. Heat the oil in a heavy 10-inch or 12-inch skillet and add the lamb; brown over high heat and remove. To the remaining oil in the skillet, add the onion, garlic, and lemon rind. Sauté this mixture for about 5 minutes, stirring frequently. Pour in the vermouth and reduce over high heat until it is just a glaze. Put the lamb back into the skillet and add the chicken stock, rosemary, and bay leaf; season lightly with salt and pepper. Simmer the lamb for 1 hour, stirring occasionally.

Drain the artichoke hearts and dry thoroughly. Add them to the lamb and continue to simmer for 25 to 35 minutes until they are tender. Add a bit of lemon juice and season to taste. Serve at once.

Lamb Hunter's Style
serves four

A celebrated Roman dish served at Eastertime. The lamb used is traditionally one month old and milk-fed; although it may be impossible to find lamb of this quality in our country, this dish can be successfully prepared with any very young lamb of good quality. It is classically served with peas. For wine, serve Pinot Noir or delicate Nebbiolo.

$2\frac{1}{2}$ pounds very young lamb, cut from the leg, boned, and cut into $1\frac{1}{2}$-inch cubes

Flour seasoned lightly with salt and freshly ground pepper

1 sprig each fresh rosemary and sage (or $\frac{1}{2}$ teaspoon each dried)

2 cloves garlic

3 tablespoons olive oil

1 tablespoon red-wine vinegar

1 cup chicken stock

3 anchovy fillets, finely chopped

Preheat the oven to 325 degrees.

Dredge the lamb cubes in the seasoned flour, shaking off any excess. Finely chop together the herbs and the garlic. Heat 2 tablespoons of the olive oil in a small Dutch oven, add the lamb cubes, and brown them over moderately high heat. Sprinkle with the finely chopped herb and garlic mixture, stirring to coat the meat, and continue to cook for 1 to 2 minutes. Pour the vinegar into the pot, immediately cover, and allow the vinegar to evaporate. Remove the cover, add the chicken stock, cover again, and place in the oven to cook for about 1 hour or until the lamb is very tender. (This depends on the age of your lamb.)

Meanwhile, heat the remaining tablespoon of olive oil in a small skillet, add the anchovy, and cook for a few minutes until the mixture resembles a paste. Stir this paste into the lamb 10 minutes before it has finished cooking.

Lamb Riblets in Lemon-Oregano Marinade
serves four

B reast of lamb marinated in a zesty lemon and oregano base and then gril-led: an inexpensive and delightful main course or appetizer. Serve with a Roasted Pepper Salad or Gazpacho. This dish calls for a big Zinfandel, or try it with Greek retsina if your taste runs that way.

3 pounds breast of lamb, cut into 3- or 4-inch lengths	Salt and freshly ground black pepper
Juice of 4 or 5 lemons	2 or 3 cloves garlic, peeled and sliced (optional)
1 tablespoon dried oregano	

Remove any excess fat from the riblets, and put them in the lemon juice, oregano, salt and pepper to taste, and garlic. Marinate for at least 3 hours or overnight, turning frequently.

Drain the meat, reserving the marinade, and grill over red-hot coals for 30 to 45 minutes, brushing frequently with the marinade, until the riblets are crisp and well browned.

This dish may also be done in a 400-degree oven; the cooking time remains the same, but you must place the riblets on a rack so the fat is allowed to drain off.

Moussaka
serves ten to twelve

T his dish has been claimed by the Greeks, the Turks, the Armenians, and a score of other nations. It is hard to imagine a handful of widely scattered cooks simultaneously devising an idea so unique; what is probably closer to the truth is that the dish arose out of a subtle intermingling of all these cultures.

A good moussaka is free from excess oil; I have suggested broiling the eggplant slices rather than frying them, since they absorb much less oil that way. Be sure also to use a very lean ground lamb; ideally, grind it yourself. Serve with the Octopus and Cucumber Salad and an Oregon Pinot Noir or a California Burgundy.

3 large unpeeled eggplants, cut into slices ½ inch thick	Olive oil

Lamb mixture

2 tablespoons each butter and
 olive oil
2½ cups onion, finely chopped
2 cloves garlic, finely chopped
3 pounds lean ground lamb
1-pound tin Italian plum
 tomatoes, drained and
 coarsely chopped
2 tablespoons tomato paste
2 bay leaves
Pinch of oregano
¼ cup golden raisins, soaked

in dry red wine to cover
 (optional)
Salt and freshly ground pepper
2 cups dry red wine
Pinch each of allspice and
 cinnamon
2 tablespoons parsley, finely
 chopped
3 tablespoons walnuts, coarsely
 chopped

Béchamel sauce with ricotta

8 tablespoons butter
6 tablespoons flour
5 cups hot milk
Salt and freshly ground pepper

Dash freshly ground nutmeg
½ cup ricotta cheese
1 cup grated Kefalotiri or
 Romano cheese

Preheat the broiler to 450 degrees.

Brush both sides of the eggplant slices with a little olive oil and put them on foil-lined baking sheets. Broil the slices 5 to 6 inches from the heat source until lightly browned; turn over and repeat the process. They should be cooked no longer than 5 minutes per side. Set the broiled eggplant aside and lower the oven temperature to 350 degrees.

Start the lamb mixture by heating the butter and olive oil in a large skillet and cooking the onion and garlic in it until golden. Add the ground lamb and cook, breaking the lumps apart with a fork, for 6 to 8 minutes. Add all remaining ingredients except the walnuts (be sure to drain the raisins), and mix well. Cook over moderately high heat until all moisture has evaporated. Remove the excess oil with a bulb baster. Mix in the walnuts and set aside.

Prepare the béchamel: melt the butter in a saucepan and add the flour, stirring constantly with a wire whisk. Cook the roux over moderate heat for

5 minutes, taking care that it does not brown. Stir in the hot milk a little at a time, and whisk well after each addition.

When the sauce thickens, remove it from the heat and season with salt, pepper, and nutmeg. Put the ricotta cheese through a sieve, stir in and set aside.

Oil or butter an ovenproof baking dish (10 by 14 by 2$\frac{1}{2}$ inches) and arrange half the eggplant slices on the bottom, sprinkling them with one-third of the grated cheese; add the lamb mixture, sprinkling again with one-third of the grated cheese; cover with the remaining eggplant slices. Pour the béchamel sauce over all and use the remaining grated cheese to dust the top.

Bake for approximately 1 hour or until the top is a golden brown. Remove from the oven and allow to stand 40 minutes before serving.

This dish should be made a day in advance in order to allow the flavors to mingle and soften. Traditionally it is served slightly warmer than room temperature, which makes it ideal fare for entertaining.

Spanish Pork Roast
serves six to eight

The pork loin is marinated for 24 hours in a mixture of orange juice, thinly sliced onion, bay leaves, and a bit of allspice. The meat is then roasted and allowed to cool, the marinade leaving behind a suggestion of citrus. Serve Curried Eggs as a first course, Salmon Seviche or Potatoes in Pesto as accompaniment. You'll need a full white wine with this: a white Côte du Rhone or Marsanne.

2 cups freshly squeezed orange
   juice
1 teaspoon salt
2 tablespoons sugar
$\frac{1}{2}$ cup onion, thinly sliced

3 bay leaves, broken up into
   pieces
Pinch of allspice
4-pound pork loin roast,
   boneless

4 cloves garlic, peeled and cut
　into slices
Salt and freshly ground pepper

to taste
Orange slices and flat-leaved
　parsley

Marinate the meat 24 hours before it is to be served. Combine the orange juice, salt, sugar, onions, bay leaves, and allspice and mix well. Cut small, deep slits in the roast with a sharp knife and insert in each of them a slice of garlic. Place the roast in a deep dish and pour the marinade over it. Refrigerate for 24 hours, turning occasionally.

Preheat the oven to 350 degrees.

Remove the pork from the marinade, dry well with paper towels, and season it with salt and pepper. Place it in a shallow open roasting pan with the fat side up and roast for about $2\frac{1}{2}$ hours or until the meat thermometer registers 170 degrees.

After the first 15 minutes, baste the meat with fat accumulated in the pan. After the first half hour, add the strained marinade and continue to baste with pan juices every 15 minutes. Remove the meat when done and allow to cool at room temperature. Slice thinly and garnish with orange slices and flat-leaved parsley.

Pork Loin Tonnato
serves six to eight

S ince fine veal is so difficult to obtain, I have adapted this Italian classic using very lean pork in its place. The sauce, a mixture of mayonnaise, lemon, tuna, and anchovy, is equally delicious with poached chicken. Serve with Raw Mushroom Salad or Potatoes in Pesto or Rice Salad. Try a Pinot Grigio as the wine.

4-pound pork loin roast,
　boneless and trimmed of
　excess fat, tied well
Salt and freshly ground pepper
2 small shallots, peeled

8 sprigs Italian (flat-leaved)
　parsley
$6\frac{1}{2}$-ounce can tuna packed in
　olive oil, drained
4 anchovy fillets, drained and

cut in half
1 1/2 tablespoons capers,
   drained, washed, and dried
1 1/2 cups mayonnaise

Lemon juice
Sprigs of Italian parsley, black
   olives, lemon slices

The night before serving, prepare the pork.

Preheat the oven to 350 degrees.

Rub the meat with salt and freshly ground pepper and place it in a shallow roasting pan. Put it in the preheated oven and roast for 2 to 2 1/2 hours or until a thermometer reads 170 degrees, basting the meat with its own juices occasionally. Remove from oven, allow to cool, and wrap tightly in foil.

The next day prepare the sauce: in a food processor, place the shallots, parsley, tuna, anchovy, and capers; blend to a paste. Remove and pour it over mayonnaise and blend well. Add a little lemon juice to taste, taste for seasoning, and chill.

Just before serving, slice the pork into slices 1/4 inch thick; arrange them on a large serving platter, pour sauce over all, and garnish with the parsley, olives, and lemon slices.

Pork Loin Braised in Cider
serves six to eight

T his succulent roast is accompanied by onions, potatoes, and apples that have also been cooked in the cider. Do not use American cider for this recipe; it is too sweet. Instead, use a dry cider from Normandy or England.

Serve with a dry fermented cider or Alsatian Riesling.

4-pound pork loin roast,
   boned and tied
Salt and freshly ground pepper
6 tablespoons butter
1 tablespoon vegetable oil

1/2 cup carrot, finely chopped
1/2 cup celery, finely chopped
1/2 cup leeks, finely chopped
1 large clove garlic, finely
   chopped

1 bay leaf
Pinch ground cloves
3 to 4 cups cider
6 large onions, quartered

14 to 16 very small new
  potatoes, unpeeled
6 large baking apples, peeled,
  cored, and quartered

Preheat the oven to to 350 degrees.

Season the pork loin with the salt and pepper. Heat 3 tablespoons of the butter with the oil in a heavy 10-inch skillet, put in the pork and brown it on all sides. Remove it and set aside.

In the oil remaining in the skillet, sauté the carrot, celery, leeks, and garlic over moderate heat for about 10 minutes; do not brown. Put them in the bottom of a 5- or 6-quart Dutch oven along with the bay leaf and ground cloves; put the pork on top and add enough cider to cover the meat by half.

Put the covered pot in the center of the oven and allow the meat to braise for 1 hour and 45 minutes, basting frequently. Add the onion wedges and the potatoes to the pot, adding a bit more cider if necessary to cover them. Cover and return the pot to the oven for 35 minutes.

Melt the remaining 3 tablespoons butter in a skillet and brown the apple wedges lightly. Add them to the pot and bake for another 10 minutes.

Remove the pork from the pot, place it in the center of a platter, and surround it with the apples, potatoes, and onions; keep warm. Completely degrease the sauce and put it through a sieve. Pour a little of the sauce over the meat and vegetables and serve the rest on the side. Serve at once.

Pork with Onions and Beer
serves six

Certain dishes may be said to warm the heart as well as the stomach. Belgium, known for its somewhat robust cooking, is the origin of carbonnade à la Flamande, a savory stew of beef braised in beer with onions. There is a similar dish called cachuse, prepared in an obscure region of northern France, that substitutes pork for the beef. This dish is a variation on the latter that I think you'll find extremely satisfying on a wintery day.

Added to the pork and sliced onions are small boiling onions; they lend another texture to the stew and are widely available. Do not, under any circumstances, use instead those tiny frozen onions which, when cooked, collapse into a pulpy mess. However, for a stew that is less refined, you may substitute country-style spareribs for the boned pork—but add another hour (approximately) to the cooking time.

Serve with Noodles with Mustard Butter, a well-flavored green salad, and a rich Scottish ale.

6 ounces bacon, cut into small cubes

2 tablespoons vegetable oil

1 pound (about 12 to 14) small boiling onions, peeled and trimmed

2 pounds pork loin, boned, trimmed of any fat or gristle and cut into $1\frac{1}{2}$-inch cubes

Flour seasoned with salt and pepper

$1\frac{1}{2}$ pounds mild onions, peeled and thinly sliced

2 to 3 cloves garlic, finely chopped

3 tablespoons flour

1 cup beef stock

3 cups dark beer (Dos Equis or Heineken are both excellent)

2 tablespoons red-wine vinegar

1 heaping tablespoon brown sugar

$\frac{1}{2}$ teaspoon each dried thyme and tarragon

1 bay leaf

Preheat the oven to 350 degrees.

Sauté the bacon with the oil in a heavy casserole. When it is crisp and its fat is rendered, remove and reserve. Add the whole onions to the fat and brown on all sides, shaking the pan occasionally so that they do not stick. Remove and reserve. Dredge the cubes of pork in the seasoned flour and brown them in the remaining fat over high heat. Remove and reserve.

To the remaining fat add the sliced onions and the garlic; cook slowly over low heat for about 15 minutes, until they are translucent but not brown. Stir in the 3 tablespoons flour and cook for 3 or 4 minutes, stirring constantly, until it is thoroughly incorporated. Pour in the stock and the beer, stirring until the liquid has thickened. Add the vinegar, sugar, thyme, and tarragon and simmer for about 5 minutes.

Add the browned whole onions, bacon, and pork cubes to the liquid, stir in, and place the bay leaf on top. Cover and place in the oven. Bake for about 1 hour, or until the pork is tender. This may be prepared a day in advance, and reheats beautifully.

Grilled Skewered Pork and Sausage
serves ten to twelve

An unusual combination of marinated pork, Italian sausage, and cubes of bread, skewered and grilled. The bread turns brown and crisp and catches the flavors from the two meats that sandwich it. This is delicious as either a main course or a first course. An appropriate wine would be a Montepulciano d'Abruzzo.

1 pound pork tenderloin, cut
   into 1-inch cubes
1/2 cup fruity olive oil
2 tablespoons lemon juice
2 cloves garlic, finely chopped
4 to 5 anchovy fillets, finely
   chopped
2 tablespoons fresh oregano or

sage, finely chopped
1 pound Italian pork sausage,
   either hot or mild
Dense white bread, crusts
   removed, cut into 1 1/2-inch
   cubes, equal to the number
   of pork cubes

Marinate the pork cubes in the olive oil, lemon juice, garlic, anchovy, and herb for a minimum of 3 hours, or overnight. Drain the pork and reserve the marinade. Put the sausages in simmering water and cook them for about 8 minutes, until firm but not completely cooked. Cool slightly and cut into thick rounds. Thread the ingredients onto skewers in the following order: pork, sausage, bread, etc., until each skewer is about three-quarters full.

Baste the skewers generously with the marinade and grill over charcoal or under an oven broiler, turning the skewers frequently and basting the meat with the remaining marinade. The cooking time will be approximately 10 minutes; if the bread cubes are browning too fast, move the skewers to a cooler part of the grill. When done, the meat should be cooked through and the bread, golden and crisp.

Barbequed Spareribs
serves two

E veryone has a favorite version of barbeque sauce; I've always favored
those which are slightly sweet, hot, and garlicky. This particular recipe
evolved from my addiction to chipolte chilies (see Beef and Pork Chili for
a description and source information). After the first taste of these smoky
extra-hot chilies, I knew they would be perfect for a barbeque sauce.

The ribs here are cooked twice. The initial simmering in water to cover
insures that the final product is moist, tender, and falling off the bone. Serve
these ribs with beer from one of the Northwest's excellent microbreweries
or with a dolcetto wine.

$^1/_3$ cup brown sugar
$^1/_2$ tablespoon dry mustard
4 to 6 large cloves garlic, finely
  chopped
2 chipolte chilies, finely
  chopped, and $1^1/_2$ tablespoons of their sauce

$1^1/_4$ cups beer (preferably
  dark)
$^1/_4$ pound butter, melted
Salt
2 pounds meaty baby back ribs

Make a sauce by combining all the ingredients except the ribs, mix well,
and season to taste with salt.

Preheat the oven to 350 degrees.

Place the ribs in a pan, cover them with water, add a little salt, and bring
to a boil. Reduce the heat immediately, and simmer the ribs for 30 minutes.

Set the ribs on a shallow baking pan large enough to hold them in a single
layer and brush generously with the sauce. Let them roast for about an hour,
basting every 15 minutes or so. After about 30 minutes, turn the ribs over,
baste, and continue to roast until the ribs are browned and glazed with the
sauce. Serve with spoonbread and coleslaw.

Roast Ham with Marmalade Glaze
for twelve (with ham left over)

It has become increasingly difficult to locate a good-flavored ham. Most of them are pulpy, oversmoked, and horribly oversalted, with a good deal of water added to boot. However, a reputable butcher should be able to supply you with a good "country-style"—that is, mildly smoked—ham with no water added.

If a whole ham is impractical, the butcher will often be able to cut it in half. This will give you a piece of ham weighing six to eight pounds. The butt end of the ham has more meat on it and is easier to carve; the shank end has more bone but is usually less expensive. A ham with the bone in allows the meat to stay moister and will add additional flavor. Also, after the meat is consumed, the bone may be used to flavor a number of different soups or bean dishes. Allow about a half a pound of ham per person when purchasing ham with the bone in. A precooked ham should be roasted for about sixteen minutes per pound.

Serve with Leeks Vinaigrette or Whipped Yams with Cognac. An almost dry Northwest Riesling would go well with ham.

6- to 8-pound precooked ham   marmalade
**   with bone in $^1/_4$ cup cognac or bourbon**
1 jar imported orange

Preheat the oven to 300 degrees.

Place the ham under cold running water and scrub the rind with a stiff brush; dry thoroughly. Put the ham in a shallow pan with the skin side up and roast without basting for $1^1/_2$ to 2 hours, until tender. Meanwhile, over low heat, melt the marmalade with the cognac or bourbon.

Remove the ham from the oven and raise the heat to 400 degrees. With a sharp knife or kitchen shears, remove the rind from the ham. Score the fat in a diamond pattern and spread the surface of the meat with the glaze. Return the ham to the oven and roast only long enough for the marmalade to glaze and the fat to turn crisp.

Remove from the oven and allow to stand 20 minutes before carving.

CHAPTER SEVEN

VEGETABLES

Artichoke Hearts
Preparation for Cooking

A rtichokes are consumed in countless forms, many of which use only the most succulent part, the heart, and that is what we are concerned with here.

Have a bowl of acidulated water (containing several drops of vinegar or lemon) in which to place the cleaned hearts. (They may be kept from darkening in this manner for an hour or two before cooking, but remember to drain them well.) To prepare the hearts, begin by bending back and snapping off close to the base each of the outer green leaves, allowing only the whitish, tender bottom of each leaf to remain (this is the edible portion). Keep snapping off leaves until you reach a center cone of leaves that are a pale greenish white. Slice this off close to the base. (I find it best to work with a stainless steel paring knife because the artichoke discolors so rapidly.)

Cut the exposed base in half to make it easy to remove any inner leaves and to cut out the choke (the fuzzy hairs growing out of the base); be careful not to cut away too much of the heart itself. Pare away the green outer parts of the leaves remaining on the outside and also peel the tough skin from the stem, which should always be left on. Slice as directed in the individual recipe and immediately drop into the acidulated water.

Baked Artichoke Hearts
serves four

I f you have never tasted a fresh artichoke heart, you have a wonderful surprise in store for you. This is a very simple way to prepare them but the results are ambrosial. It is traditionally served with roast meat, but is just as delicious with Squid and Fish Stew.

Artichokes

The artichoke holds no attraction for those who demand instant gratification: it cannot be attacked with knife and fork and devoured in two or three mouthfuls. It is an exemplification of civilized living, of satisfaction increased by anticipation and desire.

The lineage of the artichoke, if one may trust the most respected reference books, is rather obscure. One source states: "It is an improved cultivated development of the thistle." In the English language "thistle" simply means a prickly plant, but that same word does not exist in botany. The *Encyclopedia Britannica* lists seven plants under that category, of which no two belong to the same genus, and absolutely none to the genus of the artichoke, *Cynara*.

The *Oxford Book of Food Plants* states flatly that "the globe artichoke was known to ancient Greeks and Romans." Some sources say that the artichoke was first introduced into Europe in the fifteenth century, but it is more probable that it was actually a native of Sicily. As a possible alternative, it might have first been a native of Carthage, in northern Africa, and then transplanted to Carthaginian territory in Sicily well before our era. Frequent references to the artichoke in ancient literature are blithely explained away as really being references to the cardoon (*Cynara cardunculus*), a close relative of the globe artichoke.

In any case, the globe artichoke was brought to California by the conquering Spaniards. Today California produces the entire U.S. commercial crop, about 70 million pounds a year, or about three-quarters of an artichoke per person. The average Frenchman or Italian consumes more than two hundred times as many, but in those countries the artichoke is looked upon as rather a humble vegetable, and is usually inexpensive.

When choosing either the large or the small artichokes, pick those with compact heads, and crisp, tightly-closed green leaves. Only in the last few years have the tiny, young artichokes become available. Even these must be trimmed of their tough, fibrous outer leaves to be totally edible. Because artichokes discolor rapidly, use only a stainless-steel knife when trimming them, and immerse each as soon as trimmed in acidulated water (water to which lemon juice or a few drops of vinegar have been added). Keep your fingers dry when working with artichokes to avoid dark stains on your hands.

While a nicely steamed artichoke served up with a vinaigrette or lemon butter makes a satisfying dish, there is much more that can be done with this fine vegetable.

Artichoke-heart lasagne

One of the most marvelous variations on this classic that you'll ever encounter. Take large globe artichokes and trim them down to the hearts. Cut the hearts into thin slices and lightly poach them in a little water to which a good amount of butter has been added. Layer fresh pasta sheets with bits of the artichoke hearts; drizzle with béchamel sauce (see Eggplant Parmesan) and a grating of the very best Parmesan cheese. Repeat until you have reached the top layer. Spread the remaining béchamel on the last layer of pasta, dust with the cheese, dot with butter, and bake until tender.

Provence style

Lightly poach or steam tiny artichokes and add them to a simmering coulis—a mixture of oil, garlic, parsley and tomato (the tomato will first have to be peeled, seeded, chopped, and slightly cooked). Cook for five minutes until the flavors have blended.

Sauce Niçoise for pasta

Sauté a small amount of chopped garlic in olive oil, add trimmed and quartered baby artichokes, and sauté until they are tender. Add a moderate amount of blanched and pitted Calamata olives, the barest handful of chopped fresh mint, and thick julienne of sun-dried tomatoes. (Chunks of fresh, very ripe, tomato can be used instead of the sun-dried, in which case they should be peeled, seeded, and cubed. Add these at the end of the cooking; they should be warmed through but not heated so much that they lose their shape.) Season to taste with salt and pepper and toss immediately with cooked pasta.

2 large artichokes
1/4 cup fruity olive oil
4 to 5 medium cloves garlic,
   peeled

1 tablespoon fresh mint,
   minced
Salt and freshly ground pepper

Preheat the oven to 350 degrees.

See information on preparing artichoke hearts, page 133. Slice each heart into 6 thick pieces. Place them in a shallow ovenproof dish and drizzle with the olive oil, turning them to coat. Add the garlic, sprinkle with the mint, and salt and pepper to taste. Cover the dish tightly with foil and bake for 35 to 40 minutes, removing the foil for the last 10 minutes of baking to lightly brown the hearts. They should be tender enough to offer no resistance to a knife when done. Serve immediately as a first or vegetable course.

Fried Artichoke Hearts
serves four

Catherine de Medici was credited with introducing the artichoke, her favorite vegetable, to France. It is recorded that she especially doted on the hearts when fried, and on one occasion she consumed such an enormous number of the succulent morsels that she almost burst. You have been warned. This dish goes best with simple roasts.

2 large artichokes
2 tablespoons lemon juice
Flour for dredging
1 egg, lightly beaten

Light vegetable oil such as
   safflower or corn oil
Salt
Lemon wedges

Preheat the oven to 300 degrees.

Add the lemon juice to a bowl of cold water. Prepare the artichoke hearts (see page 133) and cut them into slices 1/2 inch thick and drop them immediately into the water. When you have finished slicing them all, drain well.

Have ready a skillet containing 1/2 inch of oil standing over moderately high heat. Flour each piece of the heart heavily, transfer it to the beaten egg to coat thoroughly, and drop into the hot oil. Let the hearts brown on one side, then turn over and brown the other side. The whole cooking process should take no longer than 2 to 3 minutes. Do not overcook or they will become mushy. Remove the fried hearts to a plate and keep warm in the oven until all are done. Sprinkle them with salt and serve with lemon wedges.

Stuffed Artichokes
serves four

T hese stuffed artichokes are too rich to serve as a first course; however, they make a splendid light entrée for lunch or a light supper. A good-quality canned tuna or fresh crabmeat may be substituted for the shrimp as an interesting variation.

4 large artichokes	Parmesan or mixture of Parmesan and Romano cheeses
4 tablespoons olive oil	
1 cup onion, finely chopped	Pinch dried hot pepper flakes or dash Tabasco
$\frac{1}{2}$ cup celery, finely chopped	
2 large cloves garlic, peeled and finely chopped	Salt
$\frac{1}{2}$ pound Pacific shrimp, cooked (do not use canned)	$\frac{1}{2}$ tablespoon lemon rind, finely grated
2 cups fresh bread crumbs	$\frac{1}{4}$ cup parsley, finely chopped
1 cup grated imported Italian	1 egg, lightly beaten

Trim off and discard the stems and any small bottom leaves of the artichokes. With kitchen shears, cut off about $\frac{1}{4}$ inch of each lower leaf; using a sharp knife cut off about 1 inch of the top. Bring a large pot of salted water to a boil; add 1 tablespoon olive oil, drop in the artichokes, and cook for about 20 minutes (they will not be done). Remove them, invert them in a colander to allow them to drain, and discard all but 1 cup of their cooking liquid.

When the artichokes are cool enough to handle, hold them upright and gently spread the leaves until you have reached the center. With a spoon or a grapefruit knife remove and discard the chokes. Set the artichokes aside while you prepare the stuffing.

Preheat the oven to 350 degrees.

Heat 3 tablespoons of the olive oil in a skillet, add the onion, celery, and garlic, and sauté over medium heat about 5 minutes until the vegetables are tender but not brown. Remove from the heat and stir in the shrimp meat, bread crumbs, and grated cheese and season with the hot pepper flakes, salt, lemon rind, and parsley. Stir in the beaten egg to bind.

Divide the stuffing into 4 parts. Stuff each artichoke center with half its alloted share; use the remaining stuffing as follows: gently pull each large leaf away from the body and place about 1 teaspoon of stuffing in the pocket. When finished, press the leaves back into shape. Continue until all 4 artichokes are stuffed.

Place the artichokes in a pot (with lid) large enough to hold them in one layer. Around them pour the reserved cooking liquid, cover, and bake for about 30 minutes or until just tender. Serve at once.

Asparagus with Sauce Maltaise
serves four

T his is a classic French dish, but one that is not often seen on menus in this country. What a shame, for the combination of asparagus with sauce maltaise (orange-and-sherry-flavored hollandaise) is so wonderful it must be tasted to be believed. The sauce is also absolutely superb on poached or grilled salmon.

3 egg yolks
1 tablespoon sherry-wine
  vinegar
$\frac{1}{4}$ cup fresh orange juice
1 to 2 tablespoons lemon juice
Salt
Pinch cayenne pepper

12 tablespoons unsalted
  butter, frozen and cut into
  small pieces
Zest of 1 orange, finely grated
1 to 2 tablespoons heavy cream
  (optional)
1 pound fresh asparagus

Put the yolks in a heavy-bottomed saucepan (enameled cast iron is excellent) and whisk lightly. Add the vinegar, orange juice, lemon juice, salt, and cayenne and whisk until well combined and creamy. Place the mixture over low heat and beat until it begins to thicken. Whisk in the butter, bit by bit, taking care not to let the sauce get too hot. If it does, remove the pan from the heat and whisk the sauce until it cools. Continue to add the butter until the sauce has thickened considerably. Stir in the grated orange zest, add some of the heavy cream if you wish to thin the sauce slightly, and taste for seasoning.

While the sauce is cooking, snap off the tough ends of the asparagus, and cook the stalks until they are just tender. Drain and dry thoroughly. Arrange on serving plates and pour over each portion a thick ribbon of the sauce. Serve immediately.

Asparagus with Fresh Ginger
serves two

T he Chinese technique of stir-frying may successfully be applied to fresh asparagus, which here is seasoned lightly with fresh ginger root, chicken broth, dry sherry, and sesame oil. Do not substitute the dried spice for the fresh ginger root: the flavor will not be the same. The small amount of sesame oil, a classic Chinese touch, lends the finished dish a subtle and slightly nutlike taste that is most pleasant. Try this with Fish and Cucumber Sauté.

1 pound fresh asparagus
2 tablespoons dry sherry
$\frac{1}{4}$ cup chicken stock
$\frac{1}{2}$ teaspoon cornstarch
$1\frac{1}{2}$ tablespoons vegetable oil
(peanut, safflower, corn)

10 paper-thin slices fresh
unpeeled ginger root
Salt
Pinch of finely granulated
sugar
$\frac{1}{2}$ teaspoon sesame oil

Cut off and discard the tough white ends of the stalks. Cut the spears on the bias into $1\frac{1}{2}$- to 2-inch lengths.

Combine in a small bowl or cup the sherry, stock, and cornstarch and stir well. Place all the ingredients ready and close to your cooking area.

Heat the vegetable oil in a heavy 10-inch skillet or wok; add the ginger slices and stir them in the oil for a few seconds; do not allow them to brown. Add the asparagus, seasoning stalks lightly with salt and a bit of sugar. Toss them about in the oil for about 3 minutes. Pour in the sherry-cornstarch mixture and stir constantly until it thickens (this will happen almost immediately). Stir in the sesame oil, blend thoroughly, and serve at once.

Asparagus with Egg-Lemon Sauce
serves two

Egg-lemon sauce is of Greek origin. It is an extraordinarily light concoction that somewhat resembles a hollandaise, but without the addition of butter. It can be successfully prepared in a cast-iron enameled saucepan if you are careful not to overheat it. If you have no such pan, substitute a double boiler and allow a few minutes more for the sauce to thicken. You will find the sauce just as delightful on green beans or broccoli. This will make a wonderful vegetable accompaniment to any sautéed meats.

1 pound asparagus	4 or 5 tablespoons lemon juice
2 large eggs	1 teaspoon cornstarch
$1/4$ teaspoon dry mustard	6 tablespoons chicken stock
Dash Tabasco	Salt and freshly ground pepper

Break off and discard the tough, woody ends of the stalks and, if the stalks are thick, peel them with the aid of a potato peeler. Bring a large skillet filled with salted water to a boil and add the asparagus. Allow the vegetable to cook for 4 to 7 minutes, depending on thickness. (Remove a stalk, cut a bit off the end, and taste to check for doneness.)

Meanwhile, in an enameled cast-iron saucepan place the eggs, mustard, Tabasco, and lemon juice. Combine the cornstarch with the chicken stock in a small bowl and mix thoroughly; add to the saucepan, season lightly with salt and pepper, and blend all together with a wire whisk. Place the saucepan over moderate heat and allow the sauce to thicken slowly, whisking continuously; this should take no longer than 3 to 5 minutes. Remove from heat immediately when done.

When the asparagus has cooked, drain it and dry thoroughly on paper towels. Place in a serving dish, pour the sauce over, and toss gently. Serve at once.

Asparagus Wrapped in Prosciutto
serves four

T his dish makes a dressy first course or accompaniment for a simple dish like Roast Chicken with Rosemary and Garlic.

32 asparagus spears	**3 teaspoons melted butter**
8 thin slices prosciutto	**$\frac{1}{4}$ cup grated Parmesan cheese**

Preheat the oven to 450 degrees.

Break or cut off and discard 2 to 3 inches of the asparagus stalks. Bring a 10- or 12-inch skillet filled with water and seasoned with salt to a boil, add the asparagus, and cook over high heat for 4 to 7 minutes, depending on the thickness of the stalks. (Pull one out of the water after a few minutes, cut off a bit of the end, and taste it, just as you would do for pasta.) Remove the asparagus when done and drain well. Divide into 4 groups of 8 each. Wrap each group in 2 slices of prosciutto, place on a serving platter, drizzle with melted butter, and sprinkle with the grated cheese. Place in the oven just long enough to allow the cheese to melt, and serve at once.

Brussels Sprouts with Cheese and Bread Crumbs
serves four

1 pound Brussels sprouts	**$\frac{1}{4}$ cup dry bread crumbs**
3 tablespoons butter	**Salt and freshly ground pepper**
$\frac{1}{4}$ cup freshly grated Parme- san cheese	

Cut off and discard the stems of the sprouts. Place in a pot of boiling salted water and cook for about 8 minutes, or until the sprouts are almost tender. Remove from heat, drain thoroughly, and chop coarsely.

In a 10-inch skillet melt the butter; when the foam subsides, add the chopped sprouts and sauté them over moderate heat until they begin to brown. Sprinkle with the grated cheese, the bread crumbs, and salt and pepper; toss the mixture together well for 1 to 2 minutes (only long enough to allow the cheese to melt) and serve immediately.

Brussels Sprouts in Vinegar
serves four

Here the Brussels sprouts are first blanched, then cooked in a light vinegar sauce. The vinegar specified is rice-wine vinegar, one of the most delicate; it is available in shops selling Oriental foods. This recipe complements corned beef especially well.

1 pound Brussels sprouts
$^1/_3$ cup rice-wine vinegar
$^1/_2$ cup water

$1^1/_2$ teaspoons sugar
Dash salt

Trim the stems off the sprouts and discard. Cut each sprout in half unless they are very small. Place in a pot of boiling, salted water and cook for 5 minutes. Remove to a colander and refresh under cold running water.

Combine the rice-wine vinegar, water, sugar, and salt in a pot large enough to hold all the sprouts and bring to a boil; add the sprouts and cook for about 8 minutes or until they are just tender. (Most of the vinegar mixture will be absorbed by the vegetable.) Serve at once.

Stuffed Cabbage with Mustard Sauce
serves six to eight

There are many versions of stuffed cabbage, most of them uninspired and rather pedestrian. This recipe, which makes use of Savoy cabbage and fennel, two of the finest winter vegetables, is exceptional. Savoy cabbage is more delicately flavored than the smooth-leaved head cabbage, and its lacy dark green to yellow leaves are most attractive.

The presentation of this dish is rather unusual, since the cabbage is served whole, with the filling replacing its core. Wedges are cut from it and the mustard sauce spooned over them. Serve with an hors d'oeuvre of Potted Salmon or Potted Shrimp and Leeks Vinaigrette. Instead of wine, serve a Normandy cider with this.

**1 large Savoy cabbage (about
    the size of a basketball)**

Filling

**1 small fennel bulb, leaves and
    stems removed, finely
    chopped (about 1 cup) (sub-
    stitute celery, if fennel is
    unavailable)**
**1 medium onion, peeled and
    finely chopped**
2 cloves garlic, finely chopped
**1 baking apple, peeled, cored,
    and coarsely chopped**
1½ pounds pork loin, ground
2 tablespoons fresh thyme,

minced, or 1 teaspoon dried
**¼ teaspoon ground cumin
    plus additional cumin to
    sprinkle on leaves**
**Pinch powdered saffron
    (optional)**
Salt and freshly ground pepper
**½ cup homemade bread
    crumbs**
2 tablespoons heavy cream
1 egg, lightly beaten
2 cups chicken stock

Sauce

2 tablespoons butter
1½ tablespoons flour
½ cup heavy cream
Freshly grated nutmeg

Salt and freshly ground pepper
**1 teaspoon French Pommery
    mustard, or other grainy
    French mustard**

Preheat the oven to 375 degrees.

Bring a large kettle of salted water to a boil. Put the cabbage in whole and simmer it for 10 to 15 minutes, turning it occasionally. (This removes the strong aroma from the cabbage.)

While the cabbage is blanching, place all the filling ingredients except the final 3 in a bowl and mix together by hand. Combine the heavy cream with the egg and add to filling, again blending by hand.

Remove the cabbage to a deep pan in the sink and run it under cold water to arrest the cooking process. As soon as it is cool enough to handle easily, trim away and discard most of the stem. Place the cabbage upright in the center of a large piece of cheesecloth or other clean, light cloth. Pull each leaf away from the head (but do not break them off) and press gently down until you reach the tight central core of leaves; cut the core out, mince it, and add to filling mixture, or reserve it for another use.

Season the uppermost leaves with a little salt and a sprinkling of ground cumin. Mound the filling in the hollow left by the core and, leaf by leaf, reform the entire cabbage, seasoning lightly between all the leaves. Bring the cheesecloth up over the cabbage, twist it tightly, tie with string, and cut off; discard any excess cheesecloth.

Place the stuffed cabbage in an ovenproof casserole, add the chicken stock, and bake for about 2 hours, basting occasionally so the cabbage will not dry out. Remove from casserole, reserving 1 cup of the stock. Keep cabbage warm while making the sauce.

Melt the butter in a small saucepan, stir in the flour with a wire whisk, and cook over low heat for 5 minutes; do not brown. Stir in the reserved chicken stock and cook until the mixture thickens. Add the heavy cream, the seasonings, and the mustard and cook over low heat for an additional 5 minutes to allow the flavors to blend.

Place the stuffed cabbage on a serving dish; cut and carefully remove cheesecloth. Slice into wedges, spoon sauce over, and serve immediately, or serve and pass the sauce separately.

Carrots with Bay Leaves and Sherry-Wine Vinegar
serves four

Sherry-wine vinegar has a smooth and slightly nutty flavor that enhances the natural sweetness in vegetables such as carrots and leeks, and also marries beautifully with asparagus (see Asparagus with Sauce Maltaise).

1 pound young carrots
2 to 3 bay leaves
3 tablespoons sherry-wine
  vinegar

Salt and freshly ground pepper
1 tablespoon olive oil

Peel the carrots and cut lengthwise in halves or in quarters. The carrot sticks should be no bigger around than your smallest finger.

Place in a pan; add the remaining ingredients and just enough water to cover. Bring to a boil, reduce the heat to moderate, and cook until tender. More water may be added if necessary but the end result should be tender but firm carrot sticks coated with a light glaze. Remove the bay leaves and serve at once.

Braised Celery Root
serves four

A delicate-tasting vegetable dish that complements pork or chicken especially well.

1 celery root, about 1 pound
3 cups chicken broth
Small pinch of dried thyme

Salt and freshly ground pepper
$^1/_3$ cup freshly grated Parmesan cheese

Peel the celery root with a sharp paring knife. Working quickly, cut into $^1/_2$-inch cubes and drop immediately into a bowl of water containing a dash of vinegar to prevent discoloration. Bring the chicken stock to a boil. Add the thyme and the celery root; reduce heat and simmer until you can pierce the vegetable easily with a knife (about 10 minutes). Drain, reserving the stock for future use, and place in a serving plate. Sprinkle with salt, pepper, and grated cheese. Toss well and serve immediately.

Corn with Ancho Chili Butter
serves four

2 to 3 large dried ancho chilies
1 stick unsalted butter
Lime juice to taste
Salt

4 ears very fresh corn on the
   cob
Large pinch sugar

Roast the ancho chilies in a dry skillet set over moderate heat until they are fragrant and begin to puff up, only a minute or 2. Take care not to burn the chilies—this will make them bitter and unusable. When slightly cooled, remove the stems and seeds from the chilies and cover the flesh with hot water. Allow to soak only long enough for the chilies to soften, 40 to 60 minutes. Drain the chilies and purée in a food processor. Add the butter, cut into small pieces, and blend together into a thick paste. Season with a little of the lime juice and salt to taste. Refrigerate until firm. This may be made 1 or 2 days in advance and freezes well.

Husk the corn. Bring a large pot of water, with a pinch of sugar, to the boil. Add the corn, cook no longer than 3 minutes, drain the corn thoroughly, and serve at once with the ancho butter.

Corn and Pepper Sauté
serves four

Rather than using fresh jalapeno peppers here you may wish to substitute the pickled variety. I always keep a jar of them, packed whole with strips of onion and carrot, in my refrigerator and find them useful for adding a little pizzazz to coleslaw, meatloaf, or any other dish calling for a bit of fresh bell pepper.

4 or 5 large ears of fresh corn
3 tablespoons butter
$^3/_4$ cup onion, finely chopped
2 fresh jalapeno pepppers,
   stems and seeds removed,

finely chopped
2 large cloves garlic, finely
   chopped
$^1/_4$ teaspoon dried oregano
$1^1/_2$ tablespoons lemon juice

Strip off the outer husks and the silk from the corn. Cut the corn away from the cobs. You can, if you wish, use one of those corn-cutting devices for this although it is quite simple to accomplish the task with a sharp knife; holding an end of the ear of corn over a bowl, cut downward, removing a few rows of kernels at a time. Continue until all the corn is cut off.

Melt the butter in a 10-inch skillet. Add the onion and peppers; sauté over moderate heat until the onion becomes transparent, about 5 or 6 minutes.

Add the garlic, corn, and oregano and cover. Simmer for 10 minutes, stirring occasionally.

Remove the lid, raise the heat to high, add the lemon juice, and salt and pepper to taste. Reduce any remaining liquid, cooking only a minute or 2, and serve immediately.

Eggplant Parmesan
serves four to six

My version of this dish, slightly unorthodox, covers the eggplant slices with a crisp bread crumb crust, overlaps them, fills the space in between with a dense, homemade tomato sauce, and coats the top lightly with a béchamel sauce thickened with Parmesan cheese. It is baked just long enough to allow the ingredients to heat through.

This dish may be served as a main course with the addition of a good French or Italian bread, green beans in a lemon and oil dressing, and fruit and cheese for dessert. It may also be used as a vegetable course.

Tomato sauce

1 tablespoon olive oil
2 tablespoons onion, finely
  chopped
1 clove garlic, finely chopped
3 cups tomatoes, skinned,

  peeled, and finely chopped
Pinch each of sugar, allspice,
  and mild chili powder
Salt and freshly ground pepper

Eggplant

1½-pound eggplant, un-
   peeled, cut into slices ½
   inch thick
Flour, seasoned lightly with
   salt and pepper

1 egg, lightly beaten
Bread crumbs
Vegetable oil for frying

Béchamel sauce with Parmesan cheese

1 tablespoon butter
1 teaspoon flour
1 cup milk
Pinch each of grated nutmeg

   and cayenne pepper
Scant ½ cup grated Parmesan
   cheese

First prepare the tomato sauce: heat the oil in a saucepan and sauté the onion and garlic for 5 minutes; add the tomatoes, sprinkle with a pinch of sugar, allspice, chili powder, salt, and pepper, and bring to a boil. Reduce the heat and simmer the sauce over moderate heat for about 45 minutes or until it thickens. It should be of spreading consistency. Cover and set aside.

Preheat the oven to 400 degrees.

Coat the eggplant slices with the seasoned flour, dip into the beaten egg, and then coat heavily with the bread crumbs. Repeat this procedure until all the eggplant slices are breaded. Place the slices in the refrigerator; the chilling will help the bread crumbs to adhere.

Meanwhile, prepare the Parmesan sauce. Heat the butter in a saucepan; when it is melted add the flour and blend it into the butter with a wire whisk. Cook over low heat for 5 minutes; do not allow the roux to brown. Add the milk, stirring all the while, and bring to a boil. Reduce the heat and cook until the sauce is thickened. Season with the nutmeg and cayenne, and add the cheese, stirring until it has melted. Taste and season with salt, if necessary. Cover with a round of waxed paper placed directly on the surface of the sauce and set aside.

Heat enough vegetable oil to just cover the bottom of a large heavy skillet. Add the eggplant and fry it, a few slices at a time, until golden brown (2 or

3 minutes on each side), adding more oil as needed. Drain the cooked slices on absorbent paper.

To assemble: lightly butter an ovenproof platter about 14 inches long. Place the smallest slice of eggplant at one end of the platter and spread with some of the tomato sauce; place the next largest slice overlapping on top of this and again spread with some of the tomato sauce. Continue in this manner until you have reassembled the entire eggplant.

Remove the waxed paper from the Parmesan sauce and spoon the sauce over the center of the overlapping slices of eggplant; spoon the remainder of the sauce around the sides. Bake the eggplant for about 10 minutes, running the dish under the broiler for 2 or 3 minutes to lightly brown the top. Serve at once.

Eggplant Caviar

This is actually a sort of relish; there are many different versions. It is served as an hors d'oeuvre or part of a buffet; accompany it with toasted rounds of French bread or strips of toasted pita.

1½-pound eggplant
¼ cup olive oil
1 cup onion, finely chopped
2 cloves garlic, finely chopped
1 large ripe tomato, peeled, seeded, and finely chopped
2 green bell peppers, roasted and finely chopped

Salt and freshly ground pepper
Dash Tabasco
Juice of ½ lemon
Dash red-wine vinegar
¼ cup parsley, finely chopped

Preheat the oven to 425 degrees.

Cut off and discard the green cap from the eggplant. Put the eggplant in a shallow pan and roast it, whole, for 30 to 35 minutes, until soft. Remove the eggplant from the oven and allow it to cool long enough so that it can be handled.

Heat 2 tablespoons of the olive oil in a 10-inch skillet. Add the onion and garlic and sauté over moderate heat for about 10 minutes; do not brown.

Cut the eggplant in half and scoop out the pulp. Chop it fine, add the mince to the onions, and add the tomato and the roasted peppers. Season lightly with salt and pepper and sauté for an additional 10 minutes, until most of the excess moisture is evaporated.

Remove from heat and stir in the remaining 2 tablespoons olive oil, lemon juice, vinegar, and parsley. Taste for seasoning, correct if necessary, and chill for 1 hour before serving.

Baked Eggplant Cubes
serves four

Very often it is the simplest foods that taste the best, and if the preparation also is simple, so much the better for the cook. Nothing could be more straightforward than the recipe here, which is especially good with lamb dishes.

1 firm medium-size eggplant	**pepper**
Flour seasoned with salt and	**Olive oil or melted butter**

Preheat the oven to 450 degrees and oil a large baking sheet with sides.

Peel and cut the eggplant into 1-inch-thick slices, and then into 1-inch cubes. Dust the cubes lightly with the seasoned flour—quickly done by placing the flour and the eggplant in a paper or plastic bag and shaking. Place the cubes a bit apart from each other on the prepared baking sheet. Over each piece, pour a dollop of oil, just enough to moisten the eggplant.

Bake for 20 minutes. The eggplant cubes will be slightly crisp and lightly browned on the outside and soft and custardy within.

Fennel Sauté with Prosciutto
serves four

1 small fennel bulb (about 1
   pound)
2 tablespoons butter

3 ounces prosciutto or baked
   ham cut into julienne
Salt and freshly ground pepper

Cut the stems and leaves from the fennel bulb and reserve for another use. Remove and discard any discolored outer sections of the bulb; cut the remainder into bite-size pieces and cook in boiling, salted water for 5 minutes. Remove, refresh under cold running water, and drain well.

Melt the butter in a skillet. Add the prosciutto or ham and sauté over high heat for 2 minutes. Add the fennel and continue to cook for another 5 minutes, stirring frequently. Season to taste with salt and pepper and serve.

(See fennel box on following pages)

Green Bean and Lemon Sauté
serves four

1 pound green beans, cut into
   3-inch lengths
2 tablespoons butter

Zest of 1 lemon
Juice of $\frac{1}{4}$ lemon
Salt and freshly ground pepper

Put the beans into boiling, salted water and cook for 6 to 8 minutes. Pour into a colander, refresh under cold water, and drain well. Melt the butter in a skillet, add the beans, lemon zest and juice, salt, and pepper and sauté over medium heat for 3 to 4 minutes, tossing well. Serve immediately.

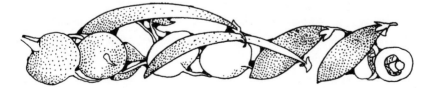

Fennel

Thomas Jefferson, who gave great attention to his extensive gardens at Monticello, received fennel seeds from Italy with this note: "The fennel is beyond every other vegetable, delicious." History does not record Jefferson's use of fennel, but successive generations of Americans have not given it the attention it deserves.

This versatile vegetable, which is considered an herb in France, has a cool, crisp licorice-tasting bulb and long stems covered with lacy dark green leaves resembling dill. Although all parts of the plant, including the flowers, can be eaten, the part most often used is the bulb; its flavor is similar to that of celery with a refreshing anise tang; the texture, too, is similar, being slightly more dense and having no "strings." It may be eaten raw or cooked, although the flavor softens when cooked, becoming slightly sweeter. Fennel is in season from October through April. In supermarkets it is sometimes mislabeled anise. Select bulbs that are firm and crisp and white to a light green in color. If the outer branches are tough or discolored, they should be removed and discarded.

To appreciate its true flavor fennel is best eaten raw, as part of a salad, a dish of crudités, or an aioli garni. It is especially pleasing with a goat cheese or a young Parmesan at the grana stage, or with a creamy French cheese. In Italy it is often served at the beginning or the end of a meal dipped in a sauce of the finest virgin olive oil seasoned with salt and pepper. Any sauce that accompanies fennel can be heightened with a bit of Pernod, which underlines the anise flavor. This applies too to recipes in which chicken or fish are being cooked with fennel; note that fennel goes particularly well with fish.

Braised fennel

Place small bulbs (trimmed and cut in two) in a pan large enough to hold them in a single layer with a dozen peeled garlic cloves, a good measure of olive oil, salt, and pepper. Sauté over low heat for about twenty minutes until lightly browned, then add about a half cup of chicken stock and continue to cook, covered, until the fennel is tender and the sauce reduced and caramelized to a rich, brown syrup.

Fennel fritters

Blanch sections of the bulb, then coat lightly with egg and flour. Fry until golden brown and serve with lemon wedges or a Pernod-flavored mayonnaise.

Roast pork with fennel

Lard a pork loin with strips of raw fennel in sufficient quantity so that when the roast is carved the cross-section will present a pattern of green. Rub the roast with fresh sage, salt, and pepper. Marinate overnight in a dry, white wine. Drain the pork, reserving the marinade. When the roast is cooked, pour the marinade into a roasting pan and reduce over high heat, adding about a teaspoon of Pernod when it is finished.

Fennel-anchovy-almond paste
(an appetizer from Provence)

Mash a cup of blanched almonds with a dozen anchovy fillets and one small fennel bulb into a paste and thin the mixture with a few tablespoons of good olive oil. Season lightly with salt, pepper, and a pinch of fresh mint. Serve atop toast points.

Fennel with anchovy-garlic-flavored oil
(from the Piedmont region of Italy)

Combine a few tablespoons butter with a good amount of olive oil in a saucepan and add a tin of finely chopped anchovy fillets as well as two or three garlic cloves, also finely chopped. Cook over low heat until the garlic and anchovies have softened and almost dissolved, and the sauce is smooth. Serve hot with strips of raw fennel and other fresh vegetables, and crusty Italian bread.

Green Bean and Pepper Sauté
serves four to six

1 pound green beans, cut into 3-inch lengths	2½ tablespoons butter
2 medium green peppers, seeded and cut into julienne	¾ cup onion, finely sliced
	Small pinch sugar

Put the beans into boiling, salted water and cook for 6 to 8 minutes, pour into a colander, refresh under cold running water, and drain well. Blanch the julienne strips of green pepper in boiling water for 1 minute, immediately plunge them into cold water, and drain well.

Melt the butter in a skillet set over medium heat, add the onions, sprinkle with a small pinch of sugar, and sauté for 5 minutes. Add the beans and the peppers and cook only long enough to heat the vegetables through; they should still be crisp. Season with salt and freshly ground pepper.

Leeks Vinaigrette
serves four

This is an extremely simple recipe. The poached leeks are dressed while they are still hot and—this is very important—with sherry-wine vinegar and a good olive oil. Something wonderful happens when the vinegar and oil come into contact with the hot vegetable; the flavors of all are intensified and the aroma emitted is sheer heaven. This dish is delicious with roast beef, lamb, or chicken.

6 or 8 leeks	shops and specialty stores)
Dash of vinegar	½ cup fruity olive oil
2 tablespoons sherry-wine vinegar (available in wine	Salt and freshly ground pepper

Cut off the green tops of the leeks and save for the soup pot all but 2 inches. Slice the remaining part of the leeks lengthwise almost to the root end. Wash them thoroughly under cold running water to remove all the sand and grit. Cut off and discard the root end, slice each leek into 2-inch lengths, and put in a pot of boiling salted water to which a dash of vinegar has been added. (The vinegar will allow the leeks to remain white and keep their flavor.) Cook over medium heat for 10 to 15 minutes or until tender. Remove, run under cold water to arrest the cooking process, and drain thoroughly.

Place the leeks in a shallow serving dish, pour the sherry-wine vinegar and oil over them, season with salt and pepper to taste, toss together gently, and serve immediately.

Gratin of Leeks
serves four

A lmost any vegetable is at home in a gratin. Here the leeks are wrapped in slices of ham or prosciutto, bathed in heavy cream, and drizzled with a mixture of grated cheese and bread crumbs. This may be served as an unusual first course or as the vegetable course.

8 leeks
Dash of vinegar
4 slices of baked ham or
   prosciutto
Enough heavy cream to cover
   bottom of gratin dish

(about $^1/_2$ cup)
3 tablespoons grated Parmesan
   or Gruyère cheese
3 tablespoons bread crumbs
$^1/_2$ tablespoon butter

Preheat the oven to 375 degrees.

Trim and clean the leeks as in the preceding recipe. Tie them together in a bunch with kitchen string and place them in a pot of boiling salted water to which a dash of vinegar has been added; simmer them for 8 minutes.

Remove leeks from the water, untie them, and drain thoroughly. Wrap each slice of ham or prosciutto around 2 leeks and place in a buttered ovenproof gratin dish large enough to hold them in a single layer. Pour the heavy cream over the rolls and sprinkle the top with the cheese and bread crumbs; dot the top with the butter cut into small bits. Bake for 20 to 30 minutes or until the top is a golden brown. Serve immediately.

Roasted Sweet (Bell) Peppers

Roasted peppers may be used in any recipe calling for cooked or sautéed peppers. They will add a more subtle flavor and a more interesting texture. Keep in mind that any of these recipes may be prepared with green bell peppers, although you will not find them as succulent as the red.

In the broiler

Preheat to highest temperature. Set broiler rack so that the tops of the peppers will be about 4 inches below the heat source. Spread foil over the oven rack and place the whole peppers on it. Roast, turning occasionally, until the skin is charred and almost black all over.

Remove the peppers, wrap them in a tea towel, and allow them to steam for about 5 minutes. Transfer the peppers from the towel to a colander and run cold water over them until they are cool enough to handle. The skins should slip off easily under running water. Remove the core and seeds and slice the flesh into strips.

On an outdoor grill

Place the rack 4 to 6 inches above very hot coals. Set the whole peppers on the rack and proceed as above. This method will take a bit longer than if done in the oven, but the peppers will take on a marvelous smoky flavor.

Piperade (Ham-Vegetable Sauté with Eggs)
serves four

A dish characteristic of the Basque country. A sauté of peppers, onions, tomatoes, and ham bound together with loosely scrambled eggs, piperade makes a wonderful lunch or light summer supper. Serve with a semi-dry Zinfandel or a white Pinot Noir.

4 tablespoons olive oil
1 cup prosciutto (or good
    baked ham), cut into thick

julienne
1 medium onion, cut in half
    and thickly sliced

2 cloves garlic, finely chopped
2 large ripe tomatoes, peeled,
    seeded, and coarsely
    chopped
Salt and freshly ground pepper
Pinch of sugar (optional)
Dash Tabasco
2 roasted red peppers (see

Roasted Sweet Peppers), cut
    into thin strips
5 eggs, lightly beaten
2 tablespoons parsley, finely
    chopped
Croutons made from French or
    Italian bread, thinly sliced
    and fried

Heat the olive oil in a heavy 10-inch skillet, add the prosciutto (or ham) and sauté until it is lightly browned around the edges. Remove with a slotted spoon and reserve.

Add the sliced onion to the skillet and sauté over moderate heat until tender but not brown, about 5 minutes. Stir in the garlic and the tomatoes and season with salt, pepper, and Tabasco; use the sugar only if your tomatoes are not very ripe.

Raise the heat and allow the juices from the tomatoes to evaporate, stirring frequently. Add the reserved prosciutto and the red pepper strips to the skillet, mixing them into the tomatoes. Reduce the heat to a simmer, pour in the eggs, and stir until they begin to thicken into soft creamy curds. Sprinkle with the parsley, surround with the fried croutons, and serve immediately.

Steamed Potatoes with Parsley Sauce
serves four

A simple dish, easily prepared, that makes a wonderful accompaniment for any roast meat, poultry, or fish.

1½ pounds small new pota-
    toes, unpeeled
6 tablespoons butter
3 tablespoons onion, finely

    minced
¼ cup parsley, finely chopped
Salt and freshly ground pepper

Steam the potatoes over low heat until they are tender; the timing will depend on their size. While the potatoes are cooking, prepare the sauce.

Melt the butter in a small saucepan, add the onion, and sauté over moderate heat for 5 minutes or until tender. Stir in the parsley and cook for another 1 to 2 minutes.

When the potatoes are ready, season with salt and pepper, pour the sauce over them, and toss until they are well coated. Serve at once.

Potatoes Sautéed with Juniper Berries
serves four

An unusual and most delicious accompaniment for any game birds. The addition of juniper berries gives the potatoes a savory and rather piquant flavor.

6 to 8 medium new potatoes
6 tablespoons butter
2 large shallots, finely chopped
1 large clove garlic, finely
    chopped

8 to 10 whole juniper berries,
    lightly bruised with a
    mortar and pestle
Salt and freshly ground pepper
$\frac{1}{4}$ cup parsley, finely chopped

Peel the potatoes and cut into thick slices. Melt the butter in a large heavy skillet; add the shallots, garlic, and juniper berries. Sauté for 1 to 2 minutes, stirring. Add the potato slices, toss to coat with the butter and spices, and sauté over moderate heat, stirring frequently, for 15 to 20 minutes. Sprinkle with the parsley, toss, and continue to cook for a few minutes more. Serve at once.

Gratin of Potatoes and Artichoke Hearts
serves four

The combination of potatoes and artichoke hearts is an especially pleasing accompaniment to roast lamb, veal, or chicken. Try it also without the artichokes but richly laced with garlic.

4 cups artichoke hearts (from
    about 4 large artichokes)
    sliced $\frac{1}{4}$ inch thick
5 cups new potatoes, peeled
    and sliced $\frac{1}{4}$ inch thick
Salt and freshly ground pepper

1 cup grated Swiss cheese (the
    imported variety has the best
    flavor)
3 tablespoons bread crumbs
1 tablespoon butter
$\frac{1}{2}$ pint heavy cream

Preheat the oven to 375 degrees.

First, prepare the artichoke hearts and keep them in acidulated water (with a few drops of vinegar or lemon juice) while you peel and slice the potatoes; then drain and dry the hearts thoroughly. Butter a shallow gratin pan (for this recipe, I use an oval one measuring 14 by 8 inches). On the bottom put a layer of 2 cups of the artichoke hearts; season them with salt and pepper and sprinkle $\frac{1}{4}$ cup cheese on them. Next, make a layer of half the potatoes, seasoning and adding cheese as before; repeat, but do not put cheese on the second layer of potatoes.

Mix the remaining cheese with the bread crumbs and coat the top heavily with this mixture. Cut the butter into small pieces and dot the top with them. Pour the cream into the dish around the edges. Place the pan in the middle level of the oven and bake for 45 to 50 minutes, until the top is crisp and brown and the vegetables are tender. Serve immediately.

Potato Pancakes
serves four

T hese crisp and delicious pancakes must be made just before serving; they cannot be reheated successfully. Top each with a small dollop of sour cream.

4 medium baking potatoes,
    peeled
1 medium onion, peeled
1 large egg
1 teaspoon salt

Freshly groupnd pepper
$\frac{1}{2}$ teaspoon baking powder
Flour
Enough vegetable oil to cover
    bottom of skillet by $\frac{1}{2}$ inch

Grate the potatoes on a fine grater into a large sieve set over a mixing bowl. Discard any liquid that accumulates in the bowl. Put the potatoes in the bowl and grate the onion directly on top of them. Add the egg, salt, pepper, and baking powder, and beat the mixture together. Stir in just enough flour to make a batter thick enough to hold its shape; this will depend largely on the quantity and character of the potatoes used.

Heat the vegetable oil in a large heavy skillet set over moderately high heat. Drop in a spoonful of the batter and flatten it to make a pancake about 3 inches in diameter. (Fry only enough pancakes at a time to just fill the skillet.) Fry the pancakes for 2 to 3 minutes per side, long enough for them to turn a golden brown; then turn carefully with a spatula and fry the other side. Continue in this fashion until all the batter is used. Drain the pancakes on paper towels and serve.

Potatoes in Pesto
serves four

The blandness of the potatoes makes a perfect background for this herb paste of fresh basil, garlic, Parmesan, olive oil, and pine nuts. Pesto may also be used to sauce pasta, poached white fish, and rice.

1 bunch fresh basil, about 3 cups
1 teaspoon salt
3 to 4 cloves garlic, peeled and cut in half
3 tablespoons pine nuts, toasted lightly over high heat in a small skillet
$\frac{1}{2}$ cup fruity olive oil
$\frac{1}{2}$ cup freshly grated Parmesan (or a combination of Parmesan and Romano)
8 medium new potatoes, peeled and cut into thick slices

Prepare the pesto: wash the basil, removing the stems, and dry well. Place in a blender or food processor with the salt, garlic, and pine nuts and purée. While the machine is running, add the olive oil in a thin stream. Remove the paste, put in a bowl, and mix in the grated cheese. Place a piece of plastic wrap directly on the surface of the pesto until serving time, or cover with $\frac{1}{4}$ inch olive oil and refrigerate. It will keep this way for 2 or 3 days.

Add the potato slices to boiling, salted water and cook until they are just tender. Drain the potatoes, reserving 1 tablespoon of the cooking liquid. Mix the pesto with the liquid, pour mixture over potato slices, and toss together. Serve immediately.

Roast Potatoes with Rosemary and Sage
serves four

T hese potatoes are as crisp and brown as if they were deep-fried, and their flavor is ambrosial, particularly with lamb or steak. Dried herbs can replace the fresh ones if absolutely necessary; in that case reduce their quantity by half.

6 medium baking potatoes, peeled
1 tablespoon each fresh rosemary and sage, finely
    chopped
Salt and freshly ground pepper
¹⁄₃ cup olive oil

Preheat the oven to 375 degrees.

Cut each of the potatoes in half, then cut each of the halves into thick wedges. Place the wedges in a mixing bowl, add the herbs, salt, pepper, and olive oil, and mix with your hands, making sure each wedge is coated with oil and herbs.

Place the potatoes with their oil in a lightweight shallow ovenproof container large enough to hold them all in a single layer. Place the pan in the middle of the oven and bake for about 1 hour, turning the potatoes occasionally so they are evenly browned.

Yams & Sweet Potatoes

The yam-versus-sweet-potato controversy seems to have been going on forever. Sweet potatoes were introduced into Europe by Columbus after the discovery of America. It is documented that he was served quite a variety of that tuber at a feast given in his honor by the King of St. Thomas. But it was the enslaved Africans who carried yams, already a staple in their diet, to the Caribbean. Since that time many historians have confused the two vegetables. Today, much of this confusion may be attributed to the looseness of popular usage. Southerners often refer to the sweet potato as a yam—even those people who organize "yam" festivals at which it is the sweet potato that is served. The situation is hardly clarified by the fact that both are grown in the same regions. One source states flatly that "all sweet potatoes and yams that are sold in the United States today are basically sweet potatoes. There are varieties of sweet potatoes which are known as yams because they are kind of copper skinned and are a deep orange color inside. In the produce business the sweet potato that is sold as a sweet potato is called a choker because it's so dry; whereas the sweet potato that is sold as a yam is sweet and juicy." If you're still in a muddle as to whether you've been eating sweet potatoes or yams, or both, you are certainly not alone.

Sweet potatoes and yams are in plentiful supply from November until early spring, yet during this time they usually appear in home kitchens only in the most predictable form: candied, mashed, or in a sweetened pie. Yet both are extremely versatile, as can be seen in the three yam recipes in this section, or in the brief recipes on the facing page.

Whipped Yams with Cognac
serves six

Having just discussed above the confusion regarding yams and sweet potatoes, I'll now add that a yam has orange-colored flesh and a more pronounced flavor than the yellow-fleshed sweet potato. The latter may be used for this recipe, but, being drier, may require more butter.

Hot sweet potato salad

Sauté cubes of bacon until crisp, and remove from pan. To the remaining fat, add chopped onion, sauté until transparent, then add vinegar and a generous amount of freshly ground pepper. Cook over high heat for a minute or two and pour over slices of boiled, still warm sweet potato, add the reserved bacon and toss together. Serve hot.

Ham and sweet potato hash

Combine small cubes of a well-flavored baked ham with diced, boiled sweet potatoes, minced onion, and green pepper. Season lightly with salt and pepper and add enough heavy cream to properly moisten the mixture. Melt butter in a heavy skillet, add the hash and cook over moderate heat until the bottom is browned and crisp. Invert the hash onto a plate, melt more butter in the skillet and slide the hash back onto it to brown the other side. Serve with poached eggs and pickled okra.

Baked and stuffed yams

Oil the skins of large yams and bake them in a hot (400-degree) oven for about an hour or until tender. While they are baking, prepare the stuffing. Heat vegetable oil in a small skillet, and add finely chopped onion and jalapeno peppers. Cook until tender, then add a few skinned Mexican chorizos and sauté until the meat is cooked. Drain off any fat. When the yams are cooked and slightly cooled, scoop the flesh from the skins, leaving a shell. Blend the cooked yam with the chorizo mixture and spoon back into the shells. Dot the tops with butter and put back into the oven to heat through.

6 medium yams	brandy
Salt	Freshly ground pepper
6 tablespoons butter	Dash fresh grated nutmeg
3 tablespoons cognac or good	

Wash the yams, but do not peel them. Cut them in quarters. Bring a pot of lightly salted water to a boil; add the yams and cover. Cook the yams until just tender, about 10 minutes.

Drain the yams and, holding each piece in a kitchen towel, peel off the skins. Cut each piece in half again and put in a food processor. Purée the yams for a few seconds, adding the butter in small pieces through the funnel while the machine is still running. Season with the cognac, salt, pepper, and nutmeg and blend for 1 to 2 seconds. Pour the whipped yams into a serving bowl and serve at once.

Baked Yams in Cream
serves four to six

4 tablespoons butter
2½ pounds yams, peeled and
   cut into slices approximately
   ¼ inch thick
Salt and freshly ground pepper
Generous ½ cup imported
   Italian Parmesan, grated (if

unavailable, substitute the
   same amount of Gruyère,
   coarsely grated)
2 cups (approximately) heavy
   unpasteurized cream
⅓ cup coarse home-made
   bread crumbs

Preheat the oven to 375 degrees.

Generously butter a shallow ovenproof baking dish large enough to hold the yams. Place a layer of yams in the bottom, season with salt and freshly ground pepper, sprinkle lightly with the cheese, and dot with butter. Continue in this fashion until the yams are used up. Pour enough of the heavy cream into the dish to come three-quarters up the side of the baking dish. Top with the bread crumbs, a bit of the grated cheese, and once again dot with butter. Bake for about 30 minutes, or until the yams are tender and the topping, crisp and brown.

South-of-the-Border Yams

serves four

2 pounds yams
4 tablespoons unsalted butter
Salt and freshly ground pepper
3 tablespoons tequila

Juice of 1 lime
2 tablespoons honey
Zest of 1 large lime

Peel the yams and cut into thick julienne. Heat the butter in a large skillet over moderate heat, add the yams and season with salt, freshly ground pepper, tequila and lime juice. Sauté the yams slowly until tender. Stir in the honey, cook for 1 or 2 minutes more to allow the flavors to meld. Garnish with the lime zest and serve.

Grated Zucchini Sauté

serves four

T he zucchini is salted to release its excess moisture, then very quickly sautéed with a bit of garlic in butter. This dish suits simple roasts of chicken or lamb as well as sautéed meats.

4 medium zucchini
Salt
2 tablespoons butter
1 teaspoon olive oil

2 large cloves garlic, finely
  chopped
Freshly ground pepper

Grate the zucchini coarsely, salt it lightly, and place it in a colander to drain for 15 minutes. Squeeze out all excess moisture from the vegetable and dry it thoroughly.

Melt the butter with the oil in a heavy 10-inch skillet. Add the garlic and stir it around in the oil for a minute, taking care not to brown it. Add the zucchini and sauté it over moderately high heat for 6 to 8 minutes, until tender but still crisp. Season with pepper and serve immediately.

CHAPTER EIGHT

PASTA & RICE

Orzo with Toasted Bread Crumbs
serves four

O rzo is a rice-shaped pasta; it's quickly cooked and can be served just as you would any rice dish. Here it's combined with butter-fried bread crumbs—the combination of textures and flavors is delicious. Another quick way with orzo is to toss it with butter, grated lemon zest, a bit of lemon juice, finely chopped garlic, and parsley—great with grilled lamb.

$^2/_3$ cup coarse home-made
   bread crumbs
5 tablespoons butter

$^3/_4$ cup orzo
Salt and freshly ground pepper
   to taste

The bread crumbs should be about the same size as the pasta for the best texture. Melt 3 tablespoons of the butter in a small skillet, add the crumbs and sauté, over low heat, until golden. Remove from heat and reserve.

Cook the orzo in plenty of salted water until al dente, about 5 to 7 minutes. Drain well, add the remaining butter, season with salt and pepper and toss. Mix in the toasted crumbs and serve immediately.

Noodles with Mustard Butter
serves six

T his is such a delightful variation on the old buttered-noodle theme that you'll wonder why you never thought of it before. If you were to serve this with a simple roast, you might wish to add a clove of pressed garlic to the noodle mixture. Also, chives complement the original idea so perfectly that you might want to remember that when they are in season again. For added texture, you could toss the seasoned noodles with bread crumbs (preferably home-made) that have been sautéed in butter until they are crisp and golden. And finally, if you have the time and the inclination, home-made noodles would place this dish in another category altogether.

8 ounces egg noodles
$\frac{1}{2}$ tablespoon salt

Mustard butter

4 tablespoons butter
2 tablespoons Dijon mustard
1 teaspoon lemon juice

Dash cayenne pepper
Small handful chopped parsley

Bring 3 or 4 quarts of water to a boil.

In the meantime prepare the mustard butter. Cream the butter with the remaining ingredients by hand, or use a food processor or blender.

Add the noodles and salt to the boiling water. Cook the noodles until al dente. (The time needed will depend greatly upon the thickness of the noodles, so the best test is to simply bite into a noodle to determine whether it is done). Drain the noodles thoroughly and toss with the prepared butter until each strand is coated. Serve at once.

Green and Yellow Pasta with Porcini Mushrooms
serves two

T he most delicious of pasta dishes are those with just a few ingredients, all of which complement each other. Simplicity should be your goal; avoid the temptation to throw any and everything into a pasta sauce.

The dried mushrooms specified here are porcini—the name means "piglets" in Italian—and they are the most delicious variety of the boletus family. Highly aromatic with a distinct meaty flavor, these richly flavored mushrooms may also be used to enhance risottos, cream sauces, or tomato sauces and are excellent when paired with game birds, veal, poultry, rabbit, and beef. Porcini mushrooms are widely available in specialty stores and some supermarkets. Accompany this dish with a wine such as Nebbiolo d'Alba.

$^1/_2$ ounce dry porcini mushrooms
8 large fresh mushrooms,
   thickly sliced and fried over
   high heat in $^1/_2$ tablespoon
   butter, seasoned with salt,
   freshly ground pepper, and a
   squeeze of lemon
2 tablespoons butter

2 ounces prosciutto, cut into
   julienne
$^3/_4$ cup heavy cream, preferably
   unpasteurized
$^1/_4$ pound each fresh egg pasta
   and spinach pasta, cooked al
   dente
$^1/_2$ cup grated imported Italian
   Parmesan cheese

Place the dry mushrooms in a sieve and rinse well under cold running water. Cover with hot tap water and soak about 45 minutes, until soft. Meanwhile, prepare the fresh mushrooms and set them aside.

When the dried mushrooms have become soft, drain them thoroughly and chop coarsely. Heat the butter in a skillet large enough to accommodate the pasta. Sauté the porcini mushrooms over low heat for a few minutes; add the prosciutto and cook just until the ham has warmed through but not browned. Add the cream, reduce over high heat until it is just beginning to thicken, and add the pasta, reducing the heat to low. Sprinkle the cheese over the pasta, toss gently until it has melted, and season to taste with salt and freshly ground pepper. Top with the sautéed mushrooms and serve at once.

Linguini Primavera
serves four to six

A version of springtime pasta with a sauce composed of sautéed onion, julienne of prosciutto, tips of fresh asparagus, heavy cream, and grated Parmesan cheese: hence, despite the delicate name, a substantial dish—too substantial for most appetites as a first course. With a green salad, it is a good light spring meal; a Pinot Grigio will turn it into a feast.

5 tablespoons butter
$^1/_4$ pound lean prosciutto, cut
   into julienne

$^1/_4$ cup onion, minced
Tips of $1^1/_2$ pounds asparagus
   (reserve stalks for another

use, such as soup)
$^1/_2$ pint heavy cream
Salt and freshly ground pepper

1 pound linguini
$^1/_4$ cup freshly grated Parmesan cheese

Melt 2 tablespoons of the butter in a small skillet; add the prosciutto and toss over medium heat for 2 minutes. Add the onion and sauté for about 5 minutes until it is soft but not brown. Add the asparagus tips and sauté briefly till they are coated with butter; pour in the heavy cream, reduce the heat, and simmer for about 5 minutes. Add salt and pepper to taste.

Cook the linguini al dente, drain, and put back into the cooking pot with the 3 tablespoons of butter cut into small pieces. Toss the pasta until the butter has melted, and put in individual heated soup plates. Stir the grated cheese into the warm sauce and pour some over each serving. Serve with additional grated cheese if desired.

Pasta Carbonara
serves four to six

For the pasta, use small shells—riccini, rotelle, or any other that will "catch" the sauce. A delicious quick meal; accompany with a tossed green salad and an Italian Merlot.

6 to 8 rashers of bacon, cut into small dice
4 tablespoons onion, finely minced
$^1/_2$ cup dry white vermouth
1 whole egg plus 2 egg yolks
1 cup heavy cream
$^1/_2$ cup freshly grated Parmesan or Romano cheese (or

combination of both)
Salt
Large pinch of cayenne pepper or dash of Tabasco
1 pound pasta
3 tablespoons butter, cut into small pieces
$^1/_4$ cup fresh parsley, minced

Bring a large pot of salted water to a full boil. While the water is heating, place the bacon in a skillet and sauté over medium heat until just crisp around the edges. Add the onion and continue to sauté for another 6 to 8 minutes until the onion is softened. Drain all but a thin film of fat from the skillet and pour the vermouth over the bacon and onion. Simmer this mixture for about

10 minutes or until the liquid is reduced to half its original amount. While this is cooking, place in a small mixing bowl the eggs, cream, grated cheese, salt, and cayenne or Tabasco and mix well. When the water is boiling, drop in the pasta and cook it until just al dente; drain well and put back in the pot.

Add the butter and parsley and blend; over the pasta pour the egg-cheese mixture, then the hot bacon mixture, tossing with forks till mixed. Place pot over very low heat, stirring contantly, until the sauce has thickened slightly. Serve at once. No additional cheese is necessary since the sauce is quite rich by itself.

Bianco e Nero (Capellini with Caviar)
serves four

For this recipe I have suggested using imported pasta because its flavor and texture are superior; the Fratelli De Cecco brand is one of the finest. The butter used must be sweet (that is, unsalted), because the salt content in caviar is so high.

The more expensive the caviar, the lower its salt content will be: since only a small amount of caviar is called for, you should choose the best you can afford. When using a pasta as fine as capellini or fedelini, time is of the essence; cook it quickly and add the sauce immediately when it is ready. If you are doubling the recipe, increase the amount of caviar to three ounces rather than four. Resist the obvious temptation to serve champagne: instead try a true Verdicchio.

1 tablespoon olive oil
$\frac{1}{2}$ cup heavy cream
2 ounces caviar, unchilled
6 tablespoons sweet butter, at
    room temperature

1 tablespoon salt
$\frac{1}{2}$ pound imported capellini
    or fedelini (very fine
    spaghetti)
Freshly ground black pepper

Place a pot filled with $3\frac{1}{2}$ quarts of water on high heat, add the olive oil, and bring to a boil. Whip the heavy cream lightly; it should not be stiff. Fold in the caviar and set aside. Cut the butter into small pieces.

When the water begins to boil, add the salt and the pasta. Cook for no longer than 4 minutes, drain into a colander, shake off excess water, and place immediately back into the pot.

Working quickly, add the softened butter bits, the cream and caviar mixture, and a good grinding of pepper. Toss the pasta gently, allowing the sauce to coat each strand. Serve immediately in heated soup plates. Grated cheese should not be served with this dish.

Note: The only salt in this dish is in the pasta water; the caviar will add sufficient salt to the final preparation.

Linguini with Mussel Sauce
serves four to six

L inguini is a particular kind of pasta, made famous by Neil Simon's *The Odd Couple*. This dish is a fine first course, but with Leeks Vinaigrette and a green salad, it serves as a main dish as well. Serve with a dry Northwest Semillon.

2 pounds mussels, cleaned
1 tablespoon butter
1 tablespoon olive oil
2 large shallots, minced
3 cloves garlic, minced
$1 \frac{1}{2}$ tablespoons flour

$\frac{1}{2}$ cup dry white vermouth
1 tablespoon fresh thyme, minced, or $\frac{1}{2}$ teaspoon dried thyme
1 pound linguini, cooked al dente

Steam 2 pounds of mussels for not longer than 5 minutes; extract the meat, chop coarsely, and reserve. Over high heat reduce the liquid the mussels were cooked in to $\frac{1}{2}$ cup and reserve it as well.

In a skillet melt the butter with the olive oil and sauté the shallots and garlic for a few minutes, taking care not to brown them. Stir in the flour with a wire whisk and cook for 5 minutes. Add the reserved broth and dry white vermouth and bring to a boil, stirring constantly until the sauce thickens. Reduce the heat, add the thyme and the chopped mussels, and cook just long enough to heat them through. Spoon some sauce over each individual bowl of pasta and pass around a mixture of grated Romano and Parmesan cheeses.

Spaghetti with Tomato-Seafood Sauce
serves four to six

T his peppery tomato sauce is filled with the bounty of the sea: mussels, octopus, shrimp, and scallops. In Italy, grated cheese is rarely used over a seafood sauce for fear it will overpower the delicate flavors of the fish. In this dish, however, an exception can be made. Celery Root Remoulade would make a good accompaniment, along with a Chianti Classico.

$4\frac{1}{2}$ tablespoons olive oil
2 cloves garlic, peeled but left whole
1 small dried hot red pepper
$\frac{1}{4}$ cup pancetta (rolled Italian bacon), cut into small dice
$\frac{1}{4}$ cup onion, finely chopped
1-pound can Italian plum tomatoes, drained and coarsely chopped
$\frac{1}{2}$ cup cooking liquid from mussels
4 ounces cooked octopus, cut into bite-size pieces
4 ounces shrimp, shelled and cut into bite-size pieces
4 ounces scallops, cut into bite-size pieces
1 pound mussels, steamed for 5 minutes, shelled, and coarsely chopped
Salt and freshly ground pepper to taste
$\frac{1}{4}$ cup parsley, minced
1 pound spaghetti, cooked al dente

In a soup pot, heat half the olive oil; add the garlic and red pepper and sauté over high heat. When both have browned, remove and discard them.

Add the pancetta and onion to the pot and sauté over medium heat for 5 minutes. Add the tomatoes and the cooking liquid from the mussels; partially cover the pot and simmer for about 20 minutes.

Meanwhile, heat the remaining olive oil in a skillet, add the octopus, shrimp, and scallops, and sauté over high heat for 3 or 4 minutes. Remove from heat and set aside.

When the tomato base has thickened slightly, add the sautéed octopus, shrimp, scallops, and mussels, and add salt and pepper if desired. Simmer for 10 minutes more, add the parsley, and serve over pasta.

Angel-Hair Pasta with Scallop Sauce
serves four

Gremalada is a piquant Milanese concoction of finely chopped lemon rind, garlic, and parsley, used primarily as a garnish for that famed dish osso bucco. Since those same flavors are highly complementary to fish, it was a simple step to combine them with olive oil and scallops. This produced a delectable sauté that could easily be served on its own, but when it was tossed with a very fine pasta, it resulted in a glorious combination. Use home-made pasta if you can, or a good imported brand like De Cecco. A good wine with this dish is a Northwest Sauvignon Blanc.

1 pound fresh bay scallops
Flour for dusting scallops, lightly seasoned with salt and pepper
$\frac{1}{3}$ cup olive oil
Zest of 1 large lemon, finely grated
1 large clove garlic, finely chopped
3 tablespoons parsley, finely chopped
1 tablespoon lemon juice
1 pound imported capellini or fedelini (very fine pasta), cooked al dente

Dust scallops lightly with the seasoned flour, shaking off any excess.

Heat the olive oil in a skillet and, when hot, add the scallops and quickly toss them in the oil for about 1 minute. Sprinkle with the lemon zest, garlic, and parsley. Continue to sauté the scallops for about 2 minutes more. Add the lemon juice and remove from heat immediately.

Place the cooked pasta in a wide shallow bowl, add the scallop sauce, and toss together. Work quickly, for the very fine pastas have a tendency to stick together if allowed to stand for any length of time. Serve immediately in heated soup plates.

Risottos

T he Italians use a particular cooking technique for risotto unlike any used in other coutries. The rice is cooked slowly in a small amount of liquid (a difficult trick with rice); when that liquid is entirely absorbed, more liquid is added, and so on until the rice is completely cooked. When you've finished cooking it, the rice will be suspended in a savory mixture of broth, butter, and quantities of Parmesan cheese. As for additional ingredients, the variations are so great, the combinations so limitless, that risotto could easily be considered a cuisine all by itself. There are vegetable risottos with spinach, asparagus, artichokes, peas, potatoes, beans, fennel, mushrooms, cabbage, zucchini, and many other different types of squash. Other risottos contain frogs' legs, tripe, chicken livers, quail, or almost anything that swims and can be eaten. True to tradition, the Venetians prefer their risottos with a touch of color, using the ink sacs of squid to dye the rice a mysterious black or a bottle of good Barolo wine to tint it a rather odd shade of purple. The marvelous flavors of both these dishes more than make up for their peculiar coloration.

A few points to watch:

Short-grained Italian rice (Arborio-type) should always be used because it alone manages to hold its texture while still producing a creamy mass. Each grain should be slightly firm in the center, much like pasta cooked al dente.

Because risotto cooks in twenty-five to thirty minutes, any ingredient that would normally be overcooked in that time (for example, asparagus tips or shellfish) should be quickly cooked separately and added to the rice at the end.

The proportions of liquid to rice are about five to one; there are just too many variables to give an exact measure.

While every recipe I've ever seen calls for the stock to be heated first, I find that a perfect risotto can be prepared even if the stock is at room temperature at the start.

Wild Mushroom Risotto
serves six to eight

S hould you be fortunate enough to have in your possession some of the Northwest's wonderful fresh wild mushrooms (chanterelles, morels, or boletus) by all means substitute them for the dried.

The porcini mushrooms suggested here are an Italian species of boletus, and they are available in most specialty stores and in many grocery stores. Serve this risotto with an old Barolo wine.

1 ounce dried porcini mushrooms or morels
4 tablespoons butter
2 tablespoons onion, finely
  chopped
1 pound Italian rice

Approximately 5 cups mildly
  flavored chicken stock
Salt and freshly ground pepper
$\frac{1}{2}$ cup grated imported Italian
  Parmesan

Rinse the dried mushrooms thoroughly in a sieve under cold running water. Soak them in hot tap water or chicken stock to cover, about 1 hour, or until softened. Drain the mushrooms, reserving the liquid to add to the risotto, and chop the mushrooms coarsely. In a pan large enough to hold the rice and the chicken stock, melt 2 tablespoons of the butter and sauté the onion and the mushrooms over moderate heat until the onion has become translucent (do not brown it). Add the rice and stir into the fat until each grain is coated. Pour in the mushroom-soaking liquid, and stir until this is absorbed into the rice. Add about 1 cup of stock to the risotto and allow this too to be absorbed, stirring frequently so that the rice does not stick.

Repeat the procedure until the rice is cooked al dente. The risotto should remain creamy, if not almost liquid; the grains should be well separated, with a light, almost puddinglike texture. When the rice is cooked, season to taste with salt, freshly ground pepper, the remaining butter, and the grated cheese. Toss gently until the cheese melts and serve immediately.

Variation: Substitute 1 cup of tomato sauce for the final cup of stock.

Risotto with Smoked Salmon

Proceed as above, omitting mushrooms. Substitute $\frac{1}{2}$ cup dry white vermouth for the mushroom-soaking liquid. Proceed as above. At the very end of the cooking, stir in about 4 tablespoons heavy cream, cook for a minute to warm, then add 3 to 4 ounces of smoked salmon (lox) cut into thick julienne. Leave on the heat only long enough to heat the salmon through. Sprinkle liberally with freshly grated black pepper and serve at once, perhaps with a Sangiovese wine.

Risotto with Vodka

Before preparing the risotto, combine $\frac{1}{2}$ teaspoon of hot red pepper flakes with 1 ounce of vodka and allow to stand. Proceed according to the master recipe (omitting the mushrooms and the onions). After cooking the risotto for 15 minutes, stir in $\frac{1}{2}$ cup of grated Parmesan cheese. When the rice is fully cooked, add the vodka mixture and a few tablespoons heavy cream (enough so the mixture becomes creamy in texture), mix well, and serve. An appropriate wine would be a Sancerre.

Seafood Risotto

For this recipe I prefer a mixture of scallops, shrimp, squid, clams, and mussels. Steam the clams and mussels until the shells just open. Strain and reserve the broth. Remove the meat from the shells, leaving a few clams or mussels in the shells for garnish. Quickly sauté and put aside the shrimp, scallops, and squid, which should be cut into thin rings. Cook the rice as above (omitting the mushrooms) using the clam and mussel stock in place of some of the chicken broth. (A mild-flavored fish broth could be used instead of the chicken broth, if you have it.)

When the rice is done, add the shellfish and a tablespoon or 2 of butter. A small amount of saffron may be added at this point as well. Serve immediately, garnished with the reserved shellfish. A wine that would go well with this would be a Pinot Grigio.

Risotto al Pesto

Proceed as usual, adding at the very end about 1 cup of freshly made pesto and $\frac{1}{4}$ cup of grated Parmesan. The mixture may be thinned with a few tablespoons of heavy cream. For wine, a Barbaresco would be a pleasant accompaniment.

Risotto with Barolo

Heat a half-bottle of good Barolo wine with an equal amount of chicken stock; when the liquid starts to boil, reduce the heat and use it to add gradually to the onion and rice mixture as described above. Cook as usual and season very lightly with salt and pepper. When the risotto is done, stir in $\frac{1}{2}$ cup of grated Parmesan cheese and a few tablespoons of butter—enough to make a creamy consistency. Serve immediately with the remaining wine.

Rice with Peanuts and Coriander
serves four

This is a version of Mexican-style rice with the added texture of fried peanuts and the zip of fresh coriander. It can take its place alongside of any entrées that call for a starch with a little pizzazz.

4 tablespoons vegetable oil
$\frac{1}{4}$ cup whole raw peanuts
3 tablespoons onion, finely
  chopped
2 large cloves garlic, finely
  chopped
2 to 3 pickled jalapeno peppers, stemmed, seeded, and
  chopped
1 cup rice
2 cups chicken stock
4 tablespoons fresh coriander,
  finely chopped

Heat the oil in a skillet over moderate heat; add the peanuts and sauté until they are brown. Remove with a slotted spoon and chop coarsely.

To the remaining oil add the onion, garlic, and peppers; sauté for a few minutes until the onion is transparent but not brown. Stir in the rice until it is coated with the oil and cook, stirring, for 1 minute. Pour in the stock, reduce the heat to low, and cover the skillet. Allow the rice to cook, without disturbing it, until it is done—10 minutes or so. When cooked, taste for seasoning and stir in the reserved peanuts and the coriander. Serve at once.

Coriander

Coriander, also known as cilantro or Chinese parsley, is common in the cuisines of China, the Middle East, India, North Africa, Central and Latin America, Spain, and Portugal. This herb has a musty, assertive flavor with a strong penetrating odor. Its name was taken from the Greek word *koris*, meaning "bed-bug," because the ancients believed coriander smelled like that insect. This herb is an acquired taste; you'll either hate it at once or become addicted forever. If you fall into the latter category, whenever you come across a bunch of the fresh herb you'll find yourself snatching it up and planning an entire meal around it. This could happen fairly often, since coriander is available year-round.

Green sauces based on fresh herbs are quite common in other countries, and the salsa verde of Mexico, flavored with coriander, is a refreshing complement to a number of traditional Mexican dishes. This cool and spicy sauce lends itself to other preparations (see Fish Salad in Salsa Verde) just as easily.

Black Beans and Rice with Salsa Verde
serves four to six

I suppose the combination of black beans and rice is quite common in South America but I doubt if it is also served with the addictive green salsa popular in Mexico. The trio is certainly a remarkable taste sensation and one that is good served with rather plain roasts—pork would be ideal. Serve with a red Rioja or a Mexican beer.

4 ounces meaty salt pork
1 medium onion, coarsely chopped
4 cloves garlic, peeled and left whole

$\frac{1}{2}$ pound black (turtle) beans, rinsed
$1\frac{1}{2}$ quarts water
Salt

After cutting off the rind, cut the salt pork into large cubes. Combine the cubes, rind, onion, and garlic with the beans in a heavy pot. Add the water, bring to a boil, reduce the heat and simmer for 1 hour. Add salt to taste and continue to cook for about 2 hours more, until the beans are tender. If the beans begin to dry out, you may add more water—their consistency should be rather soupy. Remove the rind and serve the beans over freshly cooked rice with salsa verde. The flavor of these beans improves with age, so they may be made a day or 2 in advance.

Serve this with salsa verde, page 111. The recipe calls for 4 chilies, which make a very piquant sauce, so you may want to adjust the number according to your own taste.

CHAPTER NINE

BREADS, PIZZAS, &
SAVORY TARTS

Asparagus Bread Sticks
makes about twenty sticks

An absolutely delightful conceit: bread sticks that are shaped to resemble stalks of asparagus. This recipe is adapted from *Beard on Bread* (James Beard, Knopf, 1978), one of the finest books written on that subject. The sticks are really quite simple to make, even if you're not a particularly practised bread-maker; all it takes is a pair of sharp scissors. This is a delicacy to offer to the asparagus-lovers in your life no matter what the season.

2 packages active dry yeast
1 tablespoon granulated sugar
2 teaspoons salt
$\frac{1}{4}$ cup olive oil
$1\frac{1}{2}$ cups warm water (approximately 110° to 115°)

3 to $3\frac{1}{2}$ cups all-purpose flour
1 cup grated Romano cheese
1 egg white beaten with 1 tablespoon water

In a large mixing bowl combine the yeast, sugar, and salt. Add the oil and $\frac{1}{4}$ cup of the water. Beat this mixture well with a wooden spoon for about 3 minutes. Add $\frac{1}{2}$ cup of the flour and continue beating with the wooden spoon. Alternately add flour, 1 cup at a time, and water until you have a fairly soft dough, reserving approximately $\frac{1}{2}$ cup flour. Remove the dough to a floured surface and begin to knead in the cheese and the reserved flour, a little at a time. Knead the dough for several minutes until it springs back very briskly when you press your fingers in it. It must be smooth and satiny, and all the flour on the board should be absorbed.

Preheat the oven to 300 degrees. Let the dough rest on the board, covered with a towel, for about 5 minutes, then shape it into a roll about 20 to 22 inches long. With a very sharp knife cut it into at least 20 equal pieces.

Let the dough rest again for 3 or 4 minutes. Then, using the palms of your hands, roll each piece out to a length of 10 inches, measuring about $\frac{1}{4}$ inch in diameter. Place the bread sticks on baking sheets which have been oiled and lightly sprinkled with corn meal. Arrange the bread sticks an inch apart from each other.

Using a pair of sharp scissors, cut some small, inverted Vs along the "stem" end. About $1\frac{1}{2}$ inches from the top, begin to make a series of small cuts in lines moving upward, staggering the lines so that the lines narrow at the top.

Let the sticks sit for about 5 minutes, until they just barely begin to rise. At this stage, they should be not much thicker in diameter than a pencil. Just before putting them into the oven, brush them very lightly with the egg-and-water mixture. Bake for about 30 minutes. They should be golden brown on the outside and slightly chewy on the inside.

Note: These will stay crisp for several days if stored in an airtight container.

Corn Bread Madeleines
makes one dozen

The element of surprise is an important (and little-used) component of a meal—taking a dish and moving it out of the ordinary by its presentation or its preparation. Here, corn bread is baked in the shape of small shells, only a bite or two each and the perfect size to garnish a plate of Green Gumbo or a dish of Chicken Hash, an unusual presentation I'm sure even Proust would approve of. Madeleine plaques (molds) are available in any well-stocked kitchen-supply shop.

$\frac{1}{3}$ cup white flour
$\frac{2}{3}$ cup yellow corn meal
$\frac{1}{4}$ teaspoon salt
1 teaspoon sugar

$1\frac{1}{4}$ teaspoons baking soda
1 egg (large)
$\frac{2}{3}$ cup buttermilk
1 tablespoon melted butter

Preheat the oven to 400 degrees.

Sift dry ingredients into a mixing bowl. Add the buttermilk to the egg and beat until just combined; stir this into the corn meal mixture until all lumps have dissolved. Stir in the melted butter.

Generously butter a madeleine plaque. Fill each depression in the plaque with enough batter to reach almost to the top. Place the pan in the oven and bake for 13 minutes, or until the corn bread is golden on the top and a rich brown around the edges. Remove from the mold and serve immediately.

French Toast with Jam Pockets
serves four

A variation on a much-favored breakfast staple. Here, the slices of bread are cut quite a bit thicker so that a pocket can be cut into the middle and filled with your choice of jam or marmalade—but not jelly, which is much too runny.

6 large eggs
½ cup sugar
4 tablespoons dark rum
1 day-old loaf of French bread, unsliced

Approximately 4 teaspoons orange marmalade
Vegetable oil for frying
Confectioner's sugar

Break the eggs into a bowl; add the sugar and rum and beat thoroughly until completely mixed and frothy. Trim away and discard the bread crust. Cut the bread into 4 rectangles that measure about 4 inches long, 2 inches high, and 2 inches wide. On the long side of each rectangle, cut in the center a pocket about 2 inches wide that goes halfway through the bread. Fill each pocket with a portion of the marmalade.

Pour the egg mixture into a shallow dish; add the bread and allow to soak for about 30 minutes, turning so that each side is thoroughly saturated.

In a skillet just large enough to hold the bread, heat ½ inch of vegetable oil until hot. Put the bread into the oil and fry over moderately high heat until each side is a crisp, golden brown. Remove the fried bread and drain briefly on paper towels. Dredge each piece with confectioner's sugar and serve immediately.

Bruschetta La Griglia
(Garlic-Coated Bread with Cheese Sauce)

serves six

T his uncommon recipe was given to me by the chef of La Griglia, a charming and typically New York restaurant tucked away on Mulberry Street. Its inventor, Edward Conticelli, later won the New York State lottery and disappeared from the restaurant scene, leaving behind only memories of this exquisite creation and some of the best meals I've ever been served. Any comparison between bruschetta and garlic bread would be equivalent to comparing liverwurst to paté. Imagine: a crisp loaf of bread, gilded with garlic paste and floating in a sauce of heavy cream, imported Parmesan, and sweet butter—one of the most delicious and unusual dishes you'll ever taste. Since bruschetta is so rich you will wish to serve it, on its own, as a first course, with a Tuscan wine—for example, Rosso di Brunello or Carmignnano. Follow with a simple roast or grilled meat.

8 large cloves garlic, peeled
$\frac{1}{3}$ cup olive oil
1 loaf French or Italian bread
    (avoid sourdough, it's too
    salty), approximately 12
    inches long and 3 inches
    wide

$1\frac{1}{2}$ cups heavy cream
1 cup grated imported Italian
    Parmesan cheese
3 tablespoons unsalted butter
1 tablespoon chopped parsley

Preheat the oven to 350 degrees.

Drop the garlic cloves into a food processor and purée with the olive oil until the mixture has the consistency of a thin paste. Since only a small amount of the paste is needed for this recipe, reserve the remainder, topped with a thin layer of olive oil, in a sealed jar for another purpose or another bruschetta.

Cut the bread diagonally in inch-thick slices without cutting through the bottom crust. Using a pastry brush, paint a thin coating of the garlic paste on the cut surfaces of the loaf and also on the top and side crusts. Place directly on the oven rack and heat for about 10 minutes, or until the top is crisp.

While the bread is in the oven, prepare the sauce. Heat the cream and stir in the cheese, a little at a time, so that it is allowed to melt completely into the sauce, which should be absolutely smooth. Stir in the butter and keep warm until the bread is ready.

When the bread is crisp and aromatic, remove from the oven and place in a shallow serving dish with sides. Pour the sauce over the loaf, sprinkle with parsley, and serve immediately, giving each diner a portion of bruschetta on a small plate, along with a knife and fork for eating it.

Pizza with Fresh Tomato and Pancetta Sauce
serves six to eight

Here is a dish that combines a classic Roman pasta sauce with a Neapolitan pizza dough. The results, I think, are very special. The sauce is deceptively simple: fresh tomatoes, onion, hot pepper, and pancetta (an Italian bacon cured in salt and spices and rolled into the shape of a sausage). Make the dough from your favorite recipe, or do it the really easy way and buy the dough; Italian bakeries often sell frozen pizza dough, and your local bakery will probably be able to sell you some raw bread dough. Serve with a Chianti from the Rufina district.

1-pound pizza dough
2 tablespoons olive oil
1 small onion, finely chopped
$^{1}/_{4}$ pound pancetta, sliced thin and then cut into thick julienne
Large pinch dried hot red pepper flakes
Pinch each of sugar and allspice

Salt
3 pounds fresh tomatoes, peeled, seeded, and coarsely chopped
$^{1}/_{4}$ cup grated Romano cheese
$^{1}/_{4}$ pound whole-milk mozzarella cheese, coarsely grated
$^{1}/_{4}$ pound provolone cheese, coarsely grated

While the dough is rising, prepare the sauce. Heat the oil in a 3-quart pot, add the onion, sprinkle with a pinch of sugar, and sauté 5 to 7 minutes. Add the pancetta and sauté about 3 minutes—do not brown. Add the tomatoes, red pepper flakes, allspice, and salt to taste. Cook over high heat for 5 minutes, stirring.

Reduce the heat to a simmer and cook uncovered for approximately 1 hour. Do not add tomato paste; the tomatoes act as their own thickening agent. When done, the sauce should be smooth and fairly thick. Allow the sauce to cool. (This sauce may also be used over spaghetti or bucatini.)

Preheat the oven to 500 degrees. Lightly grease an 11-by-17-inch rectangular baking sheet that has sides high enough to hold the dough. Put the dough in the pan and press and stretch it with your fingers until it not only reaches the sides of the pan but is large enough to be folded over to make a 1-inch rim that will hold the sauce. Spread the sauce over the dough, and lightly dust the sauce and rim with the Romano cheese. Cover this with the mozzarella and provolone and sprinkle a few drops of olive oil over all.

Bake in the middle of the oven until browned, 15 to 20 minutes. Cool for a few minutes, cut the pizza in half lengthwise, then crosswise 5 or 6 times. Serve immediately.

Pissaladière (Onion and Anchovy Pizza)
serves eight to ten

Pissaladière is a dish served up by the bakers and street vendors of Nice, in Provence. It is made of bread dough spread with a mixture of onions that have been cooked almost to the melting point in olive oil, garnished with a latticework of anchovies, and dotted with black olives.

There are as many different versions of this dish as there are cooks who prepare it. Sometimes a few tomatoes are added to the onions, but this is a rather recent development. You will see recipes calling for a pastry foundation, and this version is served in many restaurants and private homes. I prefer the chewy texture of a thick pizza dough or a brioche dough. Use your favorite recipe for the dough or buy raw bread dough from your local bakery or get a frozen pizza dough from an Italian bakery.

The flavor of the onion is essential to this preparation. When Walla Walla sweets are in the local markets, these lovely mild-flavored onions should be used for this dish. Serve it as a first course with a Grignolino wine.

1-pound pizza or brioche
   dough
$1/4$ cup fruity olive oil
3 pounds Walla Walla sweet
   onions, very thinly sliced
2 cloves garlic, finely chopped
   (optional)
3 to 4 sprigs fresh thyme,
   finely chopped

1 bay leaf
$1/2$ teaspoon salt
Freshly ground pepper
Scant $1/2$ cup grated Parmesan
   cheese
2 2-ounce cans anchovy fillets,
   drained and separated
Imported black olives, pitted
   and cut in half

After your dough has risen until double in bulk, punch it down and knead it several times. Shape into a rectangular form using your hands or a rolling pin and press into a 17-by-11-inch greased baking sheet with sides. Push the dough a bit higher than the sides and crimp it so it forms a rim. Cover and let rise until doubled in bulk, about 1 hour.

While the dough is rising, heat the olive oil in a heavy 4-quart Dutch oven; add the onions, garlic, thyme, bay leaf, salt, and pepper. Cover and cook over moderate heat for 5 minutes.

Remove the cover, raise the heat to high, and cook until the juice released from the onions has evaporated, about 5 minutes. Cover once again, reduce heat, and simmer for about 1 hour, until the onions have almost melted into a purée. Taste for seasoning and set aside until the dough is finished.

Preheat the oven to 350 degrees. When the dough in the baking pan has doubled in bulk, sprinkle the surface with the grated cheese and cover with the onion mixture (bay leaf and thyme sprigs removed), leaving a 1-inch border. Over this, make a lattice pattern with the anchovy fillets. (If you are not overly fond of the strong taste of anchovy, you might wish to soak the fillets in milk for about 10 minutes; this removes the too-salty flavor.) In each of the open spaces remaining, place half an olive.

Put the pan in the middle of the oven and bake for about 45 minutes. Serve just slightly warm or at room temperature.

Mushroom Tart
serves six

This delectable first course is based on memories of a similar dish served at the stand-up counter of Fauchon's in Paris. It's been entirely too many years since I've tasted that wonderful creation and I really cannot be sure just how close I've come to the original. I think you'll find this version pleasing, nonetheless. If you are fortunate enough to be in possession of fresh wild mushrooms—morels, chanterelles, boletus, or others—as we often are in the Northwest, by all means substitute them for the cultivated variety. Serve this with a soft wine from southern Bordeaux, like St. Emilion. Follow with Rabbit in Vinegar Sauce, steamed couscous, Braised Brussels Sprouts, and Plum Sorbet.

Pastry

Prepare the pastry 3 to 4 hours before serving, or make it the night before.

$1^3/_4$ cups unbleached stone-
ground white flour
$^1/_2$ teaspoon salt
10 tablespoons butter, chilled

2 tablespoons lard or vegetable
shortening, chilled
$^1/_3$ to $^1/_2$ cup icewater

Place the flour and the salt in a mixing bowl. Cut the butter and the lard (or shortening) into small pieces and add to the bowl. Using a pastry blender, combine the flour and the fat until the mixture resembles coarse corn meal. Slowly add the water, blending the pastry together with a fork. Add only enough water to hold the pastry together. Scrape the dough out of the bowl, knead lightly with the palms of the hands for a few seconds to distribute fat evenly, and reform into a ball. Dust the dough with flour, wrap in plastic and refrigerate for at least 2 hours.

Separate the pastry into 2 parts, the first being slightly larger than the other, and refrigerate the smaller half. Roll out the larger piece on a lightly floured surface until you have a circle measuring $10^1/_2$ to 11 inches in diameter and about $^1/_8$ inch thick.

Grease a baking sheet with no sides. Lightly grease the inside of a 9-inch flan ring and set it on the baking sheet. (Or use a quiche pan with a removable bottom.) Transfer the round of pastry into the flan ring, gently maneuvering the dough until it is snug on the baking sheet and on the sides of the flan ring. Trim off excess dough, leaving $\frac{1}{2}$ inch hanging over the flan ring. Refrigerate for an hour or until ready to use.

Now roll the remaining pastry into a circle about 10 inches in diameter and $\frac{1}{8}$ inch thick. Place on a baking sheet covered with waxed paper, and chill for an hour or until ready to use.

Filling

2 tablespoons vegetable oil
$1\frac{1}{4}$ pounds fresh mushrooms, cleaned and thickly sliced
3 tablespoons butter
4 large shallots (about 3 ounces), peeled and finely chopped
1 tablespoon finely chopped fresh thyme (or 1 teaspoon dried thyme)
1 heaping tablespoon flour
$\frac{1}{3}$ cup Madeira
$\frac{1}{2}$ cup heavy cream
Salt and freshly ground pepper
Dash of lemon juice
White of 1 egg mixed with 1 teaspoon water

Preheat the oven to 375 degrees.

Heat the oil in a large skillet. When very hot, add the mushrooms and sauté quickly, stirring constantly, for only a minute or 2. Remove the mushrooms and discard any remaining oil.

Add the butter to the skillet, melt it, and add the shallots and thyme. Sauté over moderate heat until aromatic, about 1 minute. Stir in the flour with a wire whisk and continue to sauté for 2 to 3 minutes. Pour in the Madeira and allow the mixture to thicken. Add the cream, stirring to combine, and season to taste with salt, pepper, and a dash of lemon juice. Allow the sauce to cool slightly.

Drain the mushrooms of any liquid that may have accumulated, and add to the sauce. Taste for seasoning, adjust if necessary, and pour the mixture into the flan ring. Place the reserved circle of pastry over the tart. Trim off any excess pastry and crimp together the edges of the top and bottom crusts, sealing them. Brush the top lightly with the egg-white glaze and cut a few decorative vents in the center.

Place the tart in the oven and bake for about an hour, or until the pastry is crisp and golden. Remove from the oven, unmold, and allow to cool slightly. Cut into wedges and serve.

Note: Fresh wild chanterelles or fresh morels can be substituted for the cultivated mushrooms, but since the wild varieties contain more liquid, they must be sautéed over very high heat for the liquid to be released. The liquid can then be reduced and used to replace part of the heavy cream.

Cheese and Onion Tart
serves ten to twelve

T his savory tart may be baked in advance and gently reheated just before serving. As a variation, you may wish to add six ounces of baked ham, cut into julienne. In this case, you should reduce the amount of grated cheese to half a pound. Serve as a first course with one of the Alsatian white varietals as an accompanying wine.

$1/_2$ **recipe for cream cheese pastry (see Kulebiaka) or your own pastry**
6 tablespoons butter
4 cups Walla Walla sweet onions, thinly sliced
Salt and freshly ground pepper
6 large eggs
$2^1/_2$ cups half-and-half

1 teaspoon Dijon mustard
Pinch freshly ground nutmeg
Dash Tabasco
$1/_2$ teaspoon salt
$3/_4$ pound grated Emmentaler cheese
3 tablespoons grated Parmesan cheese
2 tablespoons bread crumbs

Preheat the oven to 400 degrees.

Roll out the pastry and fit into a well-greased rectangular pan with high sides (10 by 14 by $2^1/_2$ inches). Spread a sheet of foil over the pastry, pressing it against the sides, and weight it down with rice or beans. Place in the center of the oven and after 10 to 12 minutes take out of the oven, remove foil and rice or beans, prick the pastry with a fork, and return to oven to bake for another 10 to 15 minutes. The pastry should be just starting to brown lightly and will have begun to shrink just slightly away from the sides of the pan when you take it out. Allow the pastry to cool.

Lower the oven temperature to 350 degrees. Melt the butter in a heavy pot, add the onions, and season them lightly with salt and pepper. Sauté the onions over moderate heat for 15 minutes, stirring frequently. Combine the eggs, half-and-half, mustard, nutmeg, Tabasco, and salt in a mixing bowl, beating well.

Spread the onions in the bottom of the cooled pastry shell. Sprinkle the grated Emmentaler cheese over them and pour the egg mixture over all. Mix the grated Parmesan with the bread crumbs and sprinkle the top of the tart with this mixture, then dot with butter.

Bake the tart in the upper third of the oven for 15 minutes, then increase the heat to 425 degrees and continue to bake for another 15 to 20 minutes, until the custard has puffed and browned and a knife inserted in the center comes out clean. Allow to stand 20 minutes before serving.

Swiss Chard Tart
serves six

T his tart is composed of blanched, shredded chard, sautéed quickly with a bit of onion, prosciutto, and garlic, then mixed into ricotta, Parmesan, and eggs and baked in a pastry shell. It has a light and zesty flavor and—for those concerned with keeping waistlines intact—can be made without the pastry: simply pour the filling into a well-greased nine-inch pie dish, bake, and serve in wedges. Either way a French or California Chardonnay is the right sort of wine.

1 bunch of Swiss chard (about 1 pound)
Squeeze of lemon juice
2 tablespoons olive oil or butter
$\frac{1}{2}$ cup onion, finely chopped
$\frac{1}{2}$ cup prosciutto, cut into julienne (substitute baked ham, if desired)
2 cloves garlic, finely chopped

Freshly grated nutmeg
Salt and freshly ground pepper
$1\frac{1}{2}$ cups ricotta cheese
$\frac{1}{2}$ cup freshly grated Parmesan cheese
$\frac{1}{2}$ cup milk
3 eggs
10-inch partially baked pastry shell

Preheat the oven to 400 degrees.

Cut the stems from the Swiss chard and discard them. Wash the greens well and reserve. Bring a large pot of salted water to a boil and add a squeeze of lemon juice and the greens. Cook for 2 to 3 minutes until tender but still green. Remove the chard to a colander and run it under cold water to stop the cooking process. Dry thoroughly (a lettuce-drier or spinner is good for this job) and chop it into shreds.

Heat the oil or butter in a skillet. Add the onion and sauté a few minutes until it is soft but not brown; add the prosciutto and sauté for a minute more. To the skillet add the chard and the garlic; sauté over moderately high heat for 5 minutes, stirring, until all the moisture is absorbed. Sprinkle this mixture with the nutmeg, salt, and pepper and reserve.

Put the ricotta through a sieve (or blend in a food processor for a few seconds) to remove the grainy texture. Place it in a mixing bowl along with all but a tablespoon of the grated cheese, add milk and eggs and blend well. Add to this the chard and prosciutto mixture; blend again and check the seasoning. Pour into the prepared pastry shell, sprinkle the top with the remaining cheese, and bake in the middle of the oven for 35 to 45 minutes or until the tart is browned and puffy. Remove from oven, let stand 15 minutes, and serve.

Leek and Sausage Tart

serves six

A savory combination of leeks and sausage baked in a crust: a good choice for lunch or supper. It is superb with a Valpolicella.

$^3/_4$ **pound link pork sausage, lightly seasoned**
2 tablespoons butter
4 cups leeks, cleaned and cut into $^1/_4$-inch slices
Salt and freshly ground pepper
4 ounces cream cheese
2 eggs
$^1/_4$ **cup milk**
$^1/_4$ **teaspoon salt**
Dash each of cayenne pepper and freshly grated nutmeg
10-inch unbaked pastry shell (for quiche or flan)
1 to 2 tablespoons bread crumbs

Preheat the oven to 375 degrees.

Blanch the sausages in boiling water for 5 minutes to stiffen them; drain, slash the skins, and remove and discard them. Cut the sausage meat into bite-sized pieces; put them in a skillet with the butter and sauté over medium heat until the sausage is cooked; remove and reserve.

Put the leeks in the remaining oil, season them with salt and pepper, and sauté them over medium heat for about 10 minutes, until tender.

While the leeks are cooking, combine the cream cheese with the eggs, milk, salt, and spices and blend well.

Mix the leeks and the sausage bits and fill the pastry shell with the mixture. Pour the cheese and egg mixture over this, top with the bread crumbs, and bake in the middle of the oven for about 1 hour or until the pastry is lightly browned. Remove and allow to cool for 10 minutes before serving.

CHAPTER TEN

SALADS

Bean Salad alla Romano
serves four to six

T his is a robust concoction of dried beans tossed with black and green olives, onion, and prosciutto, and dressed with a mixture of oil, vinegar, hot pepper, and garlic, that has been thickened with bread crumbs. Since fresh herbs have become so abundantly available, you will wish to use a judicious sprinkling of marjoram, mint, or oregano to enliven this salad. If you must substitute a dried herb for fresh, avoid basil—it is the only one of the lot that cannot successfully retain its true flavor when dried. As a variation, you might wish to add cubes of ripe tomato (peeled and seeded) and replace the prosciutto with small cubes of crisply fried bacon. This salad is a good selection for a buffet and also makes an excellent side dish for simple grilled or roasted meats or poultry.

1 cup dried cranberry beans (also known as Roman beans) or whatever dried beans you prefer

2 bay leaves

2 teaspoons salt

$\frac{1}{2}$ cup onion, chopped

$\frac{1}{2}$ cup olive oil plus $1\frac{1}{2}$ tablespoons

8 Calamata olives, pitted and coarsely chopped

6 large green olives stuffed with pimentos, thickly sliced

1 $\frac{1}{4}$-inch-thick slice prosciutto, diced

$\frac{1}{2}$ cup fresh bread crumbs soaked in $\frac{1}{4}$ cup beef stock and squeezed dry

2 cloves garlic

$\frac{1}{2}$ teaspoon dried red pepper flakes

3 tablespoons balsamic vinegar

1 teaspoon coarsely chopped fresh herb: basil, marjoram, savory, oregano, or mint

Soak the beans the night before. The next day, drain them and place in a deep pot with the bay leaves, salt, and enough water to cover by 2 inches. Bring to a boil, reduce the heat and simmer for about 40 minutes or until tender. Drain the beans and allow them to cool slightly.

While the beans are cooking, prepare the other ingredients for the salad. Sauté the onion in 1 1/2 tablespoons oil until transparent. Add to the beans, along with the olives and prosciutto. Toss together.

To prepare the dressing, purée the bread crumbs with the garlic, pepper flakes, vinegar and 1/2 cup olive oil. Season with salt to taste, pour the mixture over the beans, toss well, and garnish with the fresh herb.

Grated Carrot Salad
serves four

This salad is dressed with sherry-wine vinegar (available at specialty shops), which intensifies the natural sweetness of the carrots. If you use sherry vinegar as a substitute for another vinegar, take care to add less than usual because of its intense flavor.

5 medium carrots
1 shallot, peeled
1/2 teaspoon grated lemon peel
2 tablespoons parsley, chopped

1 tablespoon sherry-wine
  vinegar
6 tablespoons olive oil
Salt and freshly ground pepper

Peel and coarsely grate the carrots; place in a serving bowl. Chop together the shallot, lemon peel, and parsley, place in a small mixing bowl, and add the vinegar, olive oil, and salt and pepper to taste. Blend this dressing well, pour it over the carrots, and toss all together. Chill for 30 minutes before serving.

Celery Root Remoulade
serves four to six

This recipe is in the New Orleans style rather than the French. The addition of tiny Pacific shrimp gives it a unique Northwest flavor.

1 egg yolk, at room temperature
1 tablespoon Creole mustard

(or a good, grainy French
  mustard)

Celery Root

One of the more neglected root vegetables is celery root, or celeriac, a delicious winter offering usually available from November to April. Its round, knoblike shape is covered with a rough brown skin, and it is topped with an abundant mass of greenery somewhat resembling the flat-leaved Italian parsley. It has a mild celery flavor, and its texture resembles that of the potato.

Celeriac can be added to any soup or stew that calls for celery stalks (it's marvelous, for example, in a pot au feu or a chicken fricassee), it can be made into a purée along with potatoes to add a subtle flavor accent, or it can be made in a suave cream of celery root soup. It's used raw as often as it's used cooked, and either way, it's just as delicious, as you'll discover in the Celery Root Remoulade.

$1/2$ tablespoon red-wine vinegar
2 or 3 drops of Tabasco
Large pinch of salt
$3/4$ cup of oil (half vegetable oil, half olive oil)
Squeeze of lemon juice
1 tablespoon capers, finely chopped

2 tablespoons parsley, finely chopped
1 teaspoon finely grated lemon rind
1 celery root, about 1 pound
3 ounces Pacific shrimp, cooked (do not use canned)

First prepare the sauce. Place the egg yolk in a mixing bowl; add the mustard, vinegar, Tabasco, and salt and beat thoroughly with a wire whisk or an electric mixer. Then add a few drops of the oil, mixing well to allow the yolk to absorb the oil completely before adding any more. Continue beating until all the oil is absorbed; add the lemon juice to taste and blend. Add the capers, parsley, and lemon rind, mix well, taste for seasoning, and adjust if necessary. Set aside.

Peel the celery root and, working quickly, cut into julienne strips or grate coarsely. Mix immediately into the sauce, add the shrimp (reserving a few for garnish), mix well, and chill until serving time.

Dandelion Salad Mimosa
serves four

Young dandelion leaves have a pleasing piquant flavor; they should be picked before the plant has flowered to be at their most tender. The piquancy of this salad particularly suits dishes featuring lamb.

1 pound young dandelion
leaves
4 rashers thick bacon, cut into
small dice
2 tablespoons lemon juice
Pinch dried mustard

1 shallot, finely minced
Dash Tabasco
Salt and freshly ground pepper
$\frac{1}{3}$ cup fruity olive oil
1 hard-boiled egg

Gently wash the dandelion leaves, tear into bite-size pieces, and refrigerate for at least 30 minutes to crisp. Sauté the bacon until browned and crisp; remove to paper towels to drain.

Combine the lemon juice, dried mustard, minced shallot, Tabasco, salt, pepper, and olive oil, mixing well. Place the chilled dandelion leaves in a serving bowl, sprinkle with the bacon, and toss with only enough of the dressing to just moisten the leaves. Sieve the white and yolk of the egg separately and sprinkle both on top of the salad. Serve at once.

Eggplant Salad
serves four to six

I'm a fickle eater; foods and flavors that pleased me yesterday do less to excite me today. Although my tastes in specific foods seem to be undergoing a constant metamorphosis, there are a few dishes of which I'll never tire. These dishes too have, over the years, gone through changes and have emerged totally different from the original. Cooking techniques have been pared down so that they are simple and quick, and the seasonings refined so only those that truly add to the dish are kept. This eggplant salad, which is actually a very quick version of that Italian favorite, caponata, is a perfect example of such changes.

I've specified using Oriental eggplant—which is generally avaliable—for its wonderful flavor, which is never bitter like the larger varieties; for its size—perfect for cutting into bite-size rounds and quickly cooked; and for its beautiful pale-green celadon color.

1 pound Oriental eggplant
3 to 4 tablespoons olive oil
Salt and freshly ground pepper
Herbes de Provence (available in any food-specialty store)
3 to 4 cloves garlic, peeled and finely chopped
6 anchovy fillets, finely chopped
2 tablespoons tomato paste mixed with enough water to produce a soupy liquid
1 $1/_2$ tablespoons balsamic

vinegar
1 tablespoon sugar
2 large red bell peppers, roasted, peeled, and cut into strips (see Roasted Peppers)
1 cup small green olives stuffed with pimentos
2 tablespoons pine nuts, toasted in an ungreased skillet until golden blond
2 to 3 tablespoons flat-leaved parsley, coarsely chopped

Trim the stem ends from the eggplant and cut the flesh into thick, bite-size chunks. (This eggplant does not need to be peeled.) Heat about a tablespoon of the oil in a skillet; when hot, sauté the eggplant, a bit at a time, over high heat, seasoning with salt, pepper, and a generous amount of the herbes de Provence, until just tender. Remove to a colander to allow excess oil to drain off while cooking the remainder of the eggplant, adding oil when necessary.

When all the eggplant has been cooked, add a tablespoon of the oil to the skillet and cook the garlic and anchovy over low heat until the garlic has softened. Stir in the tomato paste mixture and cook for a few minutes until the liquid thickens considerably. Add the vinegar and the sugar to the sauce; cook for about a minute more, taste, and adjust the seasoning if necessary. The sauce should have a distinct and rather strong sweet-sour taste.

Combine the eggplant with the strips of pepper and the olives. Pour the sauce over all and garnish with the pine nuts and parsley. The salad can be held in the refrigerator for a day or so but tastes best when served at room temperature.

Honeydew, Watercress, and Sugar Pea Salad
serves six

A t first glance this salad seems to be missing most of its ingredients. That is emphatically not the case; the three ingredients listed in the title are all there are to this exercise in simplicity and restraint. After sampling this salad, you'll find that its combination of flavors would be difficult to improve upon.

2 large bunches watercress
$^1/_3$ pound sugar peas, the very smallest you can find

1 small very ripe honeydew melon

Wash the watercress and separate into small, bite-size branches, discarding the large thick stems. Dry thoroughly and chill.

Snap off and discard the stem ends from the sugar peas. Halve the melon, remove the seeds, and cut each half into thick wedges. Cut the wedges away from the rind and then cut the wedges into bite-size pieces. Place the melon in a bowl and refrigerate for an hour or 2 to allow the melon to release liquid, which will moisten the salad.

Combine all the ingredients, toss until well mixed, and serve at once.

Raw Mushroom Salad
serves four

T his recipe is an adaptation of a dish served at The Four Seasons restaurant in New York. The dressing used is very complementary to strong-flavored greens such as romaine, watercress, or spinach.

Dressing

$^3/_4$ cup heavy cream
1 tablespoon fine French mustard (Pommery, L'Ancienne, or Dijon)

$^1/_2$ tablespoon red-wine vinegar
3 tablespoons olive oil
Salt and freshly ground pepper
Dash Tabasco

Vegetables

$^1/_2$ **pound mushrooms, cleaned**   **strips 2 inches long**
     and thinly sliced $^1/_4$ **cup raw radish, grated**
2 stalks celery, cut into julienne

Prepare the dressing: combine the heavy cream with the mustard, vinegar, olive oil, salt, pepper, and Tabasco and mix well. Taste the mixture for seasoning; the dressing should be tangy, which depends on the type of mustard used. You may wish to add more than is called for.

Place the mushrooms, celery, and radish in a serving bowl, pour the dressing over them, and toss well. Serve immediately or marinate at room temperature for an hour or 2.

Orange and Fennel Salad
serves four

O nce again the pleasing combination of orange and fennel, which makes several appearances in this book. Here thin strips of raw fennel are paired with orange chunks to marinate briefly before being spooned over ribbons of Bibb lettuce. This is easy to prepare and a refreshing change from the ubiquitous tossed greens.

1 small fennel bulb   **Salt and freshly ground pepper**
2 large navel oranges   **8 to 10 leaves of Bibb lettuce,**
1$^1/_2$ tablespoons lemon juice   **thoroughly washed and**
1 tablespoon very mild vinegar,   **dried**
     such as rice-wine or   **Garnish: 16 to 20 small black**
     Champagne   **imported olives such as**
$^1/_4$ **cup finest olive oil**   **Nicoise**

Cut away and discard the core from the bottom of the fennel bulb. Slice the root into very thin rings across the grain. You will need about 1 heaping cup of the fennel. Place this in a small mixing bowl.

With a sharp paring knife, peel the oranges so that both the outer rind and the membrane are removed. Cut away pieces of orange by slicing between the exposed lines of membrane separating each segment. Add the orange chunks to the fennel. When you have finished cutting away the orange pieces, squeeze the juice from the remains of the orange into a mixing bowl. Add the lemon juice, vinegar, and olive oil. Season lightly with salt and add a liberal grinding of black pepper. Allow to marinate, at room temperature, for at least 1 hour.

Just before serving, cut the lettuce leaves into ribbons by piling 4 or 5 leaves on top of each other and rolling them lengthwise into the shape of a cigar. Cut crosswise into strips about $1/2$ inch wide. Mound a quarter of the lettuce strips on each of 4 individual serving plates; glass is especially lovely. Spoon some of the orange and fennel mixture over each serving, along with only enough liquid to just moisten the lettuce. Garnish with a scattering of the black olives and serve immediately.

Moroccan Orange and Radish Salad
serves four

An intriguing Moroccan creation: peeled, chopped orange sections and grated raw radish dressed with a mixture of lemon, sugar, salt, and cinnamon. This is a fresh and lively side dish, especially good with roast lamb or duck; it is particularly delicious served with couscous.

4 medium seedless oranges	2 tablespoons sugar
8 to 10 radishes, coarsely grated	$1/8$ teaspoon salt
6 tablespoons lemon juice	Powdered cinnamon

Peel the oranges with a serrated knife and cut the flesh into bite-size chunks. Mix the orange pieces with the grated radish.

Combine the lemon juice, sugar, and salt, pour the dressing over the orange mixture, and toss. Sprinkle the salad with a light dusting of the powdered cinnamon, cover tightly, and chill. The salad will keep, refrigerated, for 4 to 6 hours. Toss together well just before serving.

Sicilian Orange Salad
serves four to six

The utter simplicity of this salad doesn't prepare you for the delightful surprise of its flavors—the cold sweetness of the oranges contrasting with the bite of the hot pepper flakes, both mellowed a little by the addition of a good, extra-virgin olive oil. This is an especially pleasing dish to serve alongside the more robustly flavored fish such as salmon, sturgeon, marlin, or shark. It is also a superb accompaniment to spicy entrées such as jambalayas, gumbos, or paellas. In these cases you may wish to "cool down" the seasonings; simply substitute a good grinding of black pepper for the red pepper flakes and garnish with small imported black olives such as Nicoise or Gaeta. Another variation, wonderful with grilled lamb or pork, is layers of thinly sliced red onions and orange slices seasoned with a bit of fresh rosemary.

5 large navel oranges   **Red pepper flakes**
Salt   **Extra-virgin olive oil**

Peel the oranges with a serrated knife, taking care to remove every trace of the bitter white membrane. Slice the oranges, crosswise, into thin rounds. Place a layer of orange slices in the bottom of a gratin dish, sprinkle lightly with salt, a bit heavier with the pepper flakes, and drizzle enough olive oil over all to moisten. Continue in this fashion until the orange slices are used up. There should be enough oil in the dish to come midway up the oranges. Chill the salad only long enough to cool it throughout but not long enough for the oil to solidify—about an hour or so. Serve immediately.

Sweet Pea Salad
serves four

A most refreshing spring salad composed of fresh new peas, crisp julienne of bacon, sautéed mushrooms, and thinly sliced scallions dressed with olive oil and vinegar. With a rich dish like Crostini Roberto this is a light but full meal.

2 pounds (unshelled weight) fresh young peas	4 or 5 scallions, thinly sliced (including the green tops)
1 teaspoon sugar	1½ tablespoons red-wine vinegar
4 rashers thick-sliced bacon, cut into thick julienne	6 tablespoons olive oil
8 small mushrooms, cleaned and thickly sliced	Dash Tabasco
	Salt and freshly ground pepper

Place a little water in a saucepan (just enough to cover the peas), add the sugar, and bring to a boil. While the water is heating, shell the peas; add peas to the water and cook them for 5 to 7 minutes, until just tender. Remove peas and run under cold water, drain, and dry thoroughly.

Sauté the bacon in a small skillet until crisp and brown; remove and drain on paper towels. Quickly sauté the mushroom slices in the hot bacon fat until lightly browned; remove with a slotted spoon.

In a serving bowl, combine the peas, bacon, mushrooms, and scallions. Add the vinegar, oil, Tabasco, and salt and pepper to taste. Toss the salad well and serve at once, or chill for an hour or 2.

Roasted Pepper Salad
serves four

A simple yet satisfying dish composed only of roasted peppers mixed with slices of garlic, tossed with a good red-wine vinegar and olive oil, and left to marinate for an hour or two. This is a wonderful accompaniment to grilled fish or chicken. For roasting instructions, see Roasted Sweet Bell Peppers.

The peppers may also be used for an hors d'oeuvre: cut small slices of French or Italian bread, top them with thin slices of feta cheese, and finally add one or two slices of roasted pepper.

4 roasted red (or green) bell peppers, cut into strips ½ inch thick	1 or 2 cloves garlic, thinly sliced
	1½ tablespoons balsamic vinegar

4 tablespoons fruity olive oil
Salt and freshly ground pepper

Garnish: 2 tablespoons
parsley, finely chopped

Place the peppers in a serving dish, add the sliced garlic, vinegar, and oil, and season with salt and pepper. Toss together, check the seasoning (roasted peppers seem to need quite a bit of salt), and allow to stand at room temperature for an hour or 2 . Garnish with the chopped parsley just before serving.

Rice Salad
serves four

1 cup long-grain rice
$\frac{1}{4}$ pound green beans, cut into
  1-inch lengths
3 to 4 tablespoons red or white
  onion, coarsely chopped
1 tablespoon olive oil
1 large ripe tomato
$\frac{1}{4}$ cup pitted olives coarsely
  chopped (preferably a

mixture of green Calamata
  and green Spanish olives)
3 tablespoons parsley, minced
  together with $\frac{1}{4}$ teaspoon
  dried summer savory
2 to 3 tablespoons red-wine
  vinegar
$\frac{1}{4}$ cup olive oil
Salt and freshly ground pepper

Cook the rice, removing it when done to a platter to cool and to allow the grains to separate.

While the rice is cooking, boil the green beans in salted water until they are tender but still crisp. Sauté the onion in the olive oil for 2 to 3 minutes. Skin and seed the tomato and chop it into large dice.

When the rice is cool, mix in the beans, sautéed onion, tomato, olives, parsley, and savory. Toss with the vinegar and olive oil. Season to taste with salt and pepper. Chill for about an hour before serving.

Summer Tomato Salad with Fried Bread Cubes
serves four to six

I f you cannot obtain good, vine-ripened tomatoes for this salad you might as well pass it by and look for another dish since its success is so dependent upon the succulent sweetness found only in tomatoes picked at their peak. If you grow your own or are lucky enough to purchase some of these tomatoes, a luscious treat awaits. Any sweet white or red onion can be

---

Balsamic Vinegar

Balsamic vinegar—Modena's famous *aceto balsamico*—rightly deserves its superior reputation. In *The Food of Italy*, Waverly Root writes: "Earliest written reference to it dates from 1046, when Bonifacio di Canossa (father of Matilda, the Great Countess) presented a barrel of it to the Emperor Henry III as a coronation gift. In the 16th century this vinegar was considered so precious ... that it was disposed of specifically by will, figuring among the important bequests."

The making of balsamic vinegar is a tradition that is as rich as its history. Beginning as an herb-flavored wine vinegar, it is placed in the first of twelve kegs. It will journey from barrel to barrel until it reaches its full potential. The kegs are made of different woods: oak, chestnut, mulberry, juniper, and each of these adds new fragrances to the vinegar. This too is traditional, although today it is also obligatory; Italian law stipulates that only casks of these woods can be used in the making of *aceto balsamico*. After several years of blending, moving, and aging, the vinegar is a dense dark brown, with a pleasing characteristic aromatic odor and a flavor that combines tart and sweet. The grape used in the making of this vinegar is the white Trebbiano—a sugary variety that accounts for the sweetness.

Aceto balsamico must by law be at least ten years old, but there are homemade varieties that are aged for up to seventy years. As with fine wine, the older the vinegar the more complex is its character. The Modenese believe that their wonderful vinegar has medicinal properties, and the word, loosely translated, means "that which is good for the health."

substituted for the Walla Walla sweets, and if you cannot get fresh basil simply leave it out rather than use the dried variety.

Fried Bread Cubes

**4 to 6 thick slices of a dense
 white bread
4 cloves garlic, peeled but**

**left whole
Olive oil**

Think of vinegar as a culinary accessory—one that adds color, interest, and an amazing shot of flavor to a dish—a far cry from the concept of this condiment as only a preservative or a salad-dressing ingredient. Experiment with just a few of the vast array of vinegars; the more subtle varieties may be substituted for citrus in certain recipes, and the assertive balsamic may be used in place of a dollop of red wine in meat or poultry sauces.

The complex and full-bodied *aceto balsamico* is without exception the finest vinegar I've ever tasted. It should be used sparingly but is wonderfully versatile.

Suggestions for use:

- Brown a little diced pancetta (Italian bacon) in a skillet with a bit of olive oil and a smattering of onion; add precooked meat-filled tortellini. When warmed through, sprinkle with balsamic vinegar and dust with Parmesan cheese.

- Cut cabbage into thick ribbons, blanch, and sauté with onion in butter; when the vegetables are tender, sprinkle lightly with the vinegar.

- Sprinkle balsamic vinegar on tiny whole steamed new potatoes, garnish with bay leaves, and serve as an appetizer.

- Steam lengths of leek and dress while hot with balsamic vinegar and the best olive oil.

Trim away the crusts from the bread and cut into cubes that measure about 1½ inches square. Heat enough of the olive oil in a skillet to reach a depth of ¼ inch. Add the garlic and only as many bread cubes as will fit in a single layer; do not crowd them. Sauté over moderate heat, turning the cubes frequently to insure even browning, until they are crisp and golden. Drain on paper towels.

Salad

4 to 6 very ripe (preferably vine-ripened) tomatoes, medium size, peeled, seeded and cut into cubes

1 small Walla Walla sweet onion, cut into small dice

1 large sweet yellow or red bell pepper, cut into cubes

slightly smaller than the tomatoes

8 large leaves of fresh basil, cut into shreds

Salt and freshly ground pepper

Juice of ½ lemon

¼ cup extra-virgin olive oil

In a large bowl, combine the bread cubes with the vegetables and the basil. Season to taste with salt and a good amount of freshly ground pepper. Pour the lemon juice and olive oil over all and toss until mixed. Serve at once. Prepare only just before serving so that the fried bread will remain crisp.

Variation: Substitute a pepper with more heat for the bell: Anaheim or pasilla are both good.

Watercress and Radicchio Salad
serves four

Radicchio, which is grown locally in the Northwest and is generally available in larger cities, is a member of the chicory family, so its flavor has a little bite. The texture is a cross between that of lettuce and of cabbage; it looks a bit like red cabbage, though the heads are not so compact.

This is an excellent autumn/winter salad; I often serve it along with a small wedge of a full-flavored creamy blue cheese such as the Italian Gorgonzola Dolce, the French Pipo Crème, or our own Oregon Blue. If radicchio is unavailable, this salad is just as delicious, but not as brightly colored, without it.

1 ¹/₂ tablespoons balsamic vinegar
¹/₃ cup fruity olive oil
Salt and freshly ground pepper
1 ¹/₂ bunches watercress, rinsed, coarse stems removed, and the rest thoroughly dried
2 to 3 heads radicchio, rinsed, torn into bite-size pieces,

and dried
Scant ¹/₄ cup walnuts, coarsely chopped
1 large firm apple (peel left on), cored and cut into thin, bite-size wedges
2 to 3 medium shallots, peeled and finely chopped

Mix the vinegar and olive oil together in a small bowl; season to taste with salt and a good amount of freshly ground pepper.

In a large bowl, combine the other ingredients. Pour the dressing over all and toss well.

Watercress and Snow Pea Salad
serves four

An elegant green salad served with a slightly sweet-sour dressing that may be served with almost any meat, poultry, or fish dish.

2 bunches watercress
¹/₄ pound fresh snow peas, smallest possible, ends

trimmed off
4 to 6 scallions

Dressing

Juice of ¹/₂ lemon
¹/₄ teaspoon dry mustard
1-inch squeeze anchovy paste
1 teaspoon honey

Dash Tabasco
5 tablespoons olive oil
Salt and freshly ground pepper

Wash and trim the watercress and place it in a salad bowl. Bring 2 quarts of salted water to a boil, add the snow peas, and cook them for 3 to 5 minutes until tender but still crisp. Run under cold water, drain, and dry thoroughly. Add the blanched snow peas to the watercress. Thinly slice the scallions, including the green tops, and add them to the salad bowl. Cover with a dampened paper towel and chill until serving time.

Prepare the dressing: in a small mixing bowl, combine the lemon juice with the dry mustard, anchovy paste, and honey and stir well. Add the Tabasco and the olive oil, stirring constantly. Season with salt to taste and add a liberal grinding of black pepper.

Stir the dressing well before using, pour over the watercress and snow pea mixture, toss gently but thoroughly, and serve at once.

Caesar Salad
serves four

Romaine lettuce, fresh garlic croutons, grated Parmesan cheese tossed with an egg-and-anchovy dressing, and a whisper of fresh mint.

4 tablespoons olive oil
1 cup fresh bread cubes cut into $1/_2$-inch dice (French or sourdough bread)
2 or 3 cloves garlic, peeled but left whole
1 large head romaine lettuce, cleaned and broken into bite-size pieces
1 egg yolk
Pinch salt

$1/_2$ teaspoon dry mustard
2-inch squeeze anchovy paste
Juice of $1/_2$ lemon
4 tablespoons olive oil
Dash Tabasco
Freshly ground pepper
1 tablespoon fresh mint, chopped
4 tablespoons freshly grated Parmesan cheese

Heat the olive oil in a skillet over medium heat, add the bread cubes and the garlic cloves, and sauté, turning the cubes until they are browned and crisp. Drain on paper towels.

Place the romaine in a salad bowl, cover with a dampened paper towel, and chill.

Prepare the dressing: in a small mixing bowl put the egg yolk, a small pinch of salt, the dry mustard, and the anchovy paste and stir with a fork or a small whisk. Mix in the lemon juice and add the olive oil slowly, blending well. Season with Tabasco and pepper; taste and add more salt, if necessary. This can be made well in advance of serving time.

Remove the salad bowl from the refrigerator and sprinkle with the chopped mint, Parmesan cheese, croutons, and freshly ground pepper. Mix the dressing well and pour only enough of it over the salad to moisten the leaves. Toss gently and serve.

Chicken and Peach Salad
serves four

Although usually confined to the end of a meal, in some sort of sweet disguise, the peach should also be considered as part of a main-course salad: juicy cubes of the fruit combined with perfectly poached chicken, thinly sliced scallions, and chunks of pecan, with a dressing of mayonnaise, heavy cream, vinegar, and a touch of sugar. I've specified dark meat because it will stay more moist than breast meat. If you wish to substitute the latter, take care not to overcook it. It's best to combine this salad just before serving; if it sits for any length of time, the peaches will exude a good amount of juice, and dilute the dressing.

After scrutinizing this recipe, you might think its origins are in the Deep South; on the contrary—it was taken from the memory of one served at Demel's Café in Vienna. A wine that would go well with this would be a German sparkling wine—a Sekt.

8 chicken thighs (about 2
    pounds)
3 cups chicken stock
3 large scallions, including 3
    inches of the greens, thinly
    sliced

$^1/_2$ cup lightly toasted pecans,
    coarsely chopped
2 large ripe peaches, skinned
    (see Peach Chutney), pitted,
    and cut into small cubes

Sauce

$^1/_2$ cup mayonnaise
2 tablespoons heavy cream
2 tablespoons mild vinegar

(such as rice-wine or champagne vinegar)
1 tablespoon sugar

Poach the chicken in the stock for 15 minutes, or until tender. Remove chicken, and when cool enough to handle, remove and discard skin and bones. Cut the meat into cubes. Combine the chicken with the scallions, pecans, and peaches in a mixing bowl.

Prepare the sauce: into the mayonnaise whisk the cream and the vinegar. Add the sugar and mix again. Pour over the chicken and toss together. Serve at once mounded on beds of shredded Bibb lettuce.

Cucumber and Octopus Salad
serves four

T his salad was adapted from the Japanese sunomono—a mixture of sliced cucumber and octopus with rice-wine vinegar, sugar, and soy sauce—but it is dressed differently. You can purchase cooked octopus at many fish markets and it is usually quite tender. If it is not, it may be simmered for a while in boiling water to which has been added a dash of vinegar. Those of you who are not feeling adventurous may substitute cooked crab meat for the chewy, nutty-flavored octopus.

2 medium cucumbers
Coarse salt
$^1/_2$ pound cooked octopus, cut
  into thin slices
$1^1/_2$ tablespoons lemon juice or
  mild wine vinegar

5 tablespoons olive oil
Dash Oriental sesame oil
  (available at Oriental specialty stores and some supermarkets)
Salt and freshly ground pepper

Peel the cucumbers; slice off the ends, cut them in half lengthwise, and remove the seeds. Put the pieces in a bowl, sprinkle them liberally with coarse salt, and allow to stand at room temperature for at least $^1/_2$ hour. Rinse the cucumbers under cold running water, dry thoroughly, and cut into fine slices.

Combine the octopus with the cucumber slices, dress with the lemon juice or vinegar, olive oil, sesame oil, and salt and pepper to taste. Toss mixture together well, marinate for 1 hour or longer, and serve.

Curried Crab and Rice Salad
serves four

A savory combination of rice, crabmeat, and aromatic vegetables seasoned with curry powder. The secret of a good curry flavor lies in cooking the powder rather than using it right out of the bottle. This salad is lovely stuffed into hollowed-out tomatoes and can be served as a first course or as an accompaniment to a roast.

1 cup long-grain rice
3 tablespoons butter
$\frac{1}{2}$ cup onion, peeled and finely chopped
$\frac{1}{3}$ cup celery, cut into small dice
$\frac{1}{3}$ cup green bell pepper, cut into small dice
1 tablespoon curry powder (or to taste—depending on strength)
6 ounces crabmeat, cooked, carefully cleaned, and flaked (substitute cooked shrimp meat, if desired)
$\frac{1}{2}$ cup heavy cream
Salt and freshly ground pepper
Small handful parsley, finely chopped
Lemon slices

Cook the rice; when done, remove it to a serving bowl to cool and to allow the grains to separate. While the rice is cooking, melt the butter in a skillet, add the onion, celery, and green pepper, and sauté for 3 minutes; stir in the curry powder and continue to cook for a few minutes more until the vegetables are tender but still crisp. Remove from heat and stir the vegetables into the rice; add the crab or shrimp and toss together.

Just before serving, season the heavy cream lightly with salt and whip gently; it must not be stiff. Season the salad with pepper and parsley, fold in the whipped cream, taste for seasoning, and garnish with lemon slices.

Fish Salad in Salsa Verde
serves four to six

O ver the years, I've become addicted to the Mexican raw green salsa: a finely chopped mixture of tomatillos, onion, garlic, jalapeno peppers, and a good quantity of fresh coriander. The sauce is easily made and fantastic on black beans and rice, roast pork, quesadillas, poached or grilled fish, tacos, and nachos, among other things. Here it's used as the basis of a cool and spicy fish salad; the seafood is quickly sautéed and then combined with the salsa and wedges of cucumber for texture. This may be served as a first course, a light supper, or lunch.

4 cups salsa verde (see page 111)
Vegetable oil for frying
$\frac{3}{4}$ pound large shrimp, shelled and cleaned
Salt and freshly ground pepper
Lemon juice
$\frac{1}{2}$ pound any firm-fleshed

white fish: halibut cheeks, sturgeon, shark, monkfish, or swordfish, cut into large cubes
1 large English cucumber, cut lengthwise into quarters, then crosswise into thick wedges

Prepare the salsa verde, which may be done a day or 2 in advance, and refrigerate.

Pour enough vegetable oil into a large skillet to barely coat the bottom. Heat the oil and sauté the shrimp over high heat for only a minute or 2 until just firm. While the shrimp are cooking, season with salt, pepper, and a squeeze of lemon juice. Repeat the procedure for the fish, using slightly lower heat.

Place the cooked shrimp and the fish in a serving dish and toss with the salsa and the cucumber. Chill before serving.

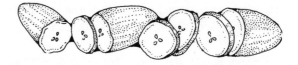

Italian Bean and Tuna Salad
serves four to six

O f Tuscan origin, this simple salad makes a lovely first course or can become part of an antipasto platter.

15-ounce can cannellini beans
  (white kidney beans)
3 tablespoons mild onion,
  finely chopped
1 small clove garlic, finely
  chopped or put through a
  press
6-ounce can tuna, packed in
  olive oil, drained

Salt and freshly ground pepper
1 teaspoon dried oregano,
  summer savory, or thyme
  chopped together with
2 tablespoons fresh parsley
Juice of $\frac{1}{2}$ lemon
Dash of red-wine vinegar
$\frac{1}{3}$ cup fruity olive oil

Refresh the beans under cold running water and drain thoroughly. Place the beans in a mixing bowl and add the onion, garlic, and tuna, separating the tuna into large flakes. Season with salt and pepper to taste, sprinkle with the herbs, and toss all together gently. Dress with the lemon juice, vinegar, and oil, mixing well. Chill slightly or serve immediately.

Salade Nicoise
serves four

T here must be hundreds of recipes purporting to be the "true" Salade Nicoise. This is definitely not one of them; it is merely a tantalizing combination of some of the best vegetables late spring has to offer. Serve it with crisp French bread and a crock of sweet butter. A Burgogne Aligoté would round out the meal.

Vinaigrette dressing

1 egg yolk
$\frac{1}{2}$ teaspoon dry mustard
Pinch of salt
2-inch squeeze anchovy paste
2 tablespoons lemon juice
Dash red-wine vinegar

$\frac{3}{4}$ cup fruity olive oil
Dash Tabasco
1 small clove garlic, put
  through a press
Freshly ground pepper

Olives

There are many different types of olives referred to in this book. In some cases they are used to add their particular flavor; at other times they are chosen as a garnish because of their size or their color. When composing a dish, scale must be taken into consideration—no single element within the dish should overpower the others. Visibly, the ingredients should blend into a harmonious whole: a salad made of ribbons of Bibb lettuce, julienne of fresh fennel root, and orange sections cries out for a delicate garnish such as small black olives. Here either the French Niçoise or the Southern Italian Gaeta may be used. Both are very tiny black olives with a mild and fruity flavor. The Gaeta is slightly sweeter and has more meat; the Niçoise is firmer and has more pit in proportion to the flesh.

For all-purpose cooking, I prefer the Greek import, the Calamata. It has an oval shape, a reddish brown color, firm flesh, and a distinct flavor caused by a red-wine vinegar brine. Their firm flesh makes them easier to work with when removing the pit, which may be done with the aid of a small paring knife or a cherry pitter. Greek olives, the ripe black variety, have a round shape and are salty with a more pronounced flavor. Because the texture of their flesh is so much softer, they are more difficult to pit. Any green olives used should be a good-quality Spanish olive, convenient because they are so commonly available pitted (and stuffed with a bit of pimento), or one of the many varieties of Italian or Greek green olives; avoid those which have a bitter taste. Green olives are the fruit in an unripened state; their flavor is sharper, more defined.

Any olive can be blanched to mellow an excessively salty flavor: boil enough water to cover the olives, add the fruit, remove from the heat, and allow to stand for up to ten minutes. Drain and use as desired. Avoid, at all costs, the canned and pitted olives processed in California, since they possess neither flavor nor texture.

Salad

2 cups new potatoes, peeled and sliced	thinly sliced
2 large green or red bell peppers, roasted (see Roasted Sweet Bell Peppers)	2 cans (7 ounces each) tuna, packed in olive oil and drained
2 large fresh artichoke hearts, prepared for cooking (see Artichoke Hearts)	2 large ripe tomatoes, cut into wedges
2 cups green beans, cut into 2-inch lengths	4 hard-boiled eggs, cut into wedges
Several lettuce leaves	2-ounce can anchovy fillets, drained and separated
1 small red onion, peeled and	½ cup imported black olives

First, prepare the dressing: in a small mixing bowl, place the egg yolk, the dry mustard, a small pinch of salt, and the anchovy paste; mix well. Add the lemon juice and vinegar, stirring, then the olive oil, Tabasco, and pressed garlic, and mix again. Season with a few grinds of pepper; taste and adjust if necessary. Set aside.

Cook the potato slices until just tender, drain them thoroughly, and dress while still hot with a little of the vinaigrette. Cut the roasted peppers into thick strips and dress them too with a little of the vinaigrette.

Cut the artichoke hearts into 8 pieces each, cook in acidulated water until just tender, drain well, and dress with a little vinaigrette.

Cook the green beans until just tender, run them under cold water to stop the cooking process, and drain thoroughly. Dress them with a little vinaigrette.

To assemble, line a large platter with the lettuce leaves, arrange on top of them first the potatoes, then the pepper strips, the artichoke hearts, and finally the green beans. Scatter the onion rings over the top and mound the tuna over them. Surround this with alternating wedges of tomato and egg, garnish the wedges with anchovy fillets, and scatter the black olives over all. Dress the tomato and egg wedges with a bit of the remaining dressing and serve.

Squid Salad
serves six

C leaning squid is not difficult, although it does take a little time: the ink
sac is usually removed by the fishmonger, making the rest a simple
procedure. Hold the squid in one hand; with the other grasp the head and
tentacles and pull. The head will come away with the contents of the body.
(If it does not, simply grasp the body at the pointed end and squeeze out the
excess with your thumb and fingers.)

Pull out the transparent, quill-like backbone and discard. There are two
flaps or "wings" on the body; pull these off under cold running water, and
all of the outside rosy-colored skin will come off easily, leaving behind a
pearly white cone of flesh. Cut the tentacles from the head just behind the
eye; restrain yourself from the impulse to discard the wormy things, for when
they are cooked, they will firm up and spread out like delicate pink flowers.

Rinse both the body and the tentacles under cold running water. Keep the
flesh of the squid in a bowl of cold water until you are ready to use it; then
drain and dry thoroughly. This would make a fine first course for a meal
whose main dish is sautéed, like Chicken Parmigiana, scallopine, or piccata,
or perhaps a Saltimbocca.

3 pounds squid, cleaned
1 1/2 cups thinly sliced celery or
  fennel
1 1/2 teaspoons dried oregano
Dash Tabasco

1 1/2 tablespoons red-wine
  vinegar
1/4 cup fruity olive oil
Salt and freshly ground pepper

Select the smallest possible squid available. Slice the cleaned bodies into
rings no more than 1 inch wide. Cut the tentacles in half if they are large.
Poach both rings and tentacles in lightly simmering salted water for about
30 minutes or until they are tender. Remove, drain well, and put in a serving
bowl.

Add remaining ingredients, seasoning to taste with salt and pepper, and
toss together until all are blended. Let the mixture marinate at room
temperature for at least an hour. Before serving, mix well again, drain off any
excess moisture, and serve as a first course.

CHAPTER ELEVEN

DESSERTS

Apples Baked in Meringue
serves six

A delightfully light dessert idea that uses one of our most famous products: apples poached in a sugar syrup flavored with lemon peel and cinnamon, then covered with meringue and quickly baked. Choose MacIntosh, Winesap, or Rome Beauty apples.

6 apples	Peel of $\frac{1}{2}$ lemon
2$\frac{1}{2}$ cups finely granulated sugar	1 cinnamon stick
1 tablespoon lemon juice	3 cloves
	3 egg whites

Peel and core the apples. In a pot large enough to hold the apples without crowding, put 2 cups sugar, 1 quart water, the lemon juice, and the lemon peel. Bring this to a boil; then add the cinnamon stick, the cloves, and the apples. Cook the apples at a rolling boil, frequently spooning the syrup over them, for about 25 minutes, until tender.

While the apples are cooking, beat the egg whites with a pinch of sugar in a stainless-steel or copper bowl. When they are firm, add the remaining $\frac{1}{2}$ cup of sugar and continue to beat until stiff.

Preheat the oven to 500 degrees.

Drain the apples thoroughly. Place the meringue in a pastry bag fitted with a star tip. Put the apples in a shallow ovenproof container and completely cover each apple with the meringue. Bake for about 5 minutes, just long enough to turn the meringue a golden brown. Serve at once.

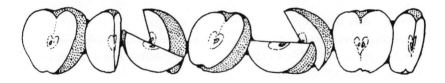

Bread Pudding with Apples
serves six to eight

T here are some who profess not to like bread pudding; you may be able to change their minds with this recipe.

1 ½ pounds baking apples
½ cup (8 tablespoons) butter
1 cup and 2 tablespoons sugar
¼ teaspoon powdered cinnamon
1-pound loaf day-old French

or Italian bread
¼ cup seedless raisins
4 large eggs
4 cups milk
2 teaspoons pure vanilla extract
Freshly grated nutmeg

Preheat the oven to 325 degrees.

Peel, core, and cut the apples into large dice. Melt 4 tablespoons butter in a heavy 10-inch skillet, add the apples, and sprinkle with 2 tablespoons sugar and the cinnamon. Sauté the apples over moderate heat for about 10 minutes, stirring frequently.

Trim off the crust of the bread and discard; cut the rest into small cubes. Using remaining butter, grease a deep ovenproof dish, add the bread cubes, the apples with their juice, and the raisins, and toss together.

Combine the eggs, milk, vanilla, and a liberal grinding of nutmeg, and beat lightly. Pour this mixture over the bread and apples. Set the dish in a pan filled with 1 inch of water and place in the oven. The custard must not be cooked too quickly or it may separate; bake the pudding for 1 ½ hours or until it is set. Serve hot with lightly whipped cream.

Fresh Figs in Blueberry Cream
serves four

8 ripe, fairly firm figs
2 tablespoons butter
1 tablespoon superfine sugar
1 ½ to 2 tablespoons blueberry

vinegar
4 tablespoons heavy cream,
   preferably unpasteurized

Trim and discard the stem ends of the figs. Halve but do not peel the figs.

Melt the butter over moderately high heat in a skillet, and add the figs, cut side down. Sprinkle them with the sugar, and cook for a minute or 2, spooning the butter and sugar over the figs until the liquid thickens and becomes syrupy. Pour in the blueberry vinegar, reduce liquid until thickened—about a minute—then add the heavy cream and cook for a few seconds more until the sauce is sufficiently thickened. Serve immediately on dessert plates.

Honeydew Melon in Anisette
serves four

A t first glance this may seem a rather unusual combination, but it is one that is most refreshing. Use a good Spanish or Italian anisette.

1 large honeydew melon
$^1/_3$ cup imported anisette liqueur

Cut the melon in half and remove the seeds. Cut the flesh into bite-size pieces (or into balls with the aid of a melon baller) and place in a serving bowl. Sprinkle with the anisette, cover, and refrigerate for at least an hour.

Gingered Honeydew
serves four

T his simple dessert is a refreshing surprise: cubes of melon in a pool of ginger-flavored syrup, a combination that is both cooling and zesty. The garnish, a very light dusting of ground amaretti (Italian macaroons), may seem unimportant, but it adds just the correct amount of flavor and finish to the dish.

$^1/_2$ cup sugar
1 cup water
Scant tablespoon fresh ginger,
  finely chopped

1 very ripe honeydew melon
Garnish: ground amaretti
  (Italian macaroons)

Fruit Vinegars

In the recipe on page 220 for Fresh Figs in Blueberry Cream the only blueberries you will find are those used to make the blueberry vinegar that flavors the cream. At first you might find the idea of adding fruit vinegar to desserts just a bit odd. But very often acid in the form of citrus is used with fruit to bring out the basic flavors, and here you are simply substituting fruit vinegar for the citrus to achieve the same effect. Fruit vinegars, as the facing page shows, can also be used to enhance fish, meat, or poultry as well as salads.

The various flavors of these vinegars (raspberry, cherry, blueberry, strawberry, peach, and even pear) are delightfully surprising: lighter than most wine vinegars, slightly sweet, and tasting intensely of the particular fruit used. There are many imported brands on the market as well as a few domestic ones. All vary widely in intensity of flavor, so adjust quantities accordingly when using them.

It is a fairly simple matter to produce these vinegars at home. Start with an already prepared vinegar; rice-wine, champagne, or white-wine vinegars are the mildest and will allow the truest flavors, while cidar vinegar may be used for extra fruitiness; avoid plain white vinegar, which is a bit too acidic. Bring the vinegar to a boil and pour it over an equal amount of whole berries or fruit. Place in glass containers, cover tightly and store in a dark place for five to seven days, then strain out the fruit or allow it to remain in the jars. For stronger flavor, the process may be repeated, straining off and discarding the first batch of berries or fruit and adding a second.

It might seem as though fruit vinegars were created specifically for use in Nouvelle Cuisine. They appeared to surface at the same time and, although suitable for many kinds of preparation, their use was confined almost totally to that genre of cooking. Actually, these flavored vinegars have been quite popular in England and France for many years, and research discloses that they were produced in home kitchens in the U.S. as early as the 1800s. In *The Virginia Housewife*, published in 1824, Mary Randolph gives a simple recipe for raspberry vinegar that is followed by this idea for a refreshing summer drink: "Fill one third of a tumbler with raspberry vinegar, add ice, a teaspoon of sugar, and top with carbonated water. Garnish with fresh berries and a mint leaf." I'm tempted to add a healthy swig of vodka to this for an unusual variation on the somewhat tired kir theme.

Following are a few quick ideas as well as a simple dessert recipe that illustrate the variety of uses of fruit vinegars.

- Sprinkle sliced strawberries with a few drops of raspberry vinegar, dust lightly with confectioner's sugar, and chill for an hour.

- Slice roast duck into thin slivers, pair with slices of ripe mango, place on a bed of escarole, and coat with a sweet-sour vinaigrette made with cherry vinegar.

- Quickly cook carrots that have been sliced into coins and dress while hot with raspberry vinegar and a little fruity olive oil. Allow to marinate for a few hours at room temperature and serve at that temperature.

- Arrange thinly sliced and peeled oranges, and coat with a vinaigrette in which strawberry vinegar is used. Garnish with imported black olives.

- Combine cooked couscous with chopped walnuts and golden raisins, and coat with a shallot-and-raspberry vinaigrette.

- Sauté small fillets of pork until just tender, and deglaze the pan with a mild mustard and the fruit vinegar of your choice.

- Use red-currant vinegar and a bit of heavy cream to deglaze the pan after roasting a duck.

- Cut a small portion of roast goose into small dice. Sauté quickly in hot fat, remove the meat, discard the fat, and deglaze the pan with equal amounts of a dry red wine and raspberry vinegar. Reduce this mixture, turn off the heat, stir in Dijon mustard, a fruity olive oil, and season to taste. Pour this dressing over young and very tender leaves of Swiss chard; add the bits of goose; toss till the greens are slightly wilted, and garnish with fresh or brandied raspberries.

Combine the sugar and water in a small saucepan. Add the ginger and put over high heat. Bring the sugar syrup to a boil, reduce the heat, and simmer for 10 minutes. Remove from the heat and allow to cool thoroughly.

Cut the melon in half, remove the seeds, and slice into wedges. Remove the rind, cut the fruit into cubes, and place the melon in a bowl. Strain off and discard the ginger, pour the syrup over the melon, and chill for 2 hours.

Serve the melon with just a little of its syrup in individual dishes, dusting the top of each serving lightly with the ground amaretti.

Peaches in Vouvray
serves four

The best peach for this dish is the white-fleshed and delicate-tasting Babcock.

4 peaches $^1\!/_4$ **to** $^1\!/_2$ **bottle of Vouvray wine**
Finely granulated sugar (op-
tional)

Bring a pot of water to a boil; immerse the peaches in it for 1 minute. Remove, run them under cold water, and slip off the skins. Remove the pits and slice the peaches into a bowl. (At this point you can sweeten the fruit with just a bit of sugar if you wish; this will largely depend on the sweetness of your wine.)

Pour enough wine over the peaches to cover them by 1 to 2 inches. Chill for at least an hour. Half an hour before serving, remove the bowl from the refrigerator and let stand at room temperature to warm slightly, since it is difficult to taste the delicacy of this dish when ice cold. Serve in deep wine glasses.

Poached Pears with Amaretto Custard
serves two

S ince perfectly ripe pears are next to impossible to find these days, I often
serve this delectable fruit poached. The underripe pears respond beautifully to this simple treatment. Choose the elegant, long-necked Bosc or the
Anjou—with long stems to facilitate handling after the pears are cooked.
The custard can be prepared in a double boiler, but that is a tedious method,
taking twice as long as the method here. The saucepan used for the final
cooking must be heavy (ideally cast iron with enamel) so that the heat is even
and the custard does not burn or stick to the bottom of the pan. You will have
a little Amaretto custard left over for which many uses can certainly be found:
over chocolate ice cream with toasted, chopped almonds; over a good,
home-made pound cake; over dessert crêpes folded around sautéed apples—
among others.

Poached pears

2 cups sugar
6 cups water
Rind of 1 lemon
1 tablespoon lemon juice
2 cloves

$^1/_2$ cinnamon stick
2 Bosc or Anjou pears, slightly
     underripe and preferably
     with long stems

Combine the sugar, water, and all other ingredients except the pears in
a pot deep enough to hold the pears without crowding. Bring to a boil. While
the poaching syrup is cooking, peel the pears with a vegetable peeler,
trimming the bottoms so they can stand upright. Immediately place them
in a bowl of cold water to which a little lemon juice has been added so that
they do not brown.

When the syrup is boiling, add the pears, cover the pot, and keep the
liquid at a rolling boil so that the pears are constantly moving and can cook
evenly throughout. The pears will be cooked in 20 to 30 minutes, depending
upon their size and state of ripeness. When finished, they should be
translucent and offer no resistance when pierced with a toothpick. Remove
the pears carefully, holding them by their stems (or failing that, with a slotted
spoon) and put them on a plate, allowing them to cool. If the pears are
prepared the day before, cover them with plastic wrap and refrigerate, but

bring them to room temperature before serving. The poaching liquid may be frozen and reused.

Amaretto custard

2 large egg yolks
3 tablespoons finely granulated
   sugar
$^1/_2$ teaspoon cornstarch
$^3/_4$ cup heavy cream
2 tablespoons Amaretto
   liqueur

$^1/_2$ to 1 teaspoon lemon juice,
   to taste
Garnish: powdered amaretti
   (Italian macaroons ground
   to a powder in a food processor)

Place the egg yolks in a mixing bowl and beat about 3 minutes, gradually adding the sugar, until the mixture is a pale yellow and has doubled in volume. Beat in the cornstarch.

Warm the cream and slowly beat into the yolk mixture. Pour the resulting mixture into a heavy enameled saucepan and set over moderate heat. Stir the custard with a wire whisk. If the custard begins to steam at any point, remove it from the heat and whisk until it has cooled slightly. It must not even reach a simmer. When the custard has thickened enough to heavily coat a wooden spoon, remove it from the heat and add the Amaretto and lemon juice to taste. Transfer to a small mixing bowl and whisk for a few minutes to cool. When the custard is completely cool, place a piece of plastic wrap directly on its surface and refrigerate until serving.

When you are ready to serve dessert, place each poached pear on a small serving plate, spoon a bit of the custard around the base and over the top, dust with the powdered amaretti crumbs, and serve.

Poached Pears with Ginger Cream
serves six

2 cups finely granulated sugar
1 tablespoon lemon juice
Peel of $^1/_2$ lemon

6 firm pears
1 cinnamon stick
3 cloves

1 cup heavy cream
1¹⁄₂ tablespoons dry sherry
3 tablespoons confectioner's

sugar
¹⁄₄ cup finely minced candied
  ginger

Combine the sugar with the lemon juice, lemon peel, and 1 quart water in a pot large enough to hold the pears without crowding, and bring to a boil. Peel the pears and add them to the sugar syrup along with the cinnamon stick and the cloves. Cook the pears at a rolling boil, frequently spooning the syrup over them, for about 25 minutes, until tender. Allow them to cool in their cooking liquid.

Beat the heavy cream until foamy; add the sherry and the confectioner's sugar and continue to beat until stiff. Fold in the candied ginger.

Place the pears on a serving platter, spoon some of the ginger cream over them, and serve immediately.

Chocolate-Coated Poached Pears in Whipped Cream
serves six

6 Bosc pears, slightly underripe, with long stems

Poaching syrup

1 tablespoon lemon juice
Peel of ¹⁄₂ lemon

3 cloves
¹⁄₂ cinnamon stick

Chocolate coating

6 ounces imported semisweet
  chocolate
2 tablespoons sweet (unsalted)
  butter

2 tablespoons Amaretto
  liqueur
3 amaretti (Italian macaroons),
  coarsely ground

Whipped cream

1 cup heavy cream   **sugar**
3 tablespoons confectioner's   **$\frac{1}{2}$ teaspoon pure vanilla extract**

Peel the pears with a vegetable peeler. Cut a thin slice off the bottom of each so they can stand upright. Drop them immediately into acidulated water (containing several drops of lemon juice) while you prepare the poaching liquid.

Combine the sugar with the remaining poaching ingredients and add to 1 quart of water in a pot large enough to hold the pears without crowding; bring to a boil. Add the pears, cover and cook at a rolling boil for about 30 minutes, until they are tender and offer no resistance when pierced with a toothpick. Remove the pears from the syrup and stand them upright on a shallow plate, well away from each other. Allow them to cool.

Cut the chocolate into slivers and place in the top half of a double boiler; melt over low heat. When no lumps are apparent, stir in the butter, bit by bit, until it is completely absorbed. Add the liqueur and mix thoroughly. Dry each pear gently with paper towels. Place a pear on a small rack set over a plate or bowl. Spoon the melted, still-warm chocolate over the pear until the entire surface is covered. Transfer the pear to a lightly buttered plate and sprinkle with enough ground amaretti to speckle the whole surface. Chill immediately. Repeat this procedure with the remaining pears. This step may be done hours in advance of serving.

To prepare the whipped cream, beat the cream, adding the sugar only after the cream has begun to thicken slightly. Add the vanilla and continue to beat until the cream forms soft peaks.

Stand each pear on an individual serving plate, top with a dollop of whipped cream, and serve.

Raspberries in Cassis
serves four

T here is very little one can do to improve on the flavor of the raspberry. This recipe combines them with the concentrated flavor of black currants and tops them with whipped cream and a sprinkling of powdered Italian amaretti cookies.

1 quart fresh raspberries
4 tablespoons crème de cassis
   liqueur
Finely granulated sugar (optional)
1 cup heavy cream
$^{1}/_{2}$ teaspoon vanilla extract

1 to 2 tablespoons confectioner's sugar
Powdered amaretti (Italian
   macaroons ground to a
   powder in a food processor
   or blender)

Clean the berries, place them in a shallow bowl, and sprinkle over them the crème de cassis (sugar may be added to sweeten them slightly if you wish). Mix the berries gently with the liqueur and chill for at least 2 hours.

Whip the cream until it begins to thicken, add the vanilla extract and the sugar to taste, and continue to whip until the cream holds its shape but is not stiff. Spoon the berries into individual serving dishes, mound the whipped cream on top, and sprinkle with the powdered amaretti.

Peach Fool
serves six

2 or 3 very ripe peaches
1 to 2 tablespoons brown sugar
1 tablespoon dark rum
$^{1}/_{2}$ pint heavy cream

1 tablespoon confectioner's
   sugar
1 teaspoon vanilla extract
A few toasted almonds

Immerse the peaches in boiling water for 1 minute. Remove and run under cold water, slipping off the skins. Cut each peach in half; remove and discard the pits. Purée the flesh in a food processor, flavoring it with the rum

Fruit Fools

The word "fool" comes from the French *fouler*, to crush. Traditionally, the fruit is crushed after light cooking, then mixed with a custard or whipped cream or both. This is a wonderful method to use for the profusion of ripe fruit available in the early Northwest summers. I have eliminated the custard in this dessert, using only whipped cream. The fruit itself need not be cooked; in fact, the raw fruit purée has a fresh and lively flavor that is most appealing. This dessert would be welcome at the end of almost any meal, but especially in summer; it is light, cool, and creamy.

The two recipes given here are for peach and strawberry fools, but you can substitute whatever fruit you fancy. The proportions are approximately one and a half cups fruit purée to a half pint whipping cream. Some fruits are more intense in flavor, so the proportions must be adjusted accordingly. You may wish to sieve a purée of raspberries or blackberries to remove the pips, although I rarely do because I find their texture pleasing.

Here is a short guide to different fruits and the flavorings that complement them:

Apricots or nectarines—apricot brandy.

Blueberries—pure maple syrup and cinnamon.

Cherries—kirsch or maraschino.

Honeydew or casaba melons—anisette or sweet Champagne.

Peaches—brown sugar and rum or bourbon or Amaretto.

Raspberries—framboise liqueur or crème de cassis.

Strawberries—crème de cassis or Grand Marnier.

and 1 tablespoon of brown sugar; taste for sweetness and add the other tablespoon of sugar if necessary. Set this mixture aside.

Whip the cream in a stainless-steel or copper bowl, adding the confectioner's sugar only after it has begun to thicken. Add the vanilla extract and whip until the cream forms stiff peaks. Measure out $1\frac{1}{2}$ cups peach purée and fold it into the whipped cream. Pour into 6 individual serving dishes and chill for at least 2 hours or overnight. Before serving, garnish the top of each serving with the toasted almonds.

Strawberry Fool
serves six

1 box very ripe strawberries	sugar
1 to 2 tablespoons finely granulated sugar	1 teaspoon pure vanilla extract (do not use imitation)
1 tablespoon crème de cassis	A few amaretti (Italian maca-
$\frac{1}{2}$ pint heavy cream	roons) ground to a powder
1 tablespoon confectioner's	

Set aside 6 whole berries to use as garnish. Stem the rest and purée in a food processor. Add the cassis and 1 tablespoon sugar, blend for 1 to 2 seconds to mix, and taste for sweetness. (You should not add too much sugar; the natural flavor of the berries should be apparent.) Add the other tablespoon of sugar if necessary and set purée aside.

Whip the cream in a stainless-steel or copper bowl, adding the confectioner's sugar only after it has begun to thicken. Add the vanilla and whip until the cream forms stiff peaks. Measure out $1\frac{1}{2}$ cups strawberry purée and fold it into the whipped cream. Pour into individual soufflé dishes and chill for at least 2 hours or overnight. (The fools may be frozen, but should be placed in the refrigerator for 30 to 45 minutes before serving to let them defrost.)

Dust the surface of each fool with the powdered amaretti and garnish with a perfect berry just before serving.

Peaches with Raspberry Fool

serves four

A variation of peach Melba that makes a light and refreshing dessert.

2 large peaches
1 cup sugar
1 cup water
$^1/_2$-inch piece of vanilla bean

$^1/_2$ recipe Raspberry Fool (see box, page 230)
Whole raspberries and toasted almond slices

Bring a pot of water to a boil; immerse the peaches for 1 minute. Remove and run them under cold water; the skins will slip off. Cut each peach in half and remove the pit. Combine the sugar, water, and vanilla bean in a pot, bring to boil, and cook for 5 minutes. Then add the peach halves, reduce the heat, and gently poach them until just tender. When done, remove the pan from the stove and allow the peaches to cool in the liquid.

Place each peach half in a coupe glass, fill the cavity generously with some of the raspberry fool, and garnish with a few whole raspberries and the toasted almonds.

Apple and Custard Tart

serves six to eight

The flavor of the apples in this tart is enhanced by only a small amount of sugar and a bit of vanilla bean. A deep tart pan with two-inch sides and a removable bottom is used for the shell.

2 pounds baking apples
5 tablespoons butter
1-inch piece of vanilla bean, split in half
4 tablespoons sugar
9-inch tart pan with deep

(2-inch) fluted sides lined with pastry shell (see Strawberry Tart)
2 large eggs
1 cup heavy cream
1 teaspoon pure vanilla extract

Preheat the oven to 400 degrees.

Peel, core, and slice the apples. Melt the butter in a 10- or 12-inch skillet, add the apple slices and vanilla bean, and sprinkle with 1 tablespoon sugar. Sauté the apple slices over moderate heat for 5 minutes, stirring frequently. Raise the heat and reduce the liquid released by the apples for about 5 minutes more.

Allow the apple slices to cool slightly. Then pour the apples into the prepared pastry shell and place in the middle of the oven. Bake the apple-filled shell for 30 minutes. Combine the eggs, cream, the remaining 3 tablespoons of sugar, and the vanilla extract in a small bowl, and beat together. Pour this custard over the apples, return to the oven, and continue to bake for an additional 20 to 30 minutes, until the custard has puffed and browned slightly. Allow to cool for about 30 minutes before serving.

Blueberry Sour Cream Tart
serves six to eight

A luscious combination of blueberries and sour cream.

10-inch pastry shell fitted into
   a quiche pan or flan ring
   (see Strawberry Tart)
3 large eggs
1 cup sour cream

$\frac{1}{2}$ cup sugar
2 cups blueberries
Large pinch cinnamon
Small pinch freshly grated
   nutmeg

Preheat the oven to 400 degrees.

Place a layer of foil over the pastry and fill it with rice or beans to keep it from puffing while baking. Put in the center of the oven, bake for 15 minutes, and remove from the oven to take out the foil and the weight. Put the pastry shell back in the oven to bake for an additional 10 minutes. Allow the shell to cool slightly before filling.

Reduce oven heat to 325 degrees.

Combine the eggs, sour cream, and $1/4$ cup of the sugar; beat well. Toss the blueberries in a mixing bowl with the remaining sugar and the spices. Place the blueberries in the bottom of the prebaked shell, cover with the egg and sour cream mixture, and bake in the center of the oven for about 45 minutes, until the crust is browned and the custard is done. Allow to cool slightly before serving.

Prune Tart
serves eight

This rich prune tart can be prepared in any season but it is especially pleasing during the winter, when there is only a limited selection of fresh fruit available. Oddly, soaking the prunes in tea (conventional, not herb tea) reinforces their flavor.

Pastry shell

Using instructions in the recipe for the Strawberry Tart, fit a pastry shell into a 10-inch quiche pan, and partially bake it (for 20 minutes at 400 degrees).

Tart filling

1 cup pitted dried prunes
1 cup steaming hot tea
$1/2$ pound cream cheese
3 large eggs
$1/4$ cup sugar
$1/2$ cup heavy cream
1 teaspoon pure vanilla extract
$1/4$ teaspoon powdered cinnamon

Pinch freshly grated nutmeg
Finely grated rind of 1 small lemon
$1/2$ cup blanched almonds, finely ground
Confectioner's sugar

Soak the prunes in the hot tea for about 45 minutes or until soft.

Preheat the oven to 350 degrees.

Beat together the cream cheese, eggs, sugar, and heavy cream until well blended. Stir in the vanilla, cinnamon, nutmeg, lemon rind, and the almonds.

Drain the prunes and chop them coarsely; stir them into the cream cheese mixture. After the partially baked pastry shell has cooled slightly, pour in the prune filling. Bake the tart in the center of the oven for 45 to 50 minutes—until the filling has set. Remove the tart from the oven, dust the top with confectioner's sugar, and allow to cool before serving.

Variation: Substitute dried apricots for the prunes and grated orange rind for the lemon rind.

Raspberry Tart
serves six to eight

A crisp pastry shell is filled with a layer of zesty lemon mousse, then topped with fresh raspberries and glazed with red currant jelly.

10-inch pastry shell, using a quiche pan or flan ring; see instructions in following recipe, and bake shell completely
2 large lemons
5 egg yolks
²⁄₃ cup sugar
2 teaspoons cornstarch

5 egg whites
Pinch salt
1 cup heavy cream, whipped until stiff
1 cup red currant jelly
1 tablespoon water
2 quarts fresh raspberries, cleaned

Grate the rind of the lemons with a zester or a fine grater. Juice the lemons, remove the pips, and reserve the juice.

Beat the egg yolks with the sugar until the mixture is thick and lemon-colored. Beat in the lemon juice and the cornstarch and pour into an enameled cast-iron saucepan. Set over moderate heat and beat constantly with a wire whisk until the mixture thickens and coats a wooden spoon lightly. Remove from heat and allow to cool.

Beat the egg whites with a pinch of salt until they are stiff. Fold them into the yolk mixture, using a rubber spatula. Sprinkle with the finely grated lemon rind and fold in the whipped cream. Allow this mousse mixture to chill for at least an hour before assembling the tart.

Melt the currant jelly with the tablespoon of water; brush the bottom and the sides of the baked tart shell with a thin layer of this glaze. Pour in the lemon mousse and spread it evenly over the bottom. Arrange the raspberries on top of the mousse, stem side down, in concentric circles. Brush the berries with the remaining glaze. Chill before serving.

Strawberry Tart
serves six to eight

T he traditional filling for most fruit tarts is a milk-sugar-egg yolks-flour combination; the one used here is a low-fat filling made with ricotta cheese. This light cheese base marries beautifully with any variety of berry and is especially good with peaches. The flavoring here (cognac or vanilla) is a simple one but there are many variations possible: grated chocolate and orange zest with Grand Marnier, coarsely ground amaretti (Italian macaroons) with Amaretto liqueur, finely powdered and toasted hazelnuts (filberts) with rum—the combinations are endless.

Pastry shell

$1\frac{1}{2}$ cups unbleached white
   flour
6 tablespoons butter, cut into
   small cubes

2 tablespoons shortening
$\frac{1}{4}$ teaspoon salt
$\frac{1}{2}$ tablespoon sugar
3 tablespoons ice water

Filling

1 ¹/₂ cups ricotta cheese
5 tablespoons finely granulated
  sugar (or to taste)
1 tablespoon cognac or 1 tea-

spoon pure vanilla extract
Ripe strawberries (about 2
  quarts), hulls removed

Glaze

1 cup red currant jelly

1 tablespoon water

Garnish

1 tablespoon finely ground
  hazelnuts (optional)

First, the pastry. In a large bowl combine the flour, butter, and shortening (both well chilled); sprinkle with the salt and sugar and work together with a pastry cutter until the texture resembles coarse cornmeal. Add the ice water, tossing with a fork until all the water is incorporated into the dough.

Form the dough into a ball, kneading lightly with the palms of the hands for a few seconds to distribute the fat evenly, and then reform into a ball. Dust the dough with a light coating of flour, wrap in waxed paper or plastic, and refrigerate for at least 2 hours.

Preheat the oven to 400 degrees.

Roll out the pastry into a 12-inch round approximately ¹/₂ inch thick; fit it into a 10-inch quiche pan or flan ring, and trim off any excess, saving for another use. Line the pastry with foil, fill with rice or beans to weight the pastry and keep the bottom from puffing up, and bake in the middle of the oven for about 10 minutes, until the pastry just begins to shrink away from the sides of the pan.

Remove the foil with the rice or beans, put the tart shell back in the oven, and bake until it is lightly browned and crisp, 10 to 15 minutes. Oven temperatures vary quite a bit so be sure the pastry is fully baked before removing it from the oven.

While the pastry shell cools in its pan, prepare the filling. Put the ricotta in a food processor and blend for a few seconds to remove the grainy texture. Add the sugar and cognac or vanilla and blend until smooth. (If not using a food processor, put the ricotta through a sieve to remove the grainy texture, then add flavorings.)

Heat the currant jelly with the water in a small saucepan until liquid. Allow the glaze to cool slightly, then paint the inside bottom and sides of the tart shell with a little of the glaze. This will ensure a crisp crust if the tart is not consumed immediately.

Pour the ricotta mixture into the coated tart shell and spread it evenly over the bottom. Arrange the strawberries on top of this, stem side down, building toward the center in concentric circles. Brush the berries with a heavy layer of glaze and sprinkle lightly with the ground hazelnuts. The tart can either be served immediately or chilled for an hour or 2.

Orange Ice
serves four

Fruit ices are such a refreshing end to warm-weather meals that it's no wonder they have become so popular. You will find that there are quite a few sorbets and ices which may be produced at home without the aid of an ice cream machine. The recipe here for orange ice may be used as a blueprint, with any citrus fruit substituted for the orange. Almost any very ripe fruit may be made into an ice, and a bit of experimenting may be done to discover whether the purée tastes best cooked or in its natural state. Lemon juice, added to taste, will balance the flavors and bring out the natural sweetness of the fruit. If an ice is being prepared a day ahead, transfer it to a bowl and cover tightly with foil. The delicate flavor of these frozen sweets seems to pale after two days, so I would not hold them any longer than that.

Orange ice may be served in the half-shells of oranges. After removing the juice, scrape the remaining pulp out with the aid of a spoon and place the shells in the freezer to help them hold their shape until serving time.

½ cup sugar
1 cup water
Peel of ½ orange, grated
1½ cups freshly squeezed

orange juice (from about 3 oranges)
3 tablespoons Grand Marnier
3 tablespoons lemon juice

Combine the sugar, water, and grated orange peel in a small saucepan. Place over moderate heat and cook until the sugar is totally dissolved and the syrup is beginning to bubble around the edges, about 10 minutes. Remove from the heat and allow to cool.

Mix this sugar syrup with the orange juice, Grand Marnier, and the lemon juice. Pour into a wide, shallow metal container and freeze for about 3 hours, or until almost solid. Remove the mixture to a mixing bowl and beat, with an electric mixer, until frothy. Pour back into the container and freeze for another hour or 2. Stir before serving.

Lemon Ice
serves four to six

A true ice should have the texture of lightly packed snow (which is why this ice would be a *granita* in Italy), so that the grains of flavored ice melt on your tongue in a delicious and seductive manner.

⅔ cup sugar
2 cups water

2 large lemons

Combine the sugar and water in a small saucepan, place over heat, and bring to a boil, cooking only long enough for the sugar to melt. Remove from the heat and allow to cool.

Finely grate the rind from the 2 lemons and set aside. Juice the lemons and strain to remove the pips.

Add the lemon rind and juice to the sugar syrup and mix. Pour into an ice tray or other shallow container and freeze for about 2 hours without stirring, until the ice has crystallized. The ice may then be put quickly through a food processor or blender to break it up, or it may be spooned directly out of the container and into serving dishes.

Plum Ice

serves six to eight

1 ½ pounds purple (Italian)
    plums, very ripe
1 ½ cups sugar
2 cups water

1 tablespoon finely chopped
    fresh or candied ginger
1 to 2 tablespoons lemon juice
1 egg white

To peel the plums, bring a 3- or 4-quart pot of water to a boil. Add about half the plums and leave in the water for 10 to 12 seconds. Take them out with a slotted spoon and continue with the remaining plums. Remove the skin from the plums; it should slide off easily. Cut the plums in half, remove the seeds, and purée the plums in a food processor. (The purée should be quite fine but there should still be some texture remaining.) Reserve.

Combine the sugar with the water and the ginger in a small saucepan. Place over moderate heat and cook until the sugar is totally dissolved and the mixture is beginning to bubble around the edges, about 10 minutes. Remove the syrup and, after it has cooled, mix it slowly into the plum purée. The amount of syrup you will use depends upon personal taste and the ripeness of the fruit. I use about 1 ¼ cups syrup for the 1 ½ pounds of plums used here. Also add lemon juice to taste; as well as balancing the flavors the lemon juice will bring out more of the fruit flavor in the plums.

Place the ice in a wide, shallow metal container and freeze for 3 hours.

Remove the ice, place in a mixing bowl and beat with an electric mixer until frothy. Pour back into the container and freeze for another 1 or 2 hours.

Beat the egg white until stiff peaks are formed. Again take out the ice, place in a mixing bowl, and beat until frothy. Combine the egg white and the ice, pour the mixture back into its container or a stainless-steel bowl, cover tightly with foil, and freeze until serving time. If held overnight, put the ice in the refrigerator an hour before serving to soften.

Watermelon Sherbet
makes one quart, serves six

T his is one of the few sherbets that can be made successfully without an
 ice cream machine. Other melons may be substituted for the watermelon, but they must be very ripe to allow for the fullest flavor. A good
greengrocer should be able to guide you in the selection of a ripe melon.
Failing that, rely on your nose, for a ripe melon gives off a faint and slightly
sweet aroma. (No amount of shaking or thumping or squeezing will tell you
anything about the ripeness of a particular melon.) A bit of lemon juice is
used in this sherbet to cut its sweetness; with another type of melon
(honeydew or casaba), you might wish to also add two or three tablespoons
of anisette.

4 to $4\frac{1}{2}$ pounds ripe watermelon
$1\frac{1}{2}$ tablespoons lemon juice
1 cup sugar

$1\frac{1}{2}$ teaspoons unflavored
   gelatin
$\frac{1}{2}$ cup heavy cream
1 large egg

Cut the flesh of the melon from the rind and remove all the seeds. Cut
the flesh into cubes about 1 inch square and purée in a food processor or
blender. Strain the purée through a sieve and reserve both pulp and liquid.
There should be about $\frac{3}{4}$ to 1 cup of pulp.

Add the lemon juice and the sugar to the pulp. Stir until the sugar is
completely dissolved. Allow the mixture to stand at room temperature for
about 2 hours or until it resembles a syrup.

Soften the gelatin in 2 tablespoons of the reserved watermelon juice; stir
until it is dissolved. Then stir in $\frac{1}{4}$ cup of the juice, heated to the boiling
point. Stir this gelatin mixture slowly into the pulp, pour into a shallow metal
container, and freeze for 1 hour.

Beat the heavy cream until stiff. Separate the egg; beat the white until stiff
and lightly beat the yolk. Remove the watermelon mixture from the freezer,
place in a chilled bowl, and beat with an electric mixer until frothy. Fold in
the whipped cream, egg white, and yolk.

Pour the sherbet back into the metal container and freeze for 4 to 5 hours, stirring the mixture 2 or 3 times during this period to break up the ice crystals. (Unlike most sherbets made in the home freezer, this one needs only to be stirred a few times during the freezing process rather than being removed from its container and beaten with a mixer.)

May be served immediately or placed in a covered container and held for future use.

Hazelnut Soufflé with Fresh Strawberry Sauce
serves four to six

Hazelnuts, or filberts, are widely grown in the Northwest and they are, to my mind, the best flavored of all nuts. When used in desserts, this beautiful flavor can be further enhanced by the addition of Frangelico, an Italian liqueur made from the hazelnut.

The recipe for the soufflé itself is based on one from chef Maurice Lecourt of Dieppe, whose own soufflés towered out of their dishes. This apple-cheeked Norman taught that one cannot overbeat egg whites when creating a soufflé. The finest results are produced when the whites are beaten by hand in a copper bowl. If one lacks either the stamina or the copper bowl, the next-best technique would be to use a stainless-steel bowl and an electric beater. Egg whites simply will not mound properly in glass or plastic bowls. The sauce may be varied with raspberries substituted for strawberries. Either fruit, when out of season, can be used in its frozen state, but there will be a considerable decline in the flavor.

Soufflé

²/₃ cup milk
4 egg yolks
¹/₂ cup sugar

2¹/₂ tablespoons flour
²/₃ cup Frangelico (hazelnut
   liqueur)

$^1/_2$ cup ground toasted hazel-   Pinch salt
  nuts (filberts)   Confectioner's sugar
5 egg whites

Preheat the oven to 325 degrees.

Liberally butter a 1$^1/_2$-quart soufflé dish and sprinkle it with sugar.

Heat the milk to boiling. Put the egg yolks and the sugar in a heavy enameled saucepan and mix well with a wire whisk. Add the flour and whisk to combine. Add the boiling milk, a little at a time, stirring constantly. Place the saucepan over moderate heat and cook until the custard base thickens enough to heavily coat a wooden spoon; it must be stirred all the time and not allowed to boil. When it has thickened sufficiently, stir in the liqueur and the nuts. This may be prepared hours in advance and left at room temperature until you are ready to use it. If you decide to do this, place a piece of plastic wrap *directly* on the surface of the custard so that it does not form a skin.

Beat the egg whites, with a pinch of salt, in either a copper or stainless-steel bowl until very firm. Stir a spoonful of the beaten whites into the custard base, then pour the custard base over the whites and fold in with a rubber spatula, taking care not to deflate the whites.

Pour the soufflé batter into the prepared dish. Bake for 10 minutes at 325 degrees, then turn the oven up to 375 and continue to bake for 10 minutes more. Sprinkle the top of the soufflé with the confectioner's sugar and bake for another 5 minutes. This soufflé should be slightly moist and cloudlike in consistency when done. Serve immediately with fresh strawberry sauce.

Fresh strawberry sauce

1 pint fresh strawberries,   framboise liqueur
  cleaned and halved   Sugar to taste
$^1/_4$ cup crème de cassis or   Squeeze of lemon juice

Purée the strawberries in a food processor, adding the liqueur of your choice and the sugar. The amount of sugar will depend on the natural sweetness of the berries and the sweetness of the liqueur chosen, and a little lemon juice will nicely balance all the flavors. Serve the sauce either chilled or at room temperature.

A Dessert Alternative: Fruit & Cheese

Completing a meal with a fruit and cheese course is a simple and appetizing alternative to the sweet that customarily appears after the entrée and salad. To put this course together, choose not a random sampling of cheeses but one or two carefully selected cheeses and a fruit that will complement them. Keep in mind that mild cheeses should be served after a lighter flavored main course such as chicken, veal, or fish, and stronger-flavored cheeses after beef, game, or lamb. Whatever is in season will largely dictate what fresh fruit is best, although you will wish to avoid any citrus or overly acidic fruits, for these marry very poorly with cheese. Following is a brief listing of fruits and the cheeses that complement them:

Apples and pears—blue cheeses: either the crumbly types like Roquefort or Stilton, or the creamy blues like Gorgonzola Dolce (an Italian blue with added butterfat—smooth-tasting and spreadable), our own Oregon Blue, or the French Pipo Crème. Aged cheddars are also an excellent choice: Vermont (especially Cabot) has an exceptionally fine fruity aroma and smooth flavor; New York cheddar is one of the sharpest available; and Black Diamond, from Canada. Well-flavored Swiss cheeses: Gruyère, nutty and smooth; and Appenzeller, not too well known here—used mainly for fondues in its country of origin, but a wonderful table cheese. Parmigiano-Reggiano from Italy, often thought of only as a grating cheese, has a superb flavor and delicious grainy texture that pairs perfectly with these two fruits. The soft, creamy goat cheeses are good too; try a Montrachet or Lezay or one of the very fine Laura Chenel goat cheeses made in California.

Berries—probably best with triple-crème cheeses like the complex-tasting Brillat-Savarin or the smooth and buttery Belletoile, both from France. Also the Italian dessert cheese that just recently appeared here, Mascarpone, which is similar to the French triple crèmes; it's a soft and delicate cow's-milk cheese that looks and tastes remarkably like freshly whipped cream.

Peaches, apricots, and figs—fresh cream cheeses, either from cow's or goat's milk; double crèmes like Brie or Camembert. Also Mascarpone and some of the milder goat cheeses.

Cherries—their crisp sweetness pairs beautifully with semisoft, creamy cheeses like the Italian Bel Paese or the French Port Salud.

Grapes—good with almost any type of cheese, but not especially interesting, flavorwise, with any one of them.

This is simply meant as a partial listing to enable you to begin experimenting with particular flavors and combinations that suit your individual taste. You need not always rely on fresh fruits, either; I'm especially partial to the combination of dried figs with goat cheeses.

At times you may wish to present this course in a more refined manner. For example, quarter fresh figs, leaving them still attached at the bottom. Spread the sections out like flower petals, spoon a dollop of Mascarpone into the center, and drizzle some Frangelico (Italian hazelnut liqueur) over all. Garnish with amarettini (small Italian macaroons).

Cheese should be stored in a cool, humid atmosphere between 42 and 50 degrees Fahrenheit; below that the cheese gets tough. Never freeze cheese. Blue cheeses, the most perishable, should be wrapped in a damp cloth, placed in a plastic box, and stored at 46 to 50 degrees. For soft cheeses with a bit of bloom on the rind (Camembert, Brie) the ideal temperature is 50 degrees. Semisoft cheeses (Port Salut, Tommes) should be tightly wrapped to avoid contact with air and stored at 46 to 50 degrees.

Always be sure to take cheese out of the refrigerator one hour before it is to be eaten, so that it will be at room temperature. An exception is Mascarpone, so rich in butterfat that it is best served cold.

Buy your cheese from a cheese shop that has a large turnover in stock and that will offer you a taste of whatever cheese may interest you. Merchants who are not afraid of taste tests are sure of the quality of their merchandise.

Chilled Lemon-Blueberry Soufflé
serves eight

S oufflés are a festive ending to almost any meal, but one is not always
ready to sacrifice time with guests to the last-minute preparations
required. If you have had any trepidation about attempting soufflés before
now, you will be overjoyed to learn that there is a species of soufflé that is
foolproof: the cold soufflé. They can be prepared hours in advance or even
the night before; they will rise majestically out of their molds, resisting any
attempt to deflate them.

A chilled soufflé can be flavored with almost anything you fancy,
including numerous spirits and liqueurs such as Benedictine, crème de cassis,
Kahlua, and anisette. Toasted almonds, hazelnuts (filberts), or pistachios are
delicious additions when the basic mixture is simply flavored with vanilla or
melted chocolate.

1 tablespoon unflavored gelatin	2 cups heavy cream
Juice of $1\frac{1}{2}$ lemons	$\frac{1}{2}$ cup confectioner's sugar
6 egg whites, chilled	Grated rind of $1\frac{1}{2}$ lemons
$\frac{1}{4}$ teaspoon cream of tartar	1 box fresh blueberries (1
$\frac{1}{4}$ cup granulated sugar	pint), puréed

Make a 3-inch-high collar of aluminum foil or waxed paper, encircle the
top of a $1\frac{1}{2}$-quart soufflé dish with it, and attach.

Combine the gelatin with the lemon juice in a small pot and set over low
heat until the gelatin has melted, about 2 to 3 minutes. Remove from heat
and allow to cool.

In a stainless-steel or copper bowl (neither egg whites nor cream will build
properly when beaten in ceramic or glass), beat the whites until they start to
froth. Add the cream of tartar and continue beating, adding the granulated
sugar gradually, until the whites form stiff peaks. Fold in the gelatin mixture
and set aside.

In another stainless-steel or copper bowl, beat the heavy cream, adding
the confectioner's sugar little by little until the cream is stiff. Sprinkle the
grated lemon rind over the top of the cream, pour in the puréed blueberries,

and fold in gently with a rubber spatula. Add the beaten egg whites to this mixture and carefully fold them in.

Pour the soufflé mixture into the collared soufflé dish. Cover with plastic wrap and freeze for at least 4 hours or overnight. Remove the collar carefully and serve.

Blueberry Upside-Down Cake
serves six to eight

What child did not grow up with memories of pineapple upside-down cake? Unfortunately the topping used was always canned, and never varied. Fresh apricots or nectarines or plums are a most delicious variation, and fresh peaches are absolutely sublime. But my favorite upside-down cake is made with fresh blueberries, incidentally a fruit that is indigenous to the Northwest.

This cake is a cinch to make even if you have an unsure hand when it comes to desserts of this ilk. If your diet permits, serve it with drifts of unsweetened whipped cream.

10 tablespoons butter at room temperature
$^1/_2$ cup light brown (or golden brown) sugar
Powdered cinnamon
1 pint fresh, plump blueberries
$^1/_2$ cup white sugar
1 teaspoon grated lemon rind

2 large eggs
2 tablespoons lemon juice
2 cups stone-ground unbleached white flour
2 teaspoons baking powder
$^1/_2$ teaspoon salt
$^3/_4$ cup heavy cream

Spread 2 tablespoons of butter on the bottom and sides of a round cake pan that is 9 inches across and 2 inches deep. Sprinkle evenly with the brown sugar, and very lightly dust with the powdered cinnamon. Add the blueberries, fitting them snugly into the bottom of the pan. Chill while you prepare the cake.

Preheat the oven to 350 degrees.

Cream the remaining 8 tablespoons of butter with the white sugar until fluffy. Mix in the lemon rind and beat in the eggs, 1 at a time, until they are thoroughly incorporated. Stir in the lemon juice.

Sift the flour, baking powder, and salt into a bowl. Add about a quarter of the dry ingredients to the butter mixture, folding together with a rubber spatula, then add a quarter of the heavy cream, again mixing with the spatula. Continue combining slowly until all the ingredients are mixed together and have formed a thick batter. Spoon the batter carefully over the prepared berries, totally covering them, and smooth the top with a spatula.

Bake for 40 to 45 minutes, or until the top of the cake is lightly browned. Test for doneness by inserting a toothpick into the middle of the cake; if it comes out without any particles clinging to it, the cake is done.

Allow to cool for $\frac{1}{2}$ hour on a wire rack, and then loosen the sides by running a knife between the cake and the pan. Place a plate on top of the cake and invert. It may be eaten warm or at room temperature.

Zuccotto (Dome-Shaped Cake)
serves eight

Zuccotto, a dessert dear to the hearts of the Florentines, is said to have been created by a pastry-maker to resemble the dome of the celebrated cathedral of Santa Maria del Fiore. In the Florentine dialect, the word *zucca* means a large squash (zucchini: small squash), or head. Any sponge cake baked in a sheet may be used to form the outside of the sweet.

Ladyfingers (see Hazelnut Charlotte) or sponge cake **baked in a sheet, for the outside**

Filling

2 cups heavy cream
$\frac{1}{4}$ cup confectioner's sugar
1 teaspoon pure vanilla extract
1 cup Italian Torrone almond
nougat, finely ground in a food processor
1 cup ricotta, forced through a sieve

3 tablespoons Frangelico liqueur	**1 tablespoon unsweetened cocoa powder**

Garnish

Unsweetened cocoa powder Confectioner's sugar	**1 to 1$\frac{1}{2}$ cups heavy cream, whipped**

Start the filling by beating the heavy cream, adding the confectioner's sugar and the vanilla extract. Fold in the ground nougat and the ricotta, sieved to remove its grainy texture.

Line a buttered round-bottomed 2-quart bowl with waxed paper. Divide and cut the ladyfingers or cooled cake into squares that will be cut in half into triangular sections. You will be lining the bowl (covering the waxed paper) with the triangular sections, fitting them in, point side down, until the bowl's inside surface has been covered. The shape of the bowl will determine the dimensions of the pieces of cake. Reserve any scraps. Sprinkle the cake sections with the Frangelico. Spread a thick layer of the cream and nougat mixture over the cake.

Mix the tablespoon of cocoa powder into the remaining cream mixture. Pour this into the bowl and smooth over the top with a spatula. Cover with the reserved pieces of cake. (Since this will be the bottom of the dessert, you needn't worry if it looks a bit irregular.) Cover the cake with a layer of waxed paper, place a plate on top, and weight it down with 1 large or several small cans of food. Refrigerate overnight.

Remove and discard the waxed paper from the top of the bowl. Place a serving plate over the top of the bowl and invert the zuccotto onto it. Remove the waxed paper and discard.

Now garnish the cake with alternating sections of cocoa powder and confectioner's sugar, like a brown and white beach ball. This is most easily done with the aid of a small sieve and waxed paper to cover the sections not being sprinkled. Pipe the whipped cream between the sections and around the bottom of the zuccotto.

Blueberry Clafouti
serves six to eight

This custardlike cake is usually baked in a shallow pan; I prefer to use a soufflé dish, which gives the clafouti an even creamier texture.

6 large eggs
2 cups milk
³/₄ cup flour
¹/₂ cup finely granulated sugar
1 teaspoon vanilla extract

1 tablespoon cognac or good brandy
3 cups fresh blueberries
Confectioner's sugar

Preheat the oven to 375 degrees.

First, prepare the batter. Beat together the eggs and milk with an electric mixer, slowly adding the flour and then the sugar. Flavor with the vanilla extract and the cognac and blend well.

Pour into a 2-quart soufflé dish enough of the batter to just coat the bottom, sprinkle in the blueberries, and cover with the remainder of the batter. Bake in the middle of the oven for about 1 hour or until the top of the clafouti is a golden brown. Dust the top lightly with confectioner's sugar and serve while still warm.

Cream Cheese Mousse with Raspberry Sauce
serves four

This cheese mousse is very much like the French coeur à la crème but much simpler to prepare. The recipe has been adapted from one in Jane Grigson's fine cookbook *Good Things*, published by Penguin Books.

1 cup ricotta cheese (put through a sieve or blended in a food processor)
2 egg yolks
¹/₄ cup finely granulated sugar
1¹/₂ tablespoons maraschino liqueur (substitute 1 tea-

spoon vanilla extract if unavailable)
¹/₂ tablespoon gelatin dissolved in 3 tablespoons boiling water
¹/₂ cup heavy cream, whipped

Sauce

1 pint fresh raspberries   **Sugar (optional)**
1 tablespoon crème de cassis

Remove the graininess from the ricotta by forcing it through a sieve or blending it in a food processor, using a plastic knife blade. Add the egg yolks, sugar, maraschino or vanilla, and dissolved gelatin. Blend well. Fold in the whipped cream. Pour into a lightly buttered 2-cup mold and chill for at least 4 hours.

To prepare the sauce, place two thirds of the berries in the food processor and purée them. Mix in the crème de cassis; a bit of sugar may be added here if you prefer a sweeter sauce. Mix the reserved whole berries into the sauce just before serving.

Unmold the mousse onto a serving plate, pour the sauce over it, and serve.

Hazelnut Charlotte
serves eight to ten

Here is another dessert based on the use of the hazelnut (or filbert) both in its natural state and in a liqueur made from the nut itself. One used to think of dessert liqueurs in terms of maiden aunts gently sipping crème de menthe frappés or other bright-colored cordials. Today, we have a great variety of these exotic spirits available to us, and Frangelico, the hazelnut liqueur imported from Italy, is one of the most versatile.

Frangelico, in addition to the way it's used here, may be used to flavor cakes or cookies; sprinkled over berries; combined with chocolate in any guise to form a superb union; or as the basis for an exquisite home-made ice cream.

The length of this recipe may seem daunting, but it is absolutely essential that home-made ladyfingers be used. If one has access to a good bakery, they can of course be purchased, but be aware that commercially prepared ladyfingers are not only artifically flavored but in most cases have the wrong texture.

As a finishing touch, a very thin length of grosgrain ribbon may be used to encircle the charlotte and tied into a bow.

Ladyfingers

3 large eggs, separated $^2/_3$ **cup all-purpose flour**
$^1/_2$ **cup superfine sugar**   **Confectioner's sugar**
$^1/_2$ **teaspoon pure vanilla extract**

Preheat the oven to 325 degrees.

Separate the eggs, and beat the whites by machine or hand. If you are not using a copper bowl for this process, a dash of salt or cream of tartar or a few drops of lemon juice can be added to the whites to aid the whipping process.

When the whites are firm, add the superfine sugar and continue beating for about a minute. Using a spatula, fold the vanilla and then the egg yolks, lightly beaten, into the egg whites.

Sift the flour on top of the mixture, folding it in as you go along. Coat 2 cookie sheets with butter and flour. Fit a pastry bag with a $^1/_2$-inch plain decorating tip, and fill it with the ladyfinger mixture. Pipe the ladyfingers onto the sheets. They should be approximately 4 inches long.

Sprinkle the ladyfingers heavily with confectioner's sugar. They should be sprinkled twice, and allowed to absorb the sugar for 5 minutes between sprinklings. Then turn the filled sheet upside down and give it a little bang with a knife to make the excess sugar fall onto the working space. This should be done rapidly. If the mixture is of the correct consistency, the ladyfingers will not change shape at all nor will they fall off the sheet. Bake for 12 to 15 minutes, and let cool for 15 minutes. The ladyfingers should be colored a pale beige and should slide easily from the baking sheet.

Charlotte mixture

2-quart charlotte mold   **unsalted butter**
12 tablespoons ($^3/_4$ cup) $^3/_4$ **cup superfine sugar**

1 cup toasted hazelnuts, ground
¼ cup ground Italian Torrone (nougat)
¼ cup (generous) Frangelico

3 cups heavy cream
3 tablespoons confectioner's sugar
½ teaspoon pure vanilla extract

Cut a round of waxed paper or parchment to fit the bottom of the charlotte mold after rubbing the bottom of the mold with a bit of butter. Put the paper on the buttered bottom—the butter will help the paper adhere. Chill the mold while preparing the filling.

Cream the butter with the sugar and beat until light and fluffy. Slowly mix in the ground hazelnuts, the Torrone and the Frangelico. Whip 2 cups of the cream with the confectioner's sugar and the vanilla. Fold into the butter and sugar mixture. Remove the mold from the refrigerator. Line the sides of the mold with the ladyfingers, fitting them tightly together. Fill the mold with the hazelnut mixture, covering the filling with any remaining ladyfingers. Cover with plastic wrap and refrigerate overnight.

When ready to serve, invert the mold onto a serving platter and remove and discard the paper that is now on top. Whip the remaining cup of cream, place in a pastry bag fitted with a star tip and decorate the top of the charlotte. Garnish with whole toasted hazelnuts.

Cannoli (Cream-Filled Pastry)
serves eight

A dessert immensely popular in Sicily: cylindrical pastry shells filled with a creamy mixture of ricotta cheese, candied fruit, and grated chocolate. The pastry shells are available readymade at Italian specialty-food stores; filling them is a simple task with the aid of a pastry bag. These delicious pastries can be prepared hours in advance and chilled. I have chosen to flavor the cheese filling with toasted hazelnuts, orange rind, and rum.

1 cup (½ pound) ricotta cheese
¼ cup confectioner's sugar

2 tablespoons dark rum
Finely grated rind of 2 oranges

¼ cup toasted hazelnuts (filberts), coarsely chopped, or
¼ cup finely grated bitter

chocolate
8 cannoli shells

Force the ricotta cheese through a fine sieve into a bowl and beat in the
sugar and the rum. Add the orange rind and hazelnuts, and blend well. Put
this mixture into a 12- or 14-inch pastry bag (not fitted with a pastry tip) and
pipe a bit of the mixture into each of the cannoli shells. Chill the cannoli for
at least 1 hour before serving.

Chocolate Truffles Grand Marnier
makes about sixty-five pieces

A luscious marriage of dark chocolate, ground almonds, orange rind, and
Grand Marnier.

1 pound semi-sweet chocolate
½ pound almonds, blanched
(skins removed), toasted,
and ground to a powder
¼ pound sweet butter
1½ tablespoons finely grated
orange rind

¼ cup Grand Marnier
1 cup unsweetened cocoa
powder mixed with
1 tablespoon powdered cinnamon and
1½ tablespoons powdered
sugar

Cut the chocolate into small pieces. Place in a double boiler and mix in
the ground almonds. Allow the chocolate to melt over simmering water.
When no lumps are apparent, stir in the butter, cut into small pieces, and
blend well. Remove from the heat and add the orange rind and Grand
Marnier and mix together. Place in the refrigerator and chill until firm, about
1 hour.

While the chocolate is cooling, mix the cocoa powder, cinnamon, and
sugar in a wide soup plate. With 2 small spoons shape the chocolate mixture
into irregular pieces about the size of chestnuts, roll them in the cocoa
mixture to coat, and freeze. They will keep for weeks if put into a tin
container fitted with a tight lid.

Variation: To make almond-flavored truffles, use the same amount of chocolate and butter, blending as above in a double boiler. After removing from the heat, stir in 1 cup finely ground Italian Torrone almond nougat and $\frac{1}{3}$ cup Amaretto liqueur. Follow remaining instructions, using only the cocoa powder to coat the truffles.

INDEX